THE DIEPPE RAID

The raid on the French port of Dieppe in
August 1942 was the first attempt by the Allies
to attack enemy-occupied Europe. It was mainly
Canadians who fought — valiantly but suicidally
on that ill-planned raid — but unfortunately
their sacrifice has too often been forgotten.
This book graphically describes the battle on
the beach and for the first time, the struggle
of those survivors who miserably found
themselves German prisoners of war.

John Mellor volunteered for the British Naval
Commandos when they were formed early in
World War II and served in a number of
combined operations including the Dieppe raid
and D-Day. Until 1953 he was a sailor with the
Royal Navy, then settled in Kitchener, Ontario.
Mr Mellor is an active member of the Royal
Canadian Legion and takes particular interest
in assisting veterans. He was recently
appointed to the *Canadian Committee for the
History of the Second World War,* which is
devoted to promoting research in several
aspects of the war.

The Dieppe Raid

John Mellor

CORONET BOOKS
Hodder and Stoughton

Copyright © 1975 by John Mellor

First published as *Forgotten Heroes*
in 1975 by Methuen (Canada)

Coronet edition 1979

Set, printed and bound in Great Britain for
Hodder and Stoughton Paperbacks, a
division of Hodder and Stoughton Ltd.,
Mill Road, Dunton Green, Sevenoaks,
Kent (Editorial Office: 47 Bedford
Square, London, WC1 3DP) by
Cox & Wyman Ltd, Reading

ISBN 0 340 22312 X

CONTENTS

PREFACE

To Canadians, the ill-fated Dieppe raid on August 19th, 1942, will always be remembered as a brave but costly sacrifice. Out of a total of 6,108 Canadian soldiers from the Second Division that set forth from England, 2,853 were killed, wounded or captured. Throughout that gruelling day there were many instances of great heroism and valour. Three Victoria Crosses were won, two by Canadians.

Was the raid worthwhile at such tremendous cost? Did the enemy have advance knowledge of the raid? Could the raid have been successful if a heavy bombardment had been used prior to the amphibious assault? Was it a mistake to concentrate on a frontal assault instead of flanking attacks? Was the raid mounted to appease critics in Moscow and Washington? These are questions that Canadians have asked themselves over the past three decades.

I have carried out research over a three-year period and queried more than 200 survivors — Canadian, British, French and German. Many have given access to private collections of memorabilia which include P.O.W. diaries, photographs and maps. Official Government sources, the Imperial War Museum, Departments of National Defence and Public Archives in Ottawa and London have generously assisted me.

To all, I wish to express my gratitude for assistance and encouragement. I owe particular thanks to Admiral of the Fleet, the Earl Mountbatten of Burma, who has given so freely of his time and has provided essential details of the planning and execution of the raid.

From the total mass of evidence gathered, I have endeavoured to give a true and factual account of the events. This is the story of ordinary citizens from Vancouver, Calgary and Winnipeg, from Windsor, Toronto and Montreal — men who faced up to their captors and emerged with high morale after suffering miserably during their long incarceration.

As a teacher, I firmly believe that our young people should

be made aware of the historical importance of the Dieppe raid and the endurance of these men who made it possible for future generations to enjoy the freedom of our democratic society. It would be well to remember that the freedom we enjoy today had to be earned at great cost by men such as the veterans of Dieppe.

The research and preparation of this book have been long and exhausting, but the many friendships I have made with the men of Dieppe make it all worthwhile. It has been an honour and a privilege to have known them.

John Mellor
November, 1974

CHAPTER ONE

A RUDE AWAKENING

At 3.50 a.m., August 19th, 1942, the citizens of the French port of Dieppe were roused by the sound of heavy gunfire out at sea.

Louis Larcheveque, who lived near the waterfront, switched on his bedside lamp. Should he seek shelter in the Passive Defence air-raid shelter nearby? Many times since the Germans had occupied his native land, M. Larcheveque had listened to similar outbursts, as hunter groups of British motor torpedo boats battled German E boats in the English Channel. Hastily donning a dressing-gown, he switched off the bedside light. Then he drew the heavy black-out curtains aside.

On the horizon to the east of the town, he saw high explosive shells bursting on the surface of the sea some distance away. Curving trajectories of multi-coloured tracer bullets added their own dazzling display as the battle raged back and forth, punctuated by the heavy rumble and crump of the shells. A few minutes later, the firing died down, then ceased. All that could be seen now was the flickering red and orange glow from burning hulks drifting aimlessly at the mercy of wind and tide before sinking from sight beneath the waves. Each ship died with a hiss of escaping steam as the cold waters snuffed the flames. For a few brief moments debris and ashes marked each site, then they too were gone with the strong Channel current. Sadly, M. Larcheveque returned to his bed to pray for the souls of those lost in battle.

The German troops garrisoned in the Dieppe area had also been alerted by the distant gunfire, but when the action ceased, they were ordered to stand down and return to their interrupted sleep.

Ten miles off the coast of Dieppe lay a German submarine chaser commanded by Lt. Bögel. Bögel vainly tried to warn the port authorities that he had intercepted a large number of Allied assault craft en route to Dieppe. Fortunately for the invading forces, a British shell had silenced the German ship's radio transmitter. The German Naval Headquarters at Dieppe had already informed the army authorities that the brief gun battle at sea was nothing more than a routine attack by the British on a German convoy.

The moon had set just after 2 a.m. At 2.30 a.m., an hour and 20 minutes prior to the sea battle, the German shore radar detector installation had reported the presence of a number of ships some 21 miles from the port of Dieppe. It could have spelled disaster for the forthcoming invasion. But it was dismissed as a normal sighting of a German convoy, which had sailed from the port of Boulogne and was expected to arrive at Dieppe at 5 a.m.

The Allied assault craft crept nearer to the beaches of Dieppe. The element of surprise, which had been of paramount importance to the success of the operation, had been diminished. But while the huge enemy coastal guns remained silent, success was still possible.

At 4.50 a.m. Dieppe was again disturbed from its sleep. The sounds of firing seemed to be much closer to Dieppe and from the east and west of the town. M. Larcheveque hastily dressed his brood of small children before hustling them into the air-raid shelter. At 5 a.m., while excitedly discussing the latest development with his friend, M. Milet, the caretaker of the town hall, he saw a group of German soldiers enter the courtyard of the town hall and make their way to an anti-tank gun post overlooking the main beach.

High on the West Headland behind the mediaeval castle that dominates the main beach of Dieppe, M. Raymond le Roy and his wife had also been awakened by the sounds of battle. Their house lay only a few kilometres from the beaches at Pourville, a little village on the western outskirts of the town of Dieppe. First came sounds of rifle and mortar fire, then voices, shouting in English. The invading assault troops clattered through the village streets in their steel-shod boots. M. le Roy was thrilled. The Tommies had arrived at last! Liberation was at hand!

After settling Madam le Roy in the air raid selter, he gazed out to sea. Gun flashes from British destroyers bombarded the German shore defences. Overhead the bombers and fighters of the Royal Air Force suddenly swooped at rooftop level to strafe and bomb the enemy gun positions. On all sides he heard the sounds of breaking glass, falling masonry, the high-pitched scream of the mortally wounded. Surely an attack would soon be mounted against the main beaches of Dieppe.

Dieppe's German defenders had also been awakened. At 4.58 a.m. the German general commanding the 302nd infantry division, Major-General Conrad Haase, ordered a general alert. From billets all over the town, German soldiers rushed to man the defences. Corporal Fritz Metzger took his post in the old castle on the western end of the beach where he was the ammunition corporal. Although he had been warned that an attack was imminent during the months of July and August, when the alarm went off it came as a complete surprise. The ancient castle had been converted into a modern, impregnable fortress, with heavy-calibre field guns aided by multiple machine guns and mortars protruding from every aperture and battlement. If an assault force attempted a landing on the main beach of Dieppe, the carefully positioned guns under Corporal Metzger would make life miserable for the invaders on the beach.

At 5.20 a.m., just before dawn, thousands of French civilians huddled in air-raid shelters and cellars heard the battle break out on their very doorstep, as Canadian troops stormed the main beaches of Dieppe. As the day passed, the sounds of battle reached an awesome peak. At times one could hear only the roar of howitzers, the whine and crump of mortar shells landing on the mile-long beach, the monotonous chatter of German machine guns and British Brens.

Occasionally, they heard or saw small parties of Canadians racing through the streets of Dieppe. Some reached the Church St. Remy, others occupied the cinema facing the promenade; a very few, greatly daring, raced through the town to reach the gas works and the great docks, Bassin du Canada. Most of these brave men were killed or wounded as they fought their way from house to house, street to street.

Throughout the long morning of horror and suffering, 48 civilians were killed and 102 wounded, including innocent women and children. Several homes were destroyed or severely damaged. R.A.F. planes had dropped thousands of leaflets at the start of the raid, informing the civilians that this was not the long-awaited invasion. It was merely a raid. They were asked to remain calm and not to attempt to aid the assault troops for fear of reprisals by their German masters at a later date. The BBC broadcast the same message repeatedly: 'We beg the population of all the sectors concerned to refrain from all action which might compromise its safety. France and her Allies will need you on the day of liberation.'

As the morning passed and a hot August sun beat down on the Dieppe beaches, the firing slowly died, became sporadic and intermittent, and finally at about 2 p.m., ceased entirely. The 'all clear' was sounded. As the civilians staggered from their cellars and air-raid shelters, they were appalled at the sight that greeted them. Long columns of Canadian and British prisoners, hundreds of them, were being forçe-marched by German guards to the courtyard of the Hôtel-Dieu, Dieppe's hospital. Many were sorely wounded and in urgent need of medical attention.

The French were puzzled. This was no ordinary commando-type raid. Almost 1,800 soldiers were assembled in the hospital grounds as prisoners of war; another 835 men lay dead on the shell-torn beaches. British tanks lay broken and battered on the beach and promenade. If it hadn't been a raid, then it must have been the Second Front! Why else would such a large force have been landed and at such a tremendous cost and sacrifice?

For the Canadain Second Division, this was the end of Oper-ration Jubilee, but its results, even in apparent defeat, were to have far-reaching effects.

Long after the Allies had finally landed in Normandy for the opening of the Second Front against Germany, Prime Minister Winston Churchill would say, 'Dieppe occupies a place of its own in the story of war and the grim casualty figures must not class it as a failure . . .'

CHAPTER TWO

COMBINED OPERATIONS

For Great Britain 1942 was the critical year of the war. After suffering humiliating defeat in the spring of 1940, when the British Expeditionary Force battled the German army as it swept through France, one catastrophe after another had followed in quick succession. Miraculously, the Royal Navy had managed to snatch the greatest part of the beaten British army out of France during the Dunkirk evacuation, but the army had been forced to leave most of its equipment behind. France and Belgium capitulated, and Britain was left on her own. Russia had signed a pact with Germany and had greedily swallowed up half of Poland and the Baltic States as she advanced to the West to meet Hitler's armies.

Britain, like most other democratic nations, had allowed her navy, army, and air force to be demobilised in 1918 after the First World War. Britain and her Dominions had lost over one million people, so it was not difficult for Prime Minister Baldwin and others to persuade Parliament to cut the defence budget during the post-war years. Unfortunately, the British armed forces were reduced to such an extent that their prime function was dangerously handicapped. Winston Churchill and Duff Cooper had warned repeatedly that the government policy of disarmament and appeasement would eventually lead to disaster, but their voices went unheeded.

Germany, Italy, and Japan had been preparing for war for almost ten years prior to the outbreak of war again in 1939, but Britain had dug her head in the sand. On the other side of the Atlantic, America had enforced her isolationist policy and refused to be either concerned or involved with European affairs.

After the debacle at Dunkirk, the British found themselves awaiting an invasion that seemed inevitable. But they would not accept defeat. Putting their factories on a war footing, they worked day and night to rebuild an efficient war machine.

In France the aged Marshal Pétain spoke to the French Cabinet which by that time comprised mainly collaborators with the German occupation. Thus the Cabinet collectively sneered at Churchill's belief that England could continue to fight alone after France had fallen. 'In three weeks, England will have her neck wrung like a chicken,' said Pétain's associate, Weygand. When Churchill addressed the Canadian Parliament on December 30th, 1941, he commented, 'Some chicken! Some neck!' The remark typified the indomitable will of the British people.

But that beleaguered nation reeled under successive defeats. In North Africa the British army had retreated before the powerful German and Italian forces. In the Far East Japan overran the vitally strategic British bases at Singapore and Hong Kong. In the Battle of the Atlantic in 1941, German U-boats sank millions of tons of British shipping; over 43.3 per cent of all the British and Allied shipping lost during the Second World War was sunk during 1941. Food was very scarce in Great Britain, and the future looked bleak.

On the credit side, a handful of gallant Spitfire and Hurricane pilots had defeated Germany in the air during the Battle of Britain. Russia became an ally after having been attacked by her former partner, Germany. America had finally entered the war after the Japanese attack on her naval base at Pearl Harbor. Unfortunately, America too had severely cut back her armed forces after 1918, and her contribution to the European war in terms of trained soldiers would not be felt until the autumn of 1942. Under the leadership of President Roosevelt, the huge American industrial machine was converted over to war production almost immediately after their entry into the war, and urgently needed arms and supplies at last began to flow across the Atlantic into Britain. The American people were demanding action after being forced into the war. President Roosevelt and the American leaders were under pressure and anxious to establish their prowess and fighting ability.

By the spring of 1942 Russia was in dire straits. The German Wehrmacht gradually advanced into Russia practically uncontested. Stalin demanded that a Second Front be opened immediately to relieve the pressure and divert some of the German divisions away from Russia.

On May 20th, Molotov, the Soviet Minister for Foreign Affairs, met Churchill in London and demanded to be told the date of the Second Front, when British troops would again land in Europe. Churchill tried to explain that the time was not opportune for an attack in force against Fortress Europe. Dunkirk was still fresh in his mind, and he had no desire to repeat the performance until Britain was strong enough in arms, men and assault craft for such a major amphibious operation. Molotov declared that he was not satisfied with the excuses put forward and reiterated his leader's recent threat, that unless the Allies came to the assistance of Russia immediately, he would be forced to come to terms with the Germans.

If Stalin had carried out this threat, there is no doubt that the opening of the Second Front on June 6th, 1944, would have been an almost impossible task, with corresponding losses. Hitler could have released millions of German soldiers from the Eastern Front and packed them into the Western Wall, forming an impregnable barrier guarding almost the whole of Europe.

Totally dissatisfied with Churchill's evasive answers, Molotov flew from London to Washington to seek American support. When he pressed the question of the Allies' opening of the Second Front, Roosevelt authorised him to notify Stalin that 'we' intend to open one this year — a categorical statement made without prior consultation with the British.

In London Roosevelt's statement to the Russians was considered imprudent and rash, especially when it was realised that such an offensive at this time would be a sacrifice of British lives, not American. What army and navy the Americans possessed at the outbreak of hostilities had been shipped out to the Pacific theatre of war to halt the Japanese advance.

A short time previous to Molotov's visit, the newly promoted American, General Eisenhower, had been ordered by his superior, General Marshall, Chief of the United States General Staff, to draw up plans for the opening of a Second Front against Germany. After much discussion with his planning staff, Eisenhower forwarded plans for an attack that involved an invasion directly across the English Channel into Nazi-occupied France. The plan called for the deliberate sacrifice of 10 divisions of British and Canadian troops to draw off a large portion of the German army from the Eastern Front and relieve the pressure on the Russians. The plan was enthusiastically adopted by Marshall and the General Staff. The date was, ironically, April 1st, 1942.

Marshall, accompanied by Harry Hopkins, President

Roosevelt's aide, flew to London to confront Churchill and the British Chiefs of Staff with their plan. Churchill finally consented to its adoption in the summer of 1942, although he was very dubious of its merits or feasibility. Marshall and Hopkins flew back to Washington to report to President Roosevelt the success of their meeting.

After the Americans had left London, Churchill's advisers, plus the General Staff, informed him that the type of attack promoted by the Americans against a heavily fortified French coast was dangerous to the point of being irresponsible, and pressed their leader to withdraw his support from the plan at once. General Sir Alan Brooke, Chief of the Imperial General Staff, declared that such an attack against Fortress Europe at this time could only end in death, capture, or ignominious re-embarkation of the forces engaged. He did not believe that it would relieve the pressure on the Russian Front, because there were already 25 German divisions stationed in France and the Low Countries to repel such an invasion. He further pointed out that even if Great Britain had sufficient landing craft and airplanes for such an assault (which she had not), only 10 British divisions and two American divisions would be available to operate in Europe against 25 German divisions.

Churchill, swayed by the powerful influences surrounding him, agreed to cancel the Second Front proposed for 1942 and on May 28th sent Lord Louis Mountbatten, the British Chief of Combined Operations, to Washington to persuade the Americans that such an operation at this stage of the war could only lead to disaster. As an alternative, he proposed a landing later in the year by Anglo-American forces in French North Africa. Churchill's instructions to Mountbatten authorised him to inform the Americans that the British would consent to mounting a Second Front in 1942 only if there was imminent danger of Russian resistance crumbling. If such a situation were to develop, the attack across the Channel would be undertaken to divert German divisions to the West Wall, away from the sorely pressed Russians. Even though such an attack at this time was considered suicidal by the British, it could be looked upon as a worthwhile sacrifice to keep Russia in the war.

This British decision not to enter into a Second Front in 1942 after all was, of course, an embarrassment to Roosevelt. Anglo-American differences of opinion on the future conduct of the war reached grave proportions. Eventually, the American

General Staff threatened to withdraw entirely from the European theatre of war and leave the British to fight alone, as indeed they had done for the previous two years. At this point, President Roosevelt interceded to prevent such a drastic move, although he was far from satisfied with the British decision. Finally on July 24th, he informed Churchill that he now accepted the British point of view and agreed that Europe was not to be invaded by a Second Front until 1943 or 1944. At the same time, he agreed to participate in the proposed Anglo-American invasion of North Africa later in the year.

After the defeated British Army had been brought back from Dunkirk, the Chiefs of Staff began to prepare for an invasion that seemed imminent. All thoughts of attack were subordinated to the more immediate problem of defence. Eventually an amphibious assault would have to be made on Hitler's Fortress Europe if the Axis powers were to be defeated, but not yet. Until then, they must build up men and arms.

In the meantime, if a continuing offensive was to be mounted against the enemy, it had to be by means of saturation bombing by R.A.F. Bomber Command in an attempt to paralyse the industrial potential on which Germany depended. Churchill decided to add a little spice to this limited offensive by forming a new Combined Operations Division to prepare raids of limited scope on the coast of occupied Europe. Under the command of Admiral Sir Roger Keyes, V.C., the nucleus of an amphibious raiding force was formed. All the men taking part had volunteered for hazardous duties, and on Churchill's suggestion they were named 'commandos', after the South African Boers who had operated so successfully against the British with similar raiding parties behind the British lines.

Unfortunately, the Chiefs of Staff of the Navy, Army, and Air Force viewed the formation of the new Combined Operations group not only as an abrogation of their own responsibilities, but also as a shameful waste of men and war materials that could be more gainfully employed in their own services. Truthfully, they were jealous of the popularity of the new group, especially after they had captured the imagination of a British public who had become accustomed to successive defeats during the course of the war.

Realising that a future amphibious landing in Europe by many thousands of men would involve a great deal of specialised training and knowledge, Churchill decided that Combined

Operations should be allowed to expand to enable it to mount raids of greater scope and ferocity if this special knowledge was to be obtained by experience. Not since the First World War at Gallipoli had Britain been involved in any large offensive, amphibious operations. If she wanted to avoid a second, and possibly fatal, Dunkirk, then all the potential problems had to be discovered prior to the invasion. Special assault landing craft and ships must be designed and built; commando training centres must be set up to inform men of the special problems inherent in such an operation; many more commando raids must be made to secure experience.

The task of building such an organisation was indeed formidable and required the appointment of a particular breed of commander. Admiral Keyes, although enthusiastic and full of the offensive spirit, was unfortunately an old man. The exacting qualities necessary for the unique position had to be sought in a younger man — a man with a propensity for organisation and the talent to develop the special tools of war required for amphibious assault on a huge scale.

Churchill appointed Lord Louis Mountbatten, the King's cousin, 41 years old, to the post. It was a wise choice. Mountbatten enjoyed great popularity in the Royal Navy and also with the British people. A career officer in the Royal Navy, he had captained H.M.S. *Kelly*, which had recently been sunk off Crete in the Mediterranean. Mountbatten and the helpless survivors had been machine-gunned by the Luftwaffe as they struggled to keep their heads above water. He possessed that rare combination of authority and responsibility with grace and humility, qualities that greatly appealed to the American Chiefs of Staff.

Reluctantly, Mountbatten accepted the post of Combined Operations. Under his guiding hand, Combined Operations grew and matured. Many of its aging staff members were replaced by younger officers from all three services — men who possessed, above all, the offensive spirit and an aptitude for planning daring operations against the enemy. Lord Louis encouraged their boldness and formulated a team spirit to combine the best brains and inventiveness in planning these forays by commando units.

Combined Operations had just celebrated a brilliantly successful operation against the French port of St. Nazaire on March 28th, 1942. The British commandos had followed a daring plan to make a surprise attack from the sea and blow up the lock-gates of the huge Normandy dock, the largest in the world.

The mighty German battleship *Tirpitz* required this dock to operate against British convoys in the North Atlantic. After its destruction, she was forced to operate from Norwegian fiords in the far north. Flushed with success, the planners were confident that similar raids against other ports would also succeed.

Coincidentally, while the Americans were trying to persuade Churchill to open up a Second Front in Europe, a plan was afoot for a raid against Dieppe in northern France. The plan was conceived by Captain John Hughes-Hallett, R.N., who had been appointed Naval Adviser to Combined Operations Head-quarters at the end of 1941. Quickly recognised as a brilliant and daring planner, he had acted as chairman of the planning committee which had executed the St. Nazaire operation. His presence on the planning committee acted as a stabilising influence over some of the more radical members, whose schemes sometimes bordered on the foolhardy.

The original plan for the raid on Dieppe had a great deal of merit. After the bitter lessons learned at great cost during the Dunkirk evacuation, air cover was deemed vital to the success of the operation. The port of Dieppe was selected after much deliberation. Only 65 miles from the British port of Newhaven, it was near enough for air cover to be supplied on a continuous basis from airfields in the south of England and to allow for the short sea passage to be made under cover of the brief summer darkness. (At this stage of the war, fighter planes had a very limited range and had not yet been fitted out with disposable fuel tanks.)

The port had a well-equipped harbour, complete with dock-side cranes and railway facilities, useful in a logistic sense to a military landing force. With the unpredictable Channel weather, a sheltered harbour was a must. A study of weather statistics had revealed that the planners could not rely on more than four successive days of calm weather on this coast.

The town of Dieppe lies within a long line of chalk cliffs very similar to those at Dover. Control of the heights at either side of the low-lying town and harbour made defence an easy task. It was known that the enemy had positioned strong gun batteries at Berneval to the east and Varengeville to the west of the town. In addition, numerous other strongpoints had been established on the east and west headlands; an amphibious landing on the main beaches would be extremely difficult, if not impossible.

The main beach of Dieppe is crescent-shaped and forms a shallow bay over a mile long. On the eastern end, a long harbour mole stretches out to sea. Along this mole, concrete pillboxes had been built to give cross-fire to the beaches. On the jetty, an old French Renault tank, Model R17-18, had been concreted into the quayside. This tank was to cause many casualties on the main beaches. All along the promenade, the enemy defenders had mounted triple rolls of dannert wire along the top of the sea wall and half-way up the beach. Hidden during the hours of darkness, the endless maze of barbed wire was designed to trap the unwary and allow the defenders to zero in with machine guns and mortar fire.

The beach was covered with round flint pebbles, two to six inches in diameter, providing a shifting, treacherous footing to men and vehicles alike. Rising steeply from the sea, the beach had a one in 30 gradient, rising to less than one in 10 under the concrete sea wall, which in places was seven to 10 feet above the beach. In several places Atlantic gales had washed pebbles up against the sea wall, so that it was possible to stand on the beach and look over the wall. An intelligent enemy had realised the danger at these low-lying points and had raised the dannert wire accordingly. All along the beach, heavy timber groynes ran out every 150 yards at right angles to the sea wall to prevent erosion from the sea. Every boarding house and hotel along the promenade beyond the sea wall had been heavily fortified with machine guns, anti-tank weapons, and mortars. Trenches and grenade pits had been dug in criss-cross fashion and led from the buildings along the sea-front to enable the defenders to move from point to point in comparative safety.

Every street leading into the town from the promenade had been effectively blocked by concrete anti-tank barriers mounted in staggered fashion; the openings between them were smothered with rolls of barbed wire to discourage infantry attacks.

Along the sea wall, forward observation officers had been installed in low concrete shelters, which were provided with long, narrow observation slits. Through these they could observe every movement along the beach and direct the fall of shell and mortar bombs. The beach had been divided into a huge checkerboard and coded. Long practice enabled the officers to pinpoint the firing area. Wooden posts had been planted at various intervals to coincide with the coded master plan.

In several places the cliffs at each end of the beach had been hollowed out to accommodate large-calibre guns, which were designed to roll back out of sight of aircraft during the daylight hours. (The air reconnaissance carried out prior to the raid was not of top standard. Although the battle maps showed numerous pillboxes along the Dieppe beach, there was no indication of their armour or of the presence of beach defences or anti-tank guns which had been mounted at each end of the beach Casino.)

Under orders issued on June 9th, the German defences in the area were organised as follows. The Berneval battery on the right formed an independent strongpoint. Dieppe itself was designated a 'defended area', subdivided into three sectors: Dieppe East, including Puys; Dieppe South; and Dieppe West, including the eastern portion of Pourville and the heights overlooking it. The Varengeville battery constituted another strongpoint, and in the Quiberville area was a 'resistance nest'. The whole Dieppe defended area was girded on the land side with a continuous barbed-wire obstacle. Puys and the heights east of Pourville were inside it, but Pourville itself lay outside. A good many pillboxes and other strongpoints had been completed by the time the raid took place.

The sector was very strong in artillery. There were three coastal batteries in the area attacked — the Varengeville battery with six 15-centimetre guns, the Berneval battery with three 17-centimetre and four 105-millimetre guns, and one near Arques-la-Bataille with four 15-centimetre howitzers. A fourth battery at Mesnil-Val, west of Le Tréport, had four 15-centimetre guns that could fire on the Berneval area. There were also sixteen 10-centimetre field howitzers divided among four battery positions, two on either side of Dieppe and all but one inside the wire barrier. In addition, eight French 75-millimetre guns were positioned on the front for beach defence. There were also a number of anti-aircraft guns in the Dieppe area.

All things considered, circumstances were not favourable to the success of a major raid on Dieppe. It is interesting to note, however, that in one of the early orders issued on the subject of defence of the Dieppe area on April 25th, 1941, the German command believed that the ports of Dieppe and Le Tréport would not be attacked directly by the enemy, but would instead be assailed by means of landing attempts at nearby points. After the raid, the Germans expressed great surprise that an assault had been attempted on the port of Dieppe by means of a frontal attack. Against such a heavy concentration of guns, the attack was analogous to the Charge of the Light Brigade.

The Germans correctly forecast that if a landing were to take place, it would probably be during the few days in July or August when nautical twilight (the hour prior to the dawn) would coincide with high-tide conditions. The invading force would not then have to cross a large expanse of open beach under fire. In addition, the faint light of nautical twilight would assist the assault troops while providing vague and hazy targets for the defenders' guns.

Accordingly, the German defenders were under a state of red alert during these very important days of the month. The day prior to the raid, the divisional command had ordered Major-General Conrad Haase to relax the alert because the danger period was considered to be over for the month. Entirely on his own initiative, he decided to prolong the alert for one extra day — the day of the raid!

CHAPTER THREE

OPERATION RUTTER

On the advice of Lord Mountbatten and Hughes-Hallett, the original Combined Operations plan avoided a frontal assault. A battalion of infantry backed by a battalion of the new Churchill Mark I tanks would land at Quiberville, six miles west of Dieppe, where the beach appeared suitable for an amphibious landing. Once ashore, they would go flat out and overrun the heights just west of Dieppe. Whoever commanded the headlands to the east and west of Dieppe controlled the movement of the landing force on the main beaches.

Two battalions of infantry would land at the village of Pourville, and another two battalions at Puys. Once ashore, they were to overrun the heights just east of Dieppe and capture the howitzer gun batteries there. The troops landed at Puys and Pourville would then advance into the outskirts of Dieppe in a hooking movement and meet up with the tanks that had landed at Quiberville. Together they would overcome all enemy resistance in Dieppe itself before destroying military installations and re-embarking from the main beaches under the protection of the Royal Air Force. Two additional battalions were to remain afloat under the land commander's control as a floating reserve to be used if and when necessary.

The original plan also called for British paratroopers and glider-borne troops to drop on the massive gun batteries at Berneval and Varengeville to immobilise the heavy coastal gun batteries. Unless these guns were put out of action initially, they could sink any or all of the ships in the invasion fleet. Heavy bomber attacks on the town and aerodrome would soften up the defences and force the enemy to keep his head down during the first precious minutes necessary for the forward assault troops to land on the beaches. These bomb attacks were to cease as soon as the troops rushed up the beaches, but fighter aircraft in great numbers were to fly at zero level to strafe the enemy, knock out gun positions, and supply a protective smoke screen. The raid was to be known as Operation Rutter.

At this stage of the planning, Lord Mountbatten submitted the scheme to his fellow members of the Chiefs of Staff Committee. They agreed that such an operation was a vital prerequisite to a major Second Front operation. Churchill enthusiastically gave his approval in principle for the raid. But the Chief of the Imperial General Staff, General Sir Alan Brooke, insisted that the Land Force planning be done under the direction of the Home Forces Command, as the number of troops involved was so much greater than for a normal commando raid. Originally, the plan also called for a division of Royal Marines, but the Commander of the Home Forces, General Paget, selected South East Command for the job, because the force would be setting forth from ports in that sector.

The man in charge of South East Command was Lt. Gen. Bernard Montgomery, who now assumed authority and responsibility for the raid. His first task was to select a division within his command to carry it out. It was not an easy task. Many of the best British regiments were serving in the North African campaign. But the Canadian 2nd Division was stationed in south-east England, and thus came directly under Montgomery's command.

The day following his appointment as Army Commander of Operation Rutter, Montgomery sent for Lt. Gen. H. D. G. Crerar, GOC 1st Canadian Army Corps, and informed him that a reconnaissance in force against the enemy was being planned and that, in his opinion, the plan was well founded. Would his Canadians like the job? Crerar accepted the offer with alacrity. His troops had been chafing at the bit for a long time. When they had first arrived in England in 1940, they had been given the responsibility of defending Britain against an imminent invasion; now, after two years of Home Guard duties, they had become bored and undisciplined.

Next Montgomery approached General McNaughton, the Canadian Army Commander in Britain, to seek official Canadian approval for the use of Canadian troops in the forthcoming operation. General McNaughton immediately consented, subject to the approval of the War Committee of the Canadian Cabinet in Ottawa.

The way was now clear, and General McNaughton formally ordered Crerar to make one infantry division, a tank battalion, and various ancillary units such as signals, engineers and field ambulance units from the 1st Canadian Corps available for the forthcoming Operation Rutter. Crerar had already selected the Canadian Second Division for the task and now issued orders for them to move to the Isle of Wight off the south coast of England to undergo an intensive programme of amphibious assault and commando training.

Commanding the Canadian 2nd Division was Major-General John Hamilton Roberts, an experienced, respected soldier. He had been a professional soldier ever since World War I, when he had been awarded the Military Cross for bravery while serving with the Royal Canadian Horse Artillery. He has best been described as 'steady and rocklike'. Chief Operations Officer of the Second Division under the command of Roberts was Lt. Col. Churchill Mann. At 36 years of age, he was acknowledged throughout the Canadian army as a brilliant staff officer whose forte was operational planning. On his shoulders rested the responsibility for the detailed planning for the operation in accordance with the plan submitted by Combined Operations.

The forces selected for Operation Rutter were regiments from the Prairies, Ontario and Quebec. The Royal Regiment of Canada commanded by Colonel Hedley Basher, the Royal Hamilton Light Infantry Regiment commanded by Lt. Col. Bob Labatt, and the Essex Scottish Regiment commanded by Lt. Col. Fred Jasperson were all Ontario regiments. From Quebec, the Regiment Fusiliers de Mont Royal was commanded by Lt. Col. Dollard Menard and was assisted by some units of the Black Watch from Montreal. From the West came the Cameron Highlanders of Canada from Winnipeg commanded by Lt. Col. Alfred Gostling, the South Saskatchewan Regiment commanded by Lt. Col. Cec Merritt, and the Calgary Tank Regiment commanded by Lt. Col. Johnny Andrews.

For the Dieppe operation, the following regiments and ancillary units were added to the force: one unit of the 1st Army Tank Brigade, the Toronto Scottish Machine Gun Regiment commanded by Lt. Col. G. S. Gostling, some Royal Canadian Artillery units plus three companies of the Royal Canadian Engineers commanded by Major B. Sucharov, the Provost Corps, the 11th Field Ambulance Brigade from Guelph, Ontario, the Canadian Corps of Signals, plus the headquarters and administrative staffs and representatives from Combined Operations Headquarters.

All Canadian Land Forces were commanded by two

Brigadiers — Bill Lett of Vancouver and Bill Southam of Toronto, with the over-all command assumed by Major-General 'Ham' Roberts.

Montgomery objected to the Combined Operations Plan on the grounds that Quiberville, where the tanks were to land in a flanking movement, was six miles from Dieppe and separated from it by two small rivers. He feared that if the enemy blew the bridges over these rivers, the tanks would be unable to reach their objectives in the town of Dieppe. He also objected to the planned two-pronged attack from the flanks. He felt that by the time the tanks had travelled the considerable distance from Quiberville to Dieppe, the enemy would have had ample time to move in their own Panzer group from outside Dieppe.

Montgomery now decided to change drastically the original plan and allow for the main attack to take place on the main beaches against the formidable array of armour and virtually impregnable defences. This decision was to have far-reaching effects on the success of the operation. Lord Mountbatten and Hughes-Hallett argued forcibly for a return to the flanking attacks, but to no avail. The tanks would land simultaneously with the infantry on the main beaches.

Another factor in the decision: British Intelligence had reported that the bridges over the Scie and Saane were not strong enough to support the weight of a Churchill tank. Such was not the case. Furthermore, at their deepest point, the rivers near the bridges were no more than 3 feet deep — the tanks could easily have forded them.

On April 25th Lord Mountbatten called a meeting to thrash out the advantages and disadvantages of the two plans. Montgomery and his staff insisted on retaining the frontal assault, and maintained that a heavy bombing attack on the forward defences immediately preceding the initial touchdown, followed by low-flying strafing attacks, would counterbalance the risks of a frontal attack.

The final authority for formulating plans for the raid had been delegated to the Home Forces Command and General Montgomery. Therefore, Lord Mountbatten and his advisers felt that they had no choice but to yield to the demand for a frontal assault. Perhaps at this point the Combined Operations group should have remained adamant and maintained that such a frontal assault was suicidal in nature. But if they had done so, the resulting stalemate could have cancelled the raid in its entirety. It was already late in the year, and little time remained to plan for another reconnaissance in force elsewhere. Without such a preliminary assault, all authorities were agreed that a major invasion to open a Second Front in 1943 would most likely be doomed. With a heavy bombing assault of maximum intensity just prior to touchdown, the assault might still succeed. The Naval Force Commander was to be Rear-Admiral Baillie-Grohman; Air Vice-Marshal T. Leigh-Mallory was appointed Air Force Commander and the Land Force Commander was General Roberts. Three men with an awesome responsibility — the lives of over 10,000 sailors, soldiers, and airmen.

CHAPTER FOUR

THE TRAINING PROGRAMME

The Isle of Wight, off the south coast of England, was the ideal site for the training ground for the forthcoming operation. Foremost of its advantages was its isolation; security was easily enforced. The island provided natural facilities for amphibious training, and its topography was similar to that of Dieppe. And so it was that early in May Roberts ordered all of the regiments involved to pack up their comfortable billets in Sussex and move at once to the island for 'exercises'.

Combined Operations and the Royal Navy supplied the special knowledge, assault craft, and naval crews to train the men for the task ahead. Practice embarkations, landings, and re-embarkations were made from the sea in all types of weather, under all manner of adverse conditions. Forced marches, assault courses under fire, and weapon training were repeated time and time again until the men were hardened and disciplined. Long days and nights of strenuous exercise and activity honed mind and body. Impatient to be let loose against the enemy, they watched their company commanders for some sign or inkling that they would soon be going into action. They had not been informed of the target but guessed with the intuition of professional soldiers that this was going to be a special mission.

Several Canadian units were selected for commando training. The men were delighted to find that the traditional parade-ground drill had been abandoned in favour of the modern method of training soldiers for close-in fighting. The men of the Royal Regiment, one of the selected commando training units, crawled on their bellies under barbed-wire entanglements with snipers firing live ammunition over their heads as a constant dreadful reminder to keep their heads down. They learned to swing across 12-foot ditches from over-hanging ropes (from which they had to jump without dropping their rifles), run, crawl, make mad, yelling bayonet charges against sandbags and life-sized dummies, climb a sheer cliff with the aid of a rope and telescopic tubular ladders, and then cross a river wearing full kit and ammunition. They practised with pistols, Sten, and Bren guns. They were taught to use a gun as a pointing finger – to fire from the hip, automatically and instinctively, without taking the valuable time to line up the target in the gun sights.

Perhaps the most valuable training was received from British commando instructors in the art of hand-to-hand combat. These rugged non-commissioned officers, often of diminutive size and weight, taught the men a dozen ways and more to kill a man with either a judo chop or a well-placed kick to tender parts.

Major Brian McCool of the Royals was selected for special training as beachmaster. As head of the military landing group, he would set up his headquarters on the main beaches. Deputy beachmasters on each flank, on Blue (Puys) and Green (Pourville) Beaches, would work directly under his command. In this special task he was to be assisted by Commander Jeff Lambert of the Royal Navy. As a team, they would signal the various boats to approach the beaches, unload their cargoes of men, ammunition, and supplies, reload with wounded and prisoners, and leave as soon as possible to make room for other boats. A powerful man, tall and heavily built, genial in nature but fierce in combat, McCool was directed to a commando training base in Scotland. He and a specially selected band of over 200 Canadian soldiers engaged in war manoeuvres with a battalion of the Royal Marine Commandos, who were also detailed for the Dieppe operation. Commanding Officer of the Royal Marines was Lt. Col. J. P. (Tigger) Phillips, a man who was greatly respected by his men and who had already seen much action.

On the Isle of Wight, training proceeded steadily. The Calgary Tank Regiment under Lt. Col. Johnny Andrews practised sea landings from specially designed tank landing craft. Ed Bennett from Woodstock, Ontario, was appointed Troop Commander of a troop of Calgary tanks named *Beefy, Bellicose,* and *Bloody.*

The Intelligence Unit was kept busy learning German orders of battle, uniforms, and insignia. Air reconnaissance photographs were studied in great detail, then precise mock-ups were built of the town and cliffs of Dieppe. Without the assistance of the engineers, the tanks would not even get off the beach. It was decided, therefore, that the engineers would sail on the tank landing craft and land with the tanks. The Royal Canadian Engineers were taught how to prepare and set demolition charges, to blow sea walls, tunnels, bridges, and tank traps. Bangalore torpedoes were included in the training of the sappers. Some were to be used for blowing up large sections of barbed wire on the beach. Others, 60 feet long and three inches in diameter, were to be used to blow up minefields; when coupled together they formed one long length of 180 feet, which could be pushed into a minefield by a tank. After detonation, the path should be clear for infantrymen to cross in safety.

A large portion of the engineers' special training was done in conjunction with the navy. Manoeuvres were performed in which the men were carried out to sea in 'parent' ships, so called because they carried in place of normal lifeboats a number of 'offspring', called assault landing craft. These were barge-shaped steel boats with blunt bows that dropped down on to the beach for the men to disembark. Powered by two Rolls-Royce engines, each would carry 35 men and a crew of three. On signal, often in total darkness, the men would pile into the boats, which would then be lowered into the water to go speeding toward the beaches until the bows grounded in the shallows off-shore. Many times when the men rushed across the dropped ramp, they would plunge into sea water, waist- or even neck-high, then wade in with weapons held high and dry above their heads to attack the 'enemy'.

Serving with the Royal Navy during the training period was a small Canadian naval team of 15 officers and 55 men. Late in 1941, Canadian naval authorities in Ottawa had formed a nucleus of a Canadian Assault Force under the command of Lt. R. F. McRae, R.C.N.V.R. of Toronto, who had transferred to the special force because he was bored with the routine task of sweeping mines from the sea lanes.

Roy Membury of Waterloo, who served under McRae, remembers the assault training programme with a shudder even after so many years. In total darkness without even the benefit of navigation lights, they had to learn how to form up into flotillas prior to making practice runs into strange beaches. Collisions were frequent, and it was only after great repetition that they managed any semblance of order.

CHAPTER FIVE

A COSTLY DECISION

Training on the Isle of Wight continued throughout the month of May. Early in June Mountbatten was sent to Washington as Churchill's special envoy to confer with President Roosevelt and the American Chiefs of Staff. He must convince the Americans that a major Second Front assault on Fortress Europe by the British during the summer of 1942 was not possible with the limited resources at hand. He was to persuade them to join the British in an assault on French North Africa later in the year.

During his absence, an additional meeting of the Force Commanders was held at Combined Operations Headquarters to finalise the details of the proposed raid on Dieppe. At the meeting, chaired by General Montgomery, it was decided to forgo the maximum-intensity bombing just prior to the raid.

It is difficult for anyone who eventually landed at Dieppe to understand the reasoning behind this catastrophic decision. The one remaining chance for success was neatly excised from the original plan. The decision was based on the argument that bombing would clutter the streets with debris, which would impede the movement of the tanks. Churchill Mann was present at this meeting, as indeed he was at all meetings pertaining to the Dieppe operation. Long after the raid was over he stated that the main reason for eliminating the bombing was political. Mr. Churchill was hoping to persuade the French to hand over their large navy before Hitler could take it, to be used for the duration of the war as an integral part of the Royal Navy. He feared that a heavy preliminary bombing would result in heavy civilian casualties which might alienate the Vichy French government and thus lose the use of their navy. Military historians disagree with Churchill on this point. Enmity between the Vichy French and the British was so bitter that French leaders such as Laval, Darlan, and Pétain would have scuttled the entire fleet rather than hand it over to the British.

Churchill Mann recalled that during the meeting General

Roberts was asked what his reaction would be if, after he had sailed beyond the half-way mark to Dieppe, he learned that the heavy bombers that were to support the landings had been cancelled due to fog or other reasons. Would he return to England or would he sail on? General Roberts did not hesitate. He was a soldier and would do his duty — sail on!

It was then recorded in the minutes that the Military Force Commander did *not* require the use of heavy bombers in support of the landings.

It appears that several factors were responsible for the decision to eliminate the heavy bombing before the actual raid. Even if political and military reasons had favoured the bombing, it is doubtful the operation would have received any co-operation from Bomber Command. Air Vice-Marshal Leigh-Mallory reported to the same meeting that he had requested 300 bombers from Air Marshal Harris, Chief of Bomber Command, for an attack on Dieppe on June 20th, one day prior to the raid, and for support of the landings the next day. 'Bomber' Harris had refused his request as a senseless interference with his night bombing programme on Germany. He termed the Dieppe raid a 'useless side-show'.

After the sad debacle of the Dardanelles campaign by British and Dominion troops in 1915, how any intelligent group of senior military and air force commanders could arbitrarily decide to eliminate the preliminary softening-up process of heavy bombardment will always remain a mystery. In his memoirs, General Montgomery writes, 'I should not myself have agreed with these changes. The demoralisation of the enemy defences by preliminary bombing was essential just before the troops touched down on the beaches.' Did Montgomery write this passage after so many years that his memory played him false? Far from disagreeing with the change in plan, he actually chaired the meeting, and according to Mountbatten, it is not on record in the minutes that he demurred.

Shortly after this meeting, General Montgomery ceased to be responsible for the raid and was posted to the British Eighth Army in North Africa. His historic victory came some time later at the Battle of El Alamein when Rommel's army was routed by the Eighth Army. Prior to commencing the assault, General Montgomery mounted hundreds of gun batteries to pound the enemy with the heaviest artillery barrage in history. The enemy was well and truly softened-up!

When Lord Mountbatten returned from his Washington visit, he learned to his consternation that the heavy bombing had been eliminated. He immediately contacted General Sir Alan Brooke to protest against this arbitrary decision. But General Brooke insisted that the Force Commanders be allowed to have their way.

In desperation Mountbatten approached the First Sea Lord, Sir Dudley Pound, to supply either a battleship or heavy cruiser to provide a frontal bombardment in support of the infantry, but he categorically refused.

'Battleships by daylight off the French coast! You must be mad, Dickie.'

Mountbatten replied quietly, 'Sir, when the Second Front Invasion comes, all your available battleships and cruisers will be used.'

The Combined Operations Plan now bore little resemblance to the original one. The flanking pincer movements by tanks and infantry had been eliminated in favour of a suicidal frontal attack in the face of heavy defences. True, there would still be landings on the flanks, but they would not be assisted by tanks, and the main body of troops would land directly in front of the town of Dieppe. Mountbatten and Hughes-Hallett had agreed to the frontal attack only under protest and only because a preliminary heavy bombing had been promised to destroy the defences and demoralise the defenders. Now that the bombing had been eliminated, the revised plan invited disaster on a large scale. At this point, military historians believe that the operation should have been abandoned as a hopeless task.

Unfortunately, Churchill had stated that he intended to proceed with the raid despite all objections. And he had good reason. At this stage of the war, he and Mountbatten were in a dilemma. It was now too late in the year to plan another reconnaissance in force elsewhere. If a Second Front Invasion was to be successful the following year, a preliminary reconnaissance in force was a vital prerequisite. Only from such an expedition would they gain the necessary experience and knowledge to mount a full-scale invasion. It was imperative to make a major landing of heavy tanks on an enemy shore to test their fighting qualities after immersion in the sea. A suitable port was a must. They had to know how difficult it would be for an amphibious force to seize a heavily defended port.

Apart from the slender cover provided by the 4-in. guns of

the eight Hunt class destoyers, the only additional protection for the troops storming the beach would be the fire protection provided by the Toronto Scottish Machine Gun Regiment. Heavy-calibre Vickers machine guns were to be mounted in the bows of the landing craft.

The raid was planned for June 21st, midsummer's day. On the night of June 11th a full dress rehearsal took place off the coast of Dorset. It was a complete shambles. The landing craft failed to beach at the correct points; one battalion was landed 22 miles from its target! The tanks were landed an hour later than the infantry; many of the boats broached-to, and in some cases the infantry were unloaded into deep water by precipitous lowering of the ramp.

Lord Mountbatten wisely insisted that another full dress rehearsal be held on June 23rd at West Bay and Bridport in Dorset, where the topography closely resembled that of Dieppe. The raid was now postponed until the first week in July.

About this time, the Naval Force Commander, Baillie-Grohman, left for another appointment. Mountbatten promoted Captain John Hughes-Hallett to the position.

The second rehearsal was better executed and Mountbatten gave his permission for the raid to proceed on one of the new dates that would provide the tide, weather, dawn, and moon conditions considered essential for a successful operation. The troops were embarked on ships, and landing craft gathered in the ports of Newhaven, Portsmouth, Southampton, Shoreham, and Yarmouth. All officers were briefed and Dieppe named as the objective.

On June 30th Churchill held a last-minute conference at 10 Downing Street to consider the forthcoming Dieppe operation. When asked if he could guarantee success, Mountbatten replied negatively. How could he? General Brooke then quickly reminded Churchill that any future Second Front Invasion must depend upon a preliminary operation such as Dieppe on a divisional scale. Churchill concurred. The raid was on!

On July 3rd all personnel taking part in the raid were briefed, and Mountbatten and Roberts visited every ship in the fleet to speak to the men. The Royal Regiment embarked at Yarmouth at the western end of the Isle of Wight. H.M.S. *Queen Astrid*, an infantry landing ship, had been detailed to carry the Royals and the Black Watch to Blue Beach at Puys with her sister ship H.M.S. *Queen Emma.* Before the war they had been busily employed on the Dover-Ostend run as passenger ferry boats. They were now fitted with 4-in. guns forward and aft and were capable of a maximum speed of 21½ knots. When refitted as infantry landing ships, they had been provided with eight infantry landing craft, hoisted and lowered by means of Wellin davits. Each landing craft carried a fully armed troop of infantry, plus a coxswain and three naval ratings with an R.N.V.R. sub-lieutenant in command. Thus, in the first wave, 200 troops could be landed from each landing ship.

Aboard every ship of the fleet, wild enthusiasm reigned. This was what they had been training for so assiduously these many months. At last they could break the monotony. How would they have reacted had they been briefed on the long, sad story of the changes in the plan and the elimination of the vitally necessary frontal bombardment?

The following day, July 4th, adverse weather conditions brought a further postponement to the last possible date in the month of July — the 8th, when weather and tide conditions would again be suitable.

Behind the scenes, the planners were furious at this latest delay. Although the sea conditions were considered favourable for an amphibious assault, cloud conditions over the Dieppe area were deemed unsatisfactory for a parachute assault on the main gun batteries of Berneval and Varengeville. Major-General Frederick Browning, commander of the first Airborne Division, refused to commit his men to the operation under what he termed dubious weather conditions. Thus despite Mountbatten's vehement protestations, the operation had to be postponed.

At the same time, Intelligence reported that the enemy had moved No. 10 Panzer (tank) Division to Amiens, only eight hours marching time from Dieppe. The plan was therefore modified to a one-tide basis, with re-embarkation set for 1100 hours, six hours after touchdown. The original plan had called for the troops to stay ashore for 15 hours.

The same evening a German reconnaissance plane dropped two bombs on two of the infantry landing ships. The *Astrid* was fortunate; the bomb crashed right through the ship without exploding. The *Josephine Charlotte* was not so lucky. A bomb exploded in the crew's quarters killing 17 sailors. Although the men were now convinced that the surprise element had been lost, they were still eager to see action. The waiting was nerve-wracking.

On the chosen day, July 8th, the weather reports were again unsuitable, and during the forenoon it was officially announced that the raid had been cancelled. All troops were returned to the mainland, and one third of each unit was sent on leave.

Plans for the raid were abandoned, and little thought was given to security. Why worry about security now that the show was off? All across south-east England, the men, proud to have been chosen to mount the first major assault against Fortress Europe, openly bragged to sweethearts, wives, and any interested listeners in the pubs over a pint of beer. The men cannot be blamed. What possible harm could there be in speaking about a raid that had been cancelled?

In actual fact, the enemy had been aware of an impending invasion for some time. The day following the bombing of the *Astrid* and *Josephine Charlotte* in the Solent by a German reconnaissance plane, Hitler issued a directive that reflected his acute concern for the Western coast defence. It spoke of the necessity for Britain to stage a large-scale invasion with the object of opening a Second Front to relieve the pressure on the Russians. He referred to the heavy concentration of ferrying vessels along the south-east coast of England and also to numerous reports from agents concerning impending enemy landings. Among these reports was one from a Portuguese sailor who gave a detailed report of the invasion fleet concentrated in the ports of south-east England.

CHAPTER SIX

THE RESURRECTION

The day Operation Rutter was cancelled, Lt. Col. Mann was promoted to Brigadier and posted to 1st Canadian Army Corps Headquarters to work directly under Lt. Gen. Harry Crerar. The next day Crerar told him that the Dieppe raid was on again and that his old commander, Major-General Ham Roberts, had requested that he be returned to his staff for the duration of the raid. He was to be the Deputy Military Commander. Churchill Mann left the next day for Fort Southwick, just north of Portsmouth, to rejoin the Canadian 2nd Division and plan the new operation. The new date set for the raid was August 19, and the name of the operation was now changed to Operation Jubilee to confuse the Germans in case there had been a security leak.

Why had the raid been resurrected? There was still immense political pressure for Combined Operations to organise another reconnaisance in strength against Fortress Europe. People in Britain were demanding action at once to relieve the pressure on the Russians. A few months before the cancellation of Operation Rutter, a pro-communist demonstration on March 29th in Trafalgar Square demanded the immediate opening of a Second Front. Even the ultra-conservative newspaper, the *Daily Express*, had demanded similar action.

Stalin too was demanding immediate action. After the unfortunate demise of Operation Rutter, Churchill had nothing left with which to placate either the Russians, the British, or the Americans. Without a raid of division strength to test the enemy defences, a major invasion in 1943 was out of the question. The final victory would be delayed by at least another year; if the Russians did not manage to hold out until then, it was doubtful if the Allies could achieve final victory.

At Combined Operations Headquarters a bitter debate followed the cancellation. The airborne command was criticised severely for refusing to allow their troops to be dropped. Hughes-Hallett pointed out that it was far too late in the year to commence planning for another raid in force. Why not re-enact the Dieppe raid? The Canadians had been trained to the hilt in their specific tasks; no further training would be required, and they could easily be reassembled and re-embarked aboard the assault craft within a matter of days.

To re-enact the raid on Dieppe after it had been cancelled, and thousands of men on leave had blown security, was a bold move. But provided that the enemy had been informed that the raid had been cancelled, there was the possibility that it might well succeed by its sheer daring. But what if the enemy had heard of the proposed raid but not of its cancellation?

Roberts, who was present at this meeting, agreed to consider the proposal in the light of a possible breach of security, and the same day gave his consent for the raid to be re-enacted using his Canadian 2nd Division.

The army chain of command was also altered now that General Montgomery had left for Africa. The over-all command was still retained by General Paget and Lord Mountbatten, but directly below them the command passed to the Canadians under McNaughton, Crerar, and Roberts.

Lord Mountbatten, Chief of Combined Operations, made the decision to call in the commandos to replace the airborne troops for the destruction of the coastal gun batteries at Varengeville and Berneval. They would attack by sea rather than by air; thus low cloud formations would no longer be a deterrent. Mountbatten advised Roberts to allow the two groups of commandos to formulate their own plans for their part in the raid. Such attacks were consistent with their previous training and experience, and they worked best alone. Roberts would still be in over-all command of all facets of the Dieppe operation, including the commando attacks on the flanks.

The broad plan, which followed the outlines of the cancelled Operation Rutter, was to capture the town of Dieppe, establish a perimeter around it, carry out extensive demolitions, remove landing barges, and operate against a Divisional Headquarters believed to be at Arques-la-Bataille on the outskirts of Dieppe.

The attack on the main beaches was set for 5.20 a.m. The four flank attacks were to be made at 4.50, half an hour earlier. It is difficult to understand the reason for a delayed landing where the defences were murderous in their intensity and where the element of surprise was of paramount importance. After the preliminary bombardment had been guillotined from the original plan, the only hope remaining was that of surprise. If the flank attacks were to hit the beaches half an hour before the main assault, surely the defenders on all sectors would be alerted and gun positions manned on *all* sectors, including that of the main beaches. General Roberts had queried this very important point but had been informed by Hughes-Hallett that the delay between assaults was necessary to give the Navy sea room for all of the different disembarkations. As a landlubber, Roberts had to accept nautical advice from the Navy, but it is noteworthy that in the later invasion off the Normandy beaches, over 5000 ships were engaged on a front that was not appreciatively longer than the combined beaches off Dieppe. Perhaps this was another of the vital lessons learned at Dieppe.

To the east of Dieppe, No. 3 Commando under Lt. Col. Durnford-Slater was to land on Yellow 1 and 2 Beaches near the village of Berneval and destroy the heavy gun battery there. On the left of the headlands overlooking the harbour (Blue Beach) the Royal Regiment of Canada and a company of the Black Watch were to land at the village of Puys and destroy the gun batteries on the headlands before swinging right and joining up with the main body of troops landing on the main beaches at 5.20.

To the west of Dieppe, No. 4 Commando under Lt. Col. the Lord Lovat was to land on Orange 1 and 2 Beaches near to the village of Varengeville and destroy the heavy coastal battery there.

The South Saskatchewan Regiment was to land on Green Beach opposite the village of Pourville, just west of Dieppe, and form a bridgehead through which the Cameron Highlanders of Canada would advance rapidly inland before hooking to the left and joining up with the tanks of the Calgary Regiment advancing from the main beaches. After joining up, they would then attack the aerodrome and the Divisional Headquarters believed to be at Arques-la-Bataille, a short distance inland.

Thirty minutes after the flank attacks, the Essex Scottish, together with tanks from the Calgary Regiment, were to land on the eastern half of the main beach facing the town of Dieppe. After consolidating their position, they were to advance rapidly into the town to secure the harbour area for the engineers to carry out demolitions.

The Royal Hamilton Light Infantry, along with tanks, were

to land on the western half of the main beach and advance rapidly through the town of Dieppe to secure exits for the tanks to join up with the Camerons advancing from Pourville.

The Fusiliers de Mont Royal in floating reserve during the assault would land to occupy the perimeter defence of the town after it had been seized by the Essex Scottish and R.H.L.I. and to act as a rear guard covering the withdrawal of all units except the two commando groups from the main beaches.

The Royal Canadian Engineers were to lay mats for the tanks to cross the main beaches, blow the sea wall to enable the tanks to get off the beach, and carry out extensive demolitions of bridges, railway tunnels, and harbour installations. The Royal Marine Commando group, led by Lt. Col. 'Tigger' Phillips, was to be in floating reserve during the assault, and then was to co-operate with the naval gunboat *Locust* commanded by Cmdr. R. E. D. Ryder.

Fifty American Rangers were attached to the force, plus another 20 men of No. 10 Inter-Allied Commando, who were to land in various spots and carry out several tasks for British Intelligence. Few were expected to return; some were to join the French Underground.

Several senior American officers who would be taking part in the Anglo-American invasion of North Africa later in the year were embarked on the headquarters destroyers as observers.

The control of the participating air forces was to be carried out from Fighter Command Headquarters at Uxbridge, under the command of Air Vice-Marshal Leigh-Mallory, with his deputy, Air Commodore A. T. Cole aboard H.M.S. *Calpe*, the headquarters destroyer. Seventy-four squadrons were to take part in the operation. In addition to the R.A.F. there were squadrons from the R.C.A.F., New Zealand, Polish, Norwegian, Czech, French, U.S.A.F. fighter squadrons, and four U.S. Fortress Bomber squadrons. Apart from the support for the invading forces, it was hoped that the enemy could be tempted to release his reserves of fighter aircraft for a large-scale air battle.

The assault armada comprised 237 vessels and craft. The expedition was to sail in 13 groups at varying speeds from four principal ports in the United Kingdom: Southampton, Portsmouth, Newhaven, and Shoreham. At a selected position out in the Channel, all of the ships and landing craft would meet and form up into one convoy. Fifteen minesweepers would lead the way sweeping a clear channel through an extensive enemy minefield and marking a path with buoys. At a point 10 miles from Dieppe, the infantry landing ships would stop to allow the troops to disembark into smaller assault craft. After forming up, each group would be led into their respective beaches by motor gunboats or motor launches.

Eight Hunt class destroyers (1,000 tons each) with four 4-in. guns on each would form the support, and targets ashore would be signalled to each destroyer from special Forward Observation Officer teams provided with portable radios.

Such was the plan. It might be considered too inflexible by some of the senior officers, but the decision had been made to proceed with the operation in spite of its shortcomings.

The attack might still have succeeded if the defenders had been subjected to a very heavy bombardment prior to and during the attack. But there would be no bombing; the element of surprise had been substituted. And a shrewd defending general had already anticipated a possible attack and was maintaining a state of red alert.

The fate of the 2nd Canadian Division was sealed.

CHAPTER SEVEN

FIREWORKS AT SEA

Several days before the raid was scheduled, messages of recall were sent to all personnel on leave. The men who had remained behind were suddenly assembled at 8 a.m. on the morning of August 18th. Ordered to dress in the skeleton equipment worn on a raid, they were told that they were going to Southampton to take part in an amphibious exercise. They went straight to the docks by truck and embarked on the infantry landing ships, which had remained there since the raid was cancelled.

The Royal Regiment embarked on the *Queen Emma* and *Princess Astrid*; the Black Watch of Canada on the *Duke of Wellington*; the Essex Scottish on *Prince Leopold* and *Prince Charles*; the Royal Hamilton Light Infantry on the *Glengyle*; The South Saskatchewan Regiment on *Princess Beatrix* and *Invicta*; and No. 4 Commando on *Prince Albert*.

The Camerons, the Royal Marine Commandos, No. 3 Commandos, and the Fusiliers de Mont Royal boarded the tiny personnel landing craft and French Chasseur boats for the 65-mile voyage.

Once aboard, the officers were called away for a briefing and on their return informed the men. Destination — Dieppe. The men were strangely subdued. With a soldier's instinct they knew that this resurrection of a cancelled raid was wrong. While they stripped and cleaned their weapons, primed grenades, there was little conversation.

Aboard the *Duke of Wellington* the Black Watch of Canada were equipped with ammunition, arms, and grenades. Each man was issued with 200 rounds of .303 ammunition, hand grenades to hang on their webbing gear, and a rifle or light machine gun such as the utility Sten or the superior Bren. They were also given naval life-belts to wear over their uniforms. The wise ones inflated theirs immediately. One of the men primed a grenade and then laid it carelessly down to get on with another chore; absent-mindedly he picked up the grenade again and started to re-prime. After two or three seconds had passed, he suddenly realised what he was doing and threw it towards the port-hole. The grenade hit the bulkhead and bounced back into the compartment, where it killed one soldier and wounded 19 others so severely that they had to be rushed ashore to hospital.

At Newhaven, all of the landing craft were concealed beneath a huge canvas screen. The infantry landing ships were disguised as merchant vessels. False funnels and bulkheads had been erected to alter their appearance, and many flew the flags of neutral countries. The German air force was obviously suspicious and flew at least 12 sorties a day, taking photographs of the huge concentration of ships assembled there.

No. 3 Commando had to queue outside the docks in the streets for half an hour before they could board their boats. The civilians left their houses and sensing the importance of the occasion, watched in silence from the curbside. The commanding officer, Durnford-Slater, boarded gun boat No. 5 with Commander D. B. Wyburd, R.N., the senior naval officer of the group. The little gun boat was to be the headquarters ship which would lead No. 3 Commando across the sea to Dieppe. She was fast, but vulnerable, her steam tubes could easily be punctured by bullet or shell fragments.

The second in command of No. 3 Commando, Major Peter Young, sailed in one of the wooden personnel landing craft skippered by Lt. Buckee, R.N.V.R., one tiny boat filled with 3 commando officers and 17 troopers. Unknowingly, they had assumed a key role in future events. In their hands rested the fate of the whole Dieppe operation.

As the shadows lengthened, Lord Mountbatten and General Crerar moved to Uxbridge to join Leigh-Mallory at Air Force Headquarters, where they would be in direct radio communication with H.M.S. *Calpe*, the headquarters ship that carried General Roberts, Captain Hughes-Hallett and Air Commodore Cole. Brigadier Mann boarded the deputy headquarters ship, H.M.S. *Fernie*, with General Truscott the American Observer.

All was ready. From seaports all along the south-east coast of England, an armada of ships quietly slipped their moorings and headed out to sea. Out of sight of land, the false funnels and neutral flags were lowered. From beneath huge canvas screens, scores of infantry and tank landing craft crept out to join the larger infantry ships threading their way carefully and silently between the numerous vessels crowding the defence boom gates at harbour mouths.

Once clear of the harbour, they were shepherded into long orderly lines and columns by the tiny Hunt class destroyers, which dashed here and there like worrying sheepdogs snapping at the heels of laggards, until finally they headed south-east towards the German-occupied coast of France.

The armada was split into 13 groups of ships and assault landing craft, escorted by eight Hunt class destroyers of the Royal Navy: *Calpe, Fernie, Brocklesby, Garth, Albrighton, Berkeley, Bleasdale,* and *Slazak,* the fleet minesweeper *Alresford,* the flat-bottomed gun-boat *Locust,* and flotillas of motor launches, motor gun-boats and flak ships.

The nine infantry landing ships on which most of the troops sailed were in the first four groups. The remainder of the vessels were assault landing craft of all sizes. Most of them were packed to the gunwales with infantry soldiers; the remainder carried the squat, ungainly Churchill tanks of the Calgary Regiment.

The 13 groups sailed at different times so that they could rendezvous at a point outside the minefield. With 15 minesweepers leading the way, the combined armada began sailing at high speed at 11.30 p.m.

Split-second timing aided by first-class seamanship and navigation brought the fleet safely through the mineswept channels just as the moon was on the wane at 2 a.m. From now on the final approach would be made in almost total darkness.

Group No. 5 containing the men of No. 3 Commando was at that moment some six miles to the west. They had successfully passed through the swept channel and were now forming up for the final run in to the beaches at Berneval. They were unaware that two separate radio messages had been sent to all units of the fleet at 1.27 a.m. and again at 2.44 a.m. from Naval Headquarters at Portsmouth, warning that a small German convoy had been detected by radar from Beachy Head on a collision course with Group 5. By a strange quirk of fate, the enemy ships had sailed from Boulogne to Dieppe at the exact time and speed that would allow them to intercept the Group some six miles from shore. Unbelievably, the first radio message was not received by any ship in the fleet, even though the ships were equipped for action stations and trained telegraphists on every ship were tuned in for just such a message. The second message was received by some units of the fleet, including *Fernie*, but the message was not relayed to *Calpe* to Hughes-Hallett or Roberts. O.R.P. *Slazak* was the ship nearest to Group 5 but did not receive either of the two messages, even though the wireless telegraphy watch was sustained by two ratings, one Polish, the other English loaned from the Royal Navy.

The final run in was cloaked by almost total darkness. Weapons were checked, webbing gear tightened. Voices were muted as the men tensed up, ready to jump on to the beach ahead.

Suddenly at 3.50 a.m. Group 5 was nakedly exposed in an artificial daylight created by star shells bursting overhead. About half a mile off the port bow, five motor vessels were approaching; they were escorted by two submarine chasers and a minesweeper. This was the German convoy en route from Boulogne to Dieppe that the British Admiralty had detected by radar. The tiny L.C.P.s were built entirely of wood, which afforded no protection whatsoever against bullets or shrapnel. They were capable of transporting 25 soldiers plus a naval crew of three. Their armament was a solitary Lewis gun, and their top speed was $9\frac{1}{4}$ knots. Obviously they had not been designed to fight a sea battle.

L.C.P. 42 came under heavy fire almost as soon as the action started. The naval officer and one of the seamen were instantly killed by a shell that smashed through the boat's windscreen. The petty officer was blinded and lay writhing in agony in the bottom of the boat. The radio was smashed beyond repair, and they drifted helplessly at the mercy of wind and tide.

Trooper Higgins from Sheffield jumped into the coxswain's seat and brought the boat under control once more. Several of the commandos aboard were severely wounded. But when Lt. Dreus asked the troop if they should go on or turn back to England, there was an instant shout of, 'We go in!' Commander Wyburd bravely turned his gun-boat toward the enemy while the landing craft scattered, but his boat was soon disabled by heavy and accurate fire. Her steam boilers were pierced by five separate shells and half the crew wounded or killed. The flak landing ship and the motor launch also engaged the enemy vessels, sinking one and leaving the other burning fiercely. By 4.07 a.m., the gun-boat was a complete shambles; her radio had been put out of action by the first shell and thus she was unable to warn the headquarters ship *Calpe* that the element of surprise had been lost.

Fortunately for the surviving assault craft, the German convoy broke off the action after losing two of her escorts. Steam Gun Boat No. 5 turned away, her speed reduced to six knots, her guns silent, her crew lying dead and mortally wounded on the decks. Amid the hiss of escaping steam and the moans of the dying, Durnford-Slater managed to reach the bridge where one of the naval officers who was badly wounded, cried, 'This is the end!' The Colonel was inclined to agree with him as he undid his boots and blew up his life-jacket. All around him, the bridge was piled with dead and wounded. There must have been ten casualties there, all hit when looking over the top of the armour plating.

Group No. 5 had been decimated and scattered. Out of a total of 23 L.C.P.s that had set out from Newhaven, four did not reach the scene of the encounter due to engine trouble and had to return to England. Of the remaining 19, four were badly hit with most of their crews killed or wounded, so that they were also forced to return to England. The remaining 15 L.C.P.s split into several groups during the action. Five of them attached themselves to the gun-boat, determined to follow the leader; three others had closed with the flak ship and were battling the German ships; the remaining seven veered away from the group and proceeded on their own to the Yellow Beaches ahead.

After the raid *Slazak* and *Brocklesby* were severely criticised for being off station by about six miles when Group No. 5 was surprised by the German convoy. It was argued that had they been closer to the group, they could have routed the German ships before they menaced the commando group. However, at 0330 hours when the landing craft had reached the lowering position some 10 miles off the beaches of Dieppe, both escorts were ordered to detach themselves from Group No. 5 and carry out an eastward sweep in the direction of Le Tréport to protect the invasion fleet from possible encroachment by enemy naval forces. Twenty minutes later they observed a brief exchange of gunfire and starshells on the horizon as Group No. 5 collided with the German convoy. It was presumed that the gunfire was directed from the shore at Berneval. Commander Pumphrey, R.N., aboard *Brocklesby* immediately turned about and fired starshells to illuminate the distant action, but was ordered to resume position by *Slazak*, the senior escort, to avoid alerting the enemy. The orders prior to sailing had been most explicit: action must be averted at all costs to enable the major landing ships to approach the coast undetected.

Wyburd and Durnford-Slater transferred to one of the L.C.P.s at 4.45 a.m. — five minutes before the vitally important assault was due on the huge coastal gun battery at Berneval by No. 3 Commando. Unless this battery was silenced, the infantry landing ships and destroyers would be in deadly peril, even at a distance of 10 miles off-shore, where they had planned to lower their assault craft. Durnford-Slater sailed at full speed in the commandeered L.C.P. to warn *Calpe* that not only had the No. 3 Commando been decimated, but also that the Berneval battery was still intact and would unleash a hellish, deadly fire on the invasion fleet at first light.

Unfortunately, they did not manage to board *Calpe* until 6.45 a.m. — one and half hours after dawn — to report news of their failure to Hughes-Hallett and Roberts. If the commando raid on Berneval had failed, why were its guns silent and the larger ships of the invasion fleet unharmed? This was a mystery that would remain unsolved until they returned to England later in the day.

CHAPTER EIGHT

THE COMMANDOS ENTER

In allowing the commandos to plan their own assault on the gun batteries, General Roberts was well aware of the nature and character of the British commando groups. All of them were graduates of Achnacarry, the ancestral home of Sir Donald Walter Cameron of Lochiel, Chief of the Clan Cameron. Situated near Spean Bridge in the highlands of Scotland, this special combined operations 'school' was run by an ex-regimental sergeant-major of the élite Coldstream Guards. Charles Vaughan had earned his King's commission the hard way, by climbing up from non-commissioned ranks. Now a lieutenant-colonel, he had previously been second in command of No. 4 Commando, but was now the 'Laird of Achnacarry'. He may not have been strictly entitled to the title 'Laird', but he ruled with an iron hand and made sure that the men passing out of his course earned the right to wear the famous green beret.

The course was designed to be extremely arduous, and in the first few weeks a great many men were rejected.

Only eight months prior to the Dieppe raid, the men of No. 3 Commando had made a successful raid on the German garrison at Vaagso in Norway. They were led by Lt. Col. John Durnford-Slater, who had already established a reputation for his No. 3 Commando. As aggressive combat troops they were matched only by their comrades in No. 4 Commando led by Lt. Col. Lord Lovat.

Both of the commando groups had been given identical tasks in the raid on Dieppe. No. 3 Commando was to assault the German gun battery at Berneval, east of the town, while No. 4 Commando assaulted its twin at Varengeville to the west, some 10 miles from Berneval. Both groups would hit the beach at the same time, 0450 hours, and scale the dark cliffs, then rush inland to silence the huge guns.

Lt. Col. Durnford-Slater's plan involved two separate landings opposite the tiny village of Berneval and Belleville-sur-

Mer. He would lead the larger group ashore at Berneval (Yellow Beach 1), while his second-in-command, Major Peter Young, landed with the remainder of the men at Belleville-sur-Mer (Yellow Beach 2). Both groups were then to move inland in a flanking movement and assemble at the rear of the gun battery, near the Berneval church. They would then attack with a force of 450 commandos. The battery contained four 5.9-in. guns and was situated on the outskirts of Berneval, about 420 yards from the edge of the cliff.

Such was the plan, sound in every detail but one — the element of luck. The encounter with the German naval group had destroyed the element of surprise. The defenders ashore had been thoroughly alerted by the noise of the action at sea and had manned all gun positions prior to the landings.

The senior N.C.O. in the group was the regimental sergeant-major of No. 3 Commando — Harry Beesley. A regular soldier in the British Army since 1926, he had served with distinction in Britain's peacetime army in India and Egypt. Although he was only 5 feet 6 inches tall, he was nevertheless strong and rugged. Since birth he had suffered from a curious malformation of the heels and on long marches he suffered greatly. But no word of complaint ever passed his lips.

Harry Beesley came from a large family in Staines, Middlesex. The family was poor and he had gone to work early as a furnaceman in a local iron foundry to help provide for them. The long, exhausting hours spent feeding and raking the raging furnaces strengthened and toughened his muscles and made him lean and hard. Intensely patriotic, Beesley has been described as unlike the 'guard'-type regimental sergeant-major. To his men, he was firm, but kindly and understanding. These human qualities proved to be invaluable.

Beesley had served with the British Expeditionary Force in France when the war started in 1939 and had fought in the rearguard action at Dunkirk before being evacuated to fight again. Within days after he had landed back in Britain, he had volunteered to join the newly formed commandos to have another crack at the foe. On July 17th, 1940, just 43 days after he had been snatched from the bloody beaches of Dunkirk, Beesley landed with Lt. Col. Durnford-Slater and 2nd Lt. Peter Young on the German-occupied island of Guernsey in the first commando raid of the war. During the next two years, he was involved in many small raids on the occupied coast of

France before landing at Vaagso with Captain Dick Wills.

The landing at Yellow Beach 1 was made quietly and went unopposed. In the eerie first light of dawn, the men rushed across the narrow beach to the shelter of the cliffs. They had landed 25 minutes late at 0515 hours and had already lost the advantage of darkness in their assault. They quickly found the gully where they hoped to climb the cliffs, but it was choked with huge coils of barbed wire interwoven with trip wires and Teller mines. Captain Wills directed some of the men to cut the wire, but it was a slow and tedious job. The remainder of the men watched the top of the cliff with taut nerves for some sign of the enemy and for the attack that must surely come.

One of their boats was hit by heavy fire as the defenders suddenly counter-attacked, and Lt. Cdr. Corke was mortally wounded. The coxswain was killed and a commando took over the wheel. The boat reached the shore barely afloat. After arranging for the badly wounded to be transferred to another vessel, Corke insisted on remaining with his boat and carrying on the fight as his life's blood drained away.

At 0535 hours, the German Armed Tanker *Franz*, one of the ships from the convoy that had surprised No. 5 group, approached the beach to lend support to the defenders but she was immediately engaged by the gallant Motor Launch 346 at a range of only 30 yards and set on fire. When she drifted ashore, the British crew removed her flag as a battle trophy.

On the beach, most of the fire seemed to be coming from two machine-gun posts and a large white house and a church on the top of the cliffs. Both of these buildings were shattered and set on fire by Motor Launch 346.

The men now gained the top of the cliff and moved inland to meet up with their comrades landing on Yellow Beach 2. The German machine-gun post again opened up and inflicted casualties. Captain Wills was shot in the neck. At last the fire was silenced by Corporal 'Banger' Hall, who captured it single-handed, after a brave, suicidal bayonet charge. Another gun post was attacked by Lt. E. D. Loustalot, commander of the small group of American Rangers in the raid. He was killed in the attempt and became the first American soldier to be killed in Europe in World War II.

L.C.P. 42 arrived at Yellow Beach 1 almost 20 minutes after Wills had landed with the other five boats. The German defenders had now manned their gun positions on the clifftop, and

Dreus and his 12 men came under heavy and accurate fire as they approached the beach. It was now broad daylight, and they were mercilessly exposed to the enemy machine guns. Their comrades who had landed earlier had already succeeded in scaling the cliff through one of the narrow gullies and had moved inland to silence the gun battery at Berneval.

Corporal Pat Habron dashed to the shelter of the cliff face, followed by his number two man on the Bren gun he was carrying. Ahead of him he could see two gullies in the cliff. The nearest was choked with an impregnable mass of dannert wire, but the next had been cleared by R.S.M. Beesley and his men as they climbed the cliff face in the earlier assault. As they now made their way along the beach, one of the men was shot dead, but the remainder succeeded in reaching the clifftop. Just ahead, they could hear the sound of heavy firing as Beesley and his men came under attack from the German defenders. Mute evidence of the accuracy of this fire was given by the body of Sergeant Mills of No. 2 troop, who lay across their path. A few yards further on, they came across Dick Wills, who had been severely wounded. Suddenly they were met with a hail of bullets from strongly defended enemy machine-gun pits.

They were also being dive-bombed by the Luftwaffe. Their position was extremely precarious. Many were dead and wounded. Ammunition was running low, and they were still only about 500 yards from the edge of the cliff. The order was given to retreat, but when the men reached the beach they found that the landing craft had become impaled on steel stakes that had been cunningly mounted on the beach, where they had been invisible at high tide. Two of the boats were beyond use, and the remaining three were forced to withdraw and watch helplessly as the men were forced to surrender.

On the way back, Pte. Lerigo hoisted Captain Wills on to his back and succeeded in climbing down the steep gully using his teeth and toenails. Once on the beach, Wills revived sufficiently to order the survivors to make their way along the beach towards Dieppe to meet up with the Canadians and continue the fight. Most of their boats had been sunk or set on fire by intensive enemy mortar and shellfire and the naval crews killed.

Pat Habron and two troopers followed Captain Clements along the beach to Dieppe but were soon thwarted by the German defenders, who threw stick grenades down on top of them from the cliff edge. They took refuge in a cave but were forced to surrender a short time later when the German troops advanced along the beach, firing into the mouth of the cave.

Sergeant Connally tried to swim out to the landing craft but was forced to return to shore exhausted; Lance-Corporal Sinclair did succeed in swimming out to one of the boats lying offshore and returned safely to England as the sole survivor. Out of a total 120 men who had landed on Yellow Beach 1, 37 were killed, 82 were taken prisoner, and one lucky soul got away.

The landing was almost a total failure. Although the survivors were glad to find themselves still alive, they felt angry and humiliated at being taken prisoner without having come near their objective — the gun batteries. As they were being searched and marched away by their captors, the men were horrified to hear the earth-shattering sound of the huge coastal guns at Berneval. The first shells had been fired at the invasion fleet only ten miles distant — stationary while they unloaded their toops into landing barges. They were sitting ducks.

While the German defenders were preparing to repulse the invaders at Yellow Beach 1, Major Young and his Lilliputian force was nearing the top of the sheer cliff at Belleville-sur-Mer. Three officers and 17 men were all that remained of the famous No. 3 Commando. The other two officers in Major Young's small party were Captain John Selwyn and Lt. Buck Ruxton. The German gun battery was strongly defended by a force of over 200 men, all of whom had been alerted and were standing by their weapons in machine-gun pits, flak posts, and trenches. The odds were impossible, yet this small boat-load of commandos moved forward with magnificent effrontery in an attempt to overcome the vastly superior force ahead. The beach where they had landed lay at the foot of a narrow gully filled with rolls of barbed wire and mines. Fortunately for the commandos, the enemy had secured the rolls of barbed wire to the sides of the cliff by means of wooden pegs. Major Young and his men expressed their sincere thanks as they used the pegs to secure hand and foot holds with their toggle ropes in the perilous climb up the cliff face.

Once they had gained the summit, they moved forward stealthily toward the village of Berneval, where they had arranged to meet their fellow commandos from Yellow Beach 1. The first indication that something had gone awry occurred when they arrived at the church. Their comrades never got there. A safer course of action at this point would have been to retreat immediately and return to the beach with all haste before the enemy became aware that a second force was in the vicinity. Instead, this small force of 20 men advanced against the heavily defended gun battery. Realising that they could not hope to overcome the battery by force, they resolved to make the defenders' task more difficult by sniping at the gun crews. The bell tower of the church overlooked the gunpits and would have made an ideal sniping position. Unfortunately, there was no way to get up there. Major Young then led his men into a cornfield adjacent to the battery. Hidden from sight, they spread out to simulate a large force, and at a distance of only 200 yards, maintained a withering and demoralising fire against the gunners.

After firing only about 20 shells at the invasion fleet, the guns fell silent, one after another, as men of the gun crews fell wounded or killed by the commandos' deadly fire. In desperation, the defenders finally swung one of the huge guns inland and fired at the men hidden in the cornfield. The guns could not be depressed sufficiently and the shells whistled harmlessly overhead before exploding about a mile inland. Thus between 0510 and 0745 hours, the gun battery was prevented from firing at the invasion fleet. These were the crucial hours when the landing ships were especially vulnerable as they unloaded smaller landing craft into the water, and provided almost perfect targets for the long-range guns of Berneval.

As ammunition began to run out, Major Young made the decision to withdraw back to the cliffs before enemy re-inforcements could arrive. They had done all that was possible to prevent the guns from firing at the fleet, and the defenders clearly believed that they faced a large force of attackers, but the bluff was running out and it was time to move before the men were massacred. As they climbed back down the cliff to the beach, the Germans counter-attacked. But Young and his little band managed to board Lt. Buckee's assault craft, which had waited patiently off-shore during the action. Only two of the men had been wounded, and it was a very happy band who sailed back to England.

Ten miles to the west, No. 4 Commando had been given the task of silencing the gun battery at Varengeville. This one battery alone was quite capable of sinking every ship in the in-vading force. Under the command of Lt. Col. Lord Lovat, the raiding force amounted to 252 officers and men, including one officer and six men of the newly formed American Rangers and four Free French commandos who had recently been trained at Achnacarry. The assault plan as designed by Lord Lovat was very similar to that of Durnford-Slater for Berneval. It called for a two-pronged attack with two separate landings taking place on Orange 1 and Orange 2 Beaches. The former was a very narrow beach in front of the tiny village of Vasterival, about four miles to the west of Dieppe. A force of 88 commandos led by Major D. Mills-Roberts would land there and scale the steep cliff prior to mounting a frontal attack against the coastal gun battery that lay about 1100 yards from the edge of the cliff.

At the same time, a larger group of 164 commandos under Lord Lovat would land on Orange 2 Beach some two miles to the west and alongside the River Saane. After landing, they would advance inland and in an encircling movement attack the gun battery from the rear.

The coastal gun battery at Varengeville formed an independent strong point. Its six 5.9. in. guns, which could sink ships even 13 miles out at sea, were protected from a possible air or land attack by flak towers containing anti-aircraft guns and machine guns. Around the perimeter, seven machine-gun emplacements, anti-tank guns, minefields, and a double line of rolled barbed wire formed an almost impregnable defence. No. 4 Commando faced a formidable task.

At 0300 hours exactly they were lowered into the water in their assault craft and quickly formed up into two columns before racing for Varengeville. They were then some 10 miles away from their landing. At the head of the two columns, a motor gunboat, No. 312, commanded by Lt. Commander Mulleneux, R.N., led the way. From then until zero hour they were in the capable hands of the navy. Many of the men curled up on the thwarts and continued their interrupted sleep. Prior to entering the boats, the men had been ordered to paint their white faces and hands with green greasepaint.

Commander Mulleneux had to land two separate bodies of men on strange beaches and pinpoint two gullies in the cliffs that he had seen only as hairline cracks on aerial photographs. No mean feat of navigation in total darkness! Fortunately, the enemy co-operated fully. The lighthouse (Phare d'Ailly), which also acted as a German artillery observation post, flashed its light on and off three times and then after a delay, another three times. Mulleneux recognised the flashes as belonging to the lighthouse on the point ahead and steered accordingly. Suddenly star shells burst overhead followed by the trajectories of tracer bullets weaving through the sky to the west of Dieppe. The men said a silent prayer for their buddies in No. 3 Commando, under attack by the German convoy off Berneval. The plan called for the landings at Berneval and Varengeville to take place simultaneously at 0450 hours. As the faces of the men were illuminated by the light cast by the star shells, Captain Dawson warned the men that it would be their turn next. But somehow they remained undetected, and some time later they were treated to the hospitable sight of the red and green navigation lights at the end of the harbour mole over to the left, winking on and off to guide the German convoy into the harbour. At the same time, and almost without warning, three blacked-out ships were sighted ahead. They could only be enemy vessels. Most likely it was the remainder of the German convoy that had attacked No. 3 Commando. A quick change of course and a confrontation was avoided without the enemy vessels sighting the low profile of the assault craft.

When the convoy reached a point three miles off-shore, it was split into two sections to allow Major Mills-Roberts to head for Orange 1 Beach with A and C troops while Lord Lovat sailed to Orange 2 Beach to the west with B, F, and H.Q. troops. As they neared the shore, each man mentally reviewed the plan. It had been rehearsed many times prior to Dieppe at Lulworth Cove in Dorset. Using scale models and aerial photographs, the area had been examined and studied in minute detail until every man had been thoroughly briefed in his own tasks.

The eerie sound of air-raid sirens floated across the water to the men as they tensed up ready for the touchdown. The lighthouse blinked once more and then blacked out as star shells burst overhead, lighting up the sea. It seemed that the surprise element had been lost, but they knew that they had to go on. They had been promised air support and they got it just as they were approaching the shore on the final run in. R.A.F. Spitfires attacked the German lighthouse to the left of their landing on Orange 1 Beach. The coastal gun battery at Varengeville had been silent up to now; obviously they did not suspect the presence of enemy vessels. German radar, like the British, was still in its infancy and could not detect the low-lying assault craft as they raced in to shore.

Major Mills-Roberts landed on Orange 1 Beach without meeting opposition. The men jumped over the sides of the boat as she grounded on the pebbly beach and raced for the shelter of the cliff as R.A.F. planes roared overhead to strafe the lighthouse and German strongpoints. Three gullies led off the beach, each filled with dense rolls of barbed wire. To add to their difficulties, they could see a German sentry silhouetted against the pre-dawn sky as he patrolled the edge of the 100-foot cliffs overhanging the beach. If the cliffs were to be scaled, it could only be through the gullies. Lt. D. C. W. Style ordered the men to place a Bangalore torpedo in the barbed wire of one of the gullies. As luck would have it, its detonation was synchronised with another explosion from above, as fighter aircraft again attacked the lighthouse with cannon. The way was now clear. Up through the gully the men rushed, into the village of Varengeville. To make their task easier, the Bangalore torpedo had unearthed a flight of steep steps leading all the way to the top, probably for use by bathers in more peaceful times.

Major Mills-Roberts advanced with the mortar section and gained the shelter of a dense wood that ran to within 200 yards of the battery forward defences. Sergeant McCarthy and his Bren gun section penetrated even further, getting within 100 yards of the battery without being detected. There was plenty of cover; the hedges were over eight feet high, and the vegetation on the ground was knee-deep. Eventually they came to an empty wooden house. Creeping up the stairs, they found that the windows were empty of glass, and they quickly set up both Bren guns through the open windows overlooking the gun pits.

Unbelievably, the landing had been made without the enemy being alerted. By now it was almost dawn and the attack had to be made against the battery before first light. Mills-Roberts ordered his men to deploy through the forest and to set up the 2- and 3-in. mortars at strategic points around the battery. The remainder of the troop crept forward as far as possible until they could aim at the German gunners in the pits. Just at that moment, the German coastal guns opened fire on the fleet, which they had at last observed in the half light on the horizon.

At the same time, the fleet opened fire and bombarded the enemy gun positions on shore. To add to the deafening bombardment, Mills-Roberts now gave the order to open fire, and a hail of Bren and rifle fire poured into the enemy machine gun outposts, silencing them.

Over on the flank, Sgt. McCarthy and his Bren gun team engaged the flak towers until they saw a stream of tracer bullets coming from the perimeter of the meadow in front of them. The commandos did not use tracer bullets because of their tell-tale effect, so it was obvious that the fire was of enemy origin. Seizing a Bren gun, McCarthy released burst after burst into the enemy gun pit, which was perfectly camouflaged to blend in with the surrounding foliage. To prove the accuracy of his fire, a group of enemy soldiers debouched suddenly from the pit and scattered throughout the meadow. They were quickly cut down. The enemy flak towers were silenced quickly in like manner.

The commando mortar groups had positioned their mortars around the gun battery. They now opened fire. One after another, the mortar bombs lobbed into the gun pits, where the German gunners were feverishly reloading and firing. With only the second salvo, a mortar bomb exploded in a pile of prepared cordite charges stacked alongside the guns for easy access. With a mighty roar and an eye-searing flash, the cordite exploded, killing or wounding members of the gun crew. Almost immediately after, a chain reaction ignited the other ammunition dumps alongside the remaining guns. Now all hell was let loose. Men were blown up into the air with arms and legs flailing like paper dolls. One blinding flash after another lit up the gruesome scene. Mingled with the screams of the burned and dying were the savage battle cries of the commandos and the harsh staccato rattle of eight-barrelled machine guns fired by Hurricanes overhead.

Sgt. McCarthy's position was rapidly becoming untenable. The enemy had mounted a counter-attack with barrages of mortar fire. Each barrage of mortar bombs crept forward 50 yards towards the old house sheltering the Bren crews. When one bomb missed flattening the house by a matter of feet, they decided to move out. When they descended the stairs, they found the body of Private Garthways, the stretcher-bearer, a victim of the near miss.

The great guns were silent. But it was known that the battery contained at least 100 men, many of whom were still armed and dangerous. If the fleet was to be safeguarded, the guns had to be destroyed. Mills-Roberts and his men continued to fire at the battery, but with the passing of every minute their position was becoming acute. If the defenders decided to counter-attack, the small force of commandos would be wiped out by the vastly superior force. Anxiously Mills-Roberts peered ahead waiting for the signal from the rear of the battery that would tell him that Lord Lovat's group was in position and ready to attack.

Lord Lovat had landed on the beach near Quiberville with six assault craft. They were not as fortunate as Mills-Roberts; they came under fire from mortars and machine guns as soon as they tried to cross the barbed wire on the beach. One of the commandos had inadvertently fired a burst from his Bren gun, alerting gunners on the clifftop.

Lord Lovat stepped ashore dressed in corduroy pants and grey sweater, with a Winchester sporting rifle tucked casually under his arm as though he were setting out on a grouse shoot on his estate. He directed the men to cross the barbed wire and make for the banks of the River Saane, a short distance to the right. Heavy enemy mortar fire descended on them from the clifftop, killing several men and wounding the others.

Most of the enemy fire seemed to be coming from a pillbox on the clifftop. Lt. Veasey coolly climbed the cliff with a squad of men using tubular ladders. Within minutes he had succeeded in silencing the pillbox fire by tossing in a few hand grenades.

Lord Lovat and his men now used the river banks as cover and advanced inland to circle around the gun battery. In the distance they could hear the sounds of battle as their comrades attacked the battery from the front. By now it was almost broad daylight, and it was with a sigh of relief that they reached the cover of Blancmesnil-le-Bas Wood, which stretched all the way to the rear of the battery defences. Here they stopped to take breath before launching the final attack.

It had been planned for B troop to attack the machine-gun positions and buildings on the right of the battery while F troop charged across open ground in a direct assault on the huge gun emplacements. As they lay quietly in the wood, they surprised a German patrol of 35 men, which was forming up ready to attack Mills-Roberts' group on the other side of the battery. The commandos slaughtered them to the last man with Bren guns. Lord Lovat then ordered Verey flares to be fired to signal Mills-Roberts that he was about to attack, and at the same time, ordered F and B troops to move forward with Bangalore torpedoes to blow the barbed wire outer defences. The Germans had cleared the brush for at least 300 yards around the battery. Any attack across the open ground would be murderous but the men had their orders *to take the battery at all costs.*

Some American Rangers had managed to climb on to the rooftops of buildings overlooking the battery. From there they sniped at the German gunners as they attempted to load the huge coastal guns. Corporal F. Koons shot one of the gunners dead, and in doing so is believed to be the first U.S. soldier to kill a German in the Second World War.

The assault was to coincide with an attack by the R.A.F., and at 0615 hours, planes arrived, blasting the gun positions with cannon and rocket fire. The order was then given to fix bayonets. The men of B and F troops charged out of the wood to race across a 300-yard gauntlet of machine-gun fire. The wire was blown by Bangalore torpedoes and the commandos roared towards the battery, screaming defiance and curses at the enemy. One after another they were systematically mowed down. Yet despite the carnage around them, Captain Pat Porteous, although wounded three times on the way in, led the men over the defence posts and into the battery gun-pits.

The German defenders seemed petrified at the sight of these screaming madmen racing forward with fixed bayonets. In a bitter hand-to-hand struggle, all but four of the defenders were killed by bayonet and rifle bursts. By 0630 hours, only 15 minutes after the mad charge, the battery was in commando hands.

Time was running out. At any moment the German reserves would come pouring into Varengeville. The order was given to spike the guns, and charges that had been prepared in England were rammed into the barrels of each of the huge guns and detonated. As the commandos prepared to leave, they laid the bodies of 11 of their comrades reverently on to the ground and hoisted the Union Jack over them.

By now there was ample evidence of a mounting German counter-attack. Bullets began to fly once more. The four German prisoners were pressed into service to carry some of the wounded, and swiftly the men returned to Orange 1 Beach, where the landing had still remained undetected. It was fortunate that they did not try to reach Orange 2 Beach, for the enemy, knowing that the commandos had landed there, had amassed strong reinforcements at the beach-head to ambush them as they returned.

On the way back to Orange 1 Beach, Sgt. McCarthy and his men picked up Lt. MacDonald who had been severely wounded by a mortar shell. Making an improvised stretcher from a door, they lowered him to the beach only to find that the tide had ebbed so that the assault craft were unable to sail right in to the foot of the cliffs.

Wading out up to their necks, the men succeeded in passing along the wounded in Goatley collapsible boats until all were safely aboard the assault craft. Sgt. McCarthy handed over Lt. MacDonald to a naval doctor on one of the larger tank landing craft for immediate surgery. Sadly, the ship was sunk later in the action, and Lt. MacDonald and the crew were drowned.

No. 4 Commando had suffered about 45 casualties, including 12 dead. But they had succeeded in removing the threat to the invasion fleet. From now on the landings could go ahead as planned. In this textbook attack, Captain Pat Porteous was awarded the Victoria Cross and Sgt. Peter McCarthy the military medal.

On the way back to the fleet, Lord Lovat sent a signal to Lord Mountbatten, 'Every one of gun crews finished off with bayonet. O.K. by you?' It was now only 0730 hours. They had been ashore for two hours and 40 minutes.

Two other flanking attacks had also been planned for 0450 hours. The Royals were to land at the village of Puys to the east of Dieppe and the South Saskatchewan Regiment at the village of Pourville to the west. The attack by the Royals was crucial. The success of the landings on the main beach by the Essex Scottish and Royal Hamilton Light Infantry regiments depended almost entirely on overpowering the enemy defences on the East Headland, which towers above the town and harbour of Dieppe. Once the Royals had landed at Puys, they were to overrun the many German guns trained on the main beaches. Here too success depended upon the element of surprise under the cloak of darkness. Obviously, the four attacks at Berneval, Puys, Pourville and Varengeville 40 minutes before the landing on the main beach had to be synchronised for any element of surprise to be effective.

CHAPTER NINE

GREEN BEACH

Two miles to the west of Dieppe lies the sleepy little village of Pourville. Its beach is dominated by cliffs on both sides, and these effectively isolate Pourville from the Dieppe beaches. The village lies in the valley of the River Scie, which divides the beach into two parts. Looking east towards Dieppe, one faces a lofty and overpowering rampart, the eastern ridge of the valley of the Scie. The Germans had strongly fortified this headland, which commands the beach. Their defences were to prove insuperable throughout the long morning of August 19th, 1942.

The South Saskatchewan Regiment was to land astride the River Scie and quickly establish a bridgehead through which the Queen's Own Camerons of Canada could pass in order to attack selected strongpoints inland. The Camerons would then hook to the left and join up with the Royal Hamilton Light Infantry and Calgary Tanks, who should by then have been breaking out of Dieppe in two directions — east to Puys and west to Pourville. The South Saskatchewan Regiment was carried aboard the infantry landing ships *Princess Beatrix* and *Invicta*. The men disembarked into their assault landing craft at 0300 hours and set sail for Green Beach at Pourville. The disembarkation was smoothly completed in total darkness, but as the *Invicta* and *Princess Beatrix* were forming up to return to England before daylight exposed them to enemy bombers, they collided. Both ships were heavily damaged. Fortunately they managed to make the port of Southampton without further mishap.

At 0450 hours the Battalion landed on the gravel beaches in front of the sea wall at Pourville. The clatter of steel-shod boots across the heavy shingle sounded like thunder after the silence of the sea voyage. But the German garrison was taken by surprise. It was a few moments before enemy gun positions opened up; by then, most of the troops had cut the barbed wire and were safely over the sea wall.

A and D Companies on the left flank were to secure the high ground surrounding a large German radio direction finder station (radar) and to overcome the German strongpoint at Quatre Vents Farm. With these companies was a small special force under Lt. Les England. Its task was classified 'most secret'; after capturing the radar station, this force was to secure vital pieces of equipment and records to take back to England to be examined by scientists. To assist these men, a radar specialist had been included in the assault group. The planners had not told him of the somewhat macabre instructions issued to England just prior to the raid: 'If capture seems imminent, shoot him. On no account must the enemy capture him alive to extract his knowledge of radar.'

In the near darkness of twilight hour, A and D Companies had been mistakenly put ashore on the west side of the river instead of the east and initially, a great part of the surprise element had been lost to them. Instead of proceeding directly to their objectives on the high ground overlooking the battle-ground from the east, they now had to fight their way through the enemy-occupied village before crossing the River Scie over a long, narrow bridge prior to assaulting the defences to the west. This bridge, which was to assume great importance at a later stage of the action, was exposed to enemy gunfire and lacked even the most basic cover.

On the other side of the bridge the advance was halted by a patch of swampy ground, but with the use of a local smoke screen to mask their movements, the companies bypassed it. Then they were halted by heavy fire from a German pillbox. In an act of great bravery, Pte. Charlie Sawden raced forward, lobbing several hand grenades through the firing aperture. He killed all six of the gun crew.

Meanwhile, C Company, operating to the west of Pourville, advanced up the terraces, silencing enemy strong points on the way and killing a great number of the defenders. They soon cleared the right half of the village of enemy troops and captured 'La Maison Blanche', which had been used as an enemy control centre.

The first prisoner to be brought into Battalion Headquarters was a German stretcher-bearer who had had his arm blown off by a grenade. As the men of the S.S.R. slowly advanced, a steady stream of prisoners was brought back to headquarters for questioning by Intelligence personnel. They were then marched into a yard at the back and closely guarded by huge members of the Provost Corps. When the fighting became intense, a German mortar bomb landed in the middle of the yard and a large number of prisoners was killed.

Prior to the raid, the BBC had agreed to broadcast a warning to the French people as soon as the assault began. The announcer appealed to the civilians not to attempt to participate in the raid. Any attempt by civilians to assist the assault troops would surely lead to reprisals later. To make doubly sure, all troops had been issued with wads of pamphlets in French to distribute to the French civilians encountered. During the course of the action, the troops were amused to find small boys chasing them in their advance through the village to beg for more and more of the pamphlets. It was very heartening to feel that these civilians were friends and allies, anxiously awaiting the day of liberation. The fact that the same pamphlets had been made from very thin, flimsy tissue paper could have also been a reason for the great interest in acquiring them. Toilet paper was almost impossible to obtain in France during the war!

After advancing through the village, Lt. Kempton's platoon in C Company established itself on the high ground to the right. A short time later, C Company was attacked by a large detachment of the enemy attempting to dislodge them from their favourable position. They held on grimly against overwhelming odds until ordered to withdraw back to the village. As they slowly retreated, Lt. Kempton was killed as he tried to cover the withdrawal of his wounded sergeant.

B Company had been given the task of clearing the enemy out of the left half of the village. They joined up with D Company, which had landed on the wrong side of the river, and quickly advanced through the village of Pourville until they reached the bridge over the River Scie. The first troops managed to cross the bridge safely, but those following were stopped cold by a barrage of extremely heavy fire from machine guns and mortars. Soon the bridge was carpeted with dead and wounded men. The advance of the South Saskatchewans ground to a halt. The commanding officer, Merritt, came forward to assess the situation. Then he walked calmly across the bridge, waving his steel helmet and calling to his men, 'Come on over, there's nothing to it.' Time after time, he led parties of men over the suicidal crossing. He seemed to live a charmed life; with bullets whistling all around him, he set a magnificent example to his men. On the other side of the bridge, he then led a series of charges against concrete gun positions to open up the road for the Camerons who would advance later towards the town of Dieppe. For these and other valiant acts, Colonel Merritt was awarded the Victoria Cross, becoming the first Canadian to win this coveted award in the Second World War.

B and D Companies now pressed on, fighting savagely all the way. They delivered a number of attacks on Quatre Vents Farm, knocking out many of the numerous pillboxes defending the approaches. One particularly offensive pillbox was destroyed by Pte. Fenner, who walked straight up to it firing his heavy Bren gun from the hip in pinpoint accuracy through the firing ports. Not far away, a platoon of the enemy with four machine guns and a mortar were successfully defending a hill. Lance-Corporal Bertelot in charge of a platoon of the S.S.R. talked over the situation with his chum, Pte. Haggard. Under cover of fire provided by Pte. Haggard, Bertelot walked up the hill firing *his* Bren gun from the hip and, as he reached the gun pits, emptied his magazine into the defenders until all were silenced. Single-handedly, he had killed 25 Germans and taken 30 prisoners.

Lt. England had managed to get within a short distance of the radar station but was forced to retire in the face of heavy fire. The station was surrounded with rings of barbed wire, mortar, and machine-gun posts and could only have been eliminated by heavy supporting fire from the destroyer *Albrighton*, which had been assigned to Green Beach. Unfortunately, the Forward Observation Officer, Capt. H. B. Carswell, R.A., was not in an advantageous position and was unable to direct the shell-fire correctly. During the action Lt. England was severely wounded; after he had been carried a short distance by stretcher-bearers, Colonel Merritt picked him up in his arms and carried him through machine-gun fire until he could safely entrust him to Pte. Earl Williams, who then carried him to the Regimental aid post. During the evacuation, he was carried aboard the destroyer *Berkeley* and placed in a bunk below decks. Under sedation, he dozed off, only to awake suddenly to find water lapping at his feet and a great hole in the ship's side through which the sea gushed in. Calmly rolling off his bunk, he swam through the hole in the side of the ship and was picked up by another vessel.

Forty minutes after the S.S.R. had landed and firmly secured the beach-head, the Queen's Own Camerons landed on
Green Beach astride the River Scie. On the leading assault
craft, Alec Graham, Piper of B Company, raised himself to his
full height in the bow and, in full view of the enemy, played his
bagpipes in a soul-rending skirl. As the eerie sound of Scottish
pipes playing 'A Hundred Pipers' floated over the water, the
men responded with rousing cheers. When the leading boats hit
the beach, they rushed over the lowered ramps and across the
shingle, which was by then covered with a murderous fire.

The commanding officer, Lt. Col. Alfred Gostling, touched
down near the eastern end of the beach; as he leapt on to the
shingle, he was shot dead. (Over to the left, his brother, Lt. Col.
Guy Standish Gostling, commanding officer of the Toronto
Scottish Regiment, was at that very moment sailing in to the
main beach at Dieppe.) The second-in-command, Major A. T.
Law, assumed command and the advance continued without
pause. The largest body of troops landed west of the river and
consisted of A Company, two platoons of B and most of C
Company. Under the command of Major Law, they moved
quickly inland and advanced toward the tiny hamlet of Petit
Appeville. Here they hoped to meet up with the Calgary Tanks
advancing from Dieppe.

Unfortunately, after they had advanced so far inland, there
was no sign of the tanks. They were now coming under increas-
ingly heavy German fire, and Law decided to give the order for
a withdrawal back to the beach. On the way, a message was
received from Headquarters, advising of the intention to evacuate Green Beach at 10 o'clock. Law and his Camerons returned
to Pourville just before 10.00, but by this time the enemy had
mounted counter-attacks and fierce shelling against the
beaches. A withdrawal across the open beaches invited disaster.
The tide was reaching its low ebb, and the small landing craft
sailed in through a curtain of fire. The evacuation was delayed
until shortly before noon, but of the 12 assault landing craft
that approached the beach, five were hit by shell-fire and sunk.
Many of the men of the S.S.R. and the Camerons were killed or
wounded as they ran across the beach. Mortar fire was coming
from all directions at once.

By now, the Germans had become thoroughly alarmed at the
situation in Pourville. Major Law had achieved the deepest
penetration of all the Canadian battalions involved in the raid.

General Haase, the German commander, ordered a reserve regiment to move up from the rear and repel the invaders. By the time the Camerons had reached the beach, the enemy had again manned the beach defences. Machine guns and mortars were mowing the men down.

Under the sea wall, over 250 wounded were given first aid by the medical officer, Captain Frank Hayter, while they patiently waited for the boats to arrive. Merritt and Law established a combined Battalion Headquarters in the Grand Central Hotel in Pourville, and from there they organised a defensive ring around the town as the Germans advanced.

Until the evacuation, casualties had been comparatively light, but this picture changed drastically once the boats arrived after 11.00 a.m. The beach was saturated with fire from the headlands to the east and west. Bullets and shell fragments seemed to fill the air on every square foot of beach. To leave the shelter of the sea wall was to invite death or wounding. Yet once the boats arrived, the men surged forward in a mad, blinding rush for safety. In that first wild charge, scores of men were killed, their blood staining the pebbles on all sides. The line of men faltered, then broke, as they fled back to the safety of the sea wall. Even several of those who were lucky enough to clamber aboard were later hit or killed as enemy shells holed the boats in a score of places.

Again and again the brave naval crews approached the beach. German fighter bombers now appeared over the beaches to strafe and bomb the survivors. Some Junkers 88's had been fitted with flame throwers, and long streams of smoky red flame flicked out of their bellies.

Merritt led many death-daring attacks against German machine-gun nests and pillboxes that were slaughtering his men on the beaches. He repeatedly succeeded in silencing them until, at approximately 12.30 p.m., the rear guard withdrew to a point just behind the sea wall. Valiantly they fought to keep the enemy at bay until the last men had been evacuated. They must have realised that their own chances of survival were slight, but they stuck to their posts. Merritt had suffered a flesh wound in the shoulder by this time, but continued to lead his men in mad counter-attacks.

The radar specialist had been evacuated earlier on. He would not learn of his brush with death until many years later.

The last survivors had been evacuated from the beach, but

still the rear guard continued to fight. The situation was becoming desperate. After being strafed by R.A.F. fighters, which caused many casualties among the Canadian troops, Merritt realised that he must soon surrender. He asked if anyone had a white flag. Major E. W. (Lefty) White spoke up; it was very much against his principles to show a white flag. He suggested instead that Corporal Joe Waner act as interpreter and give instructions to a German prisoner to return to his own lines and tell the enemy to come in peaceably to take the surrender. Merritt agreed and finally surrendered. But the valiant rear-guard action he had led had allowed hundreds of men to escape.

The assault through Pourville by Merritt's South Saskatchewan Regiment and Gostling's Queen's Own Camerons had been an outstanding success. They had defeated the enemy forces in the Pourville area and advanced inland as far as the German strongpoint at Quatre Vents Farm. If the General Staff back in Britain had not decided to eliminate the flanking attacks by the Calgary Tanks as originally suggested by Mountbatten and his planners from Combined Operations, there is little doubt that this one assault followed by a swing to the left towards the city of Dieppe could have turned the tide and overcome the German defences facing the main beaches.

CHAPTER TEN

BLUE MURDER

The Royal Regiment of Canada will land on Blue Beach and secure the headland east of Jubilee (Dieppe) with a minimum of delay. There they will destroy the local objectives which consist of machine-gun posts, heavy and light flak installations and a 4-gun howitzer battery south and east of the town. The battalion will then come into reserve and detach a company to protect an engineer demolition party operating in the gasworks and power plant.

Attached to the Royal Regiment were three platoons of the Royal Highland Regiment of Canada (the Black Watch) plus some detachments of the 3rd Light Anti-Aircraft Regiment and the 4th Field Regiment of the Royal Canadian Artillery. The Artillery men were to take over the heavy German battery of 105-mm guns beyond the village of Puys, with the help of B Company, Royal Regiment, and to turn the guns around to shell the huge torpedo dump believed to be hidden under the East Headland. The Black Watch, which had been placed under the temporary command of Capt. R. C. Hicks of the Royal Regiment, was ordered to land on the eastern end of Blue Beach to protect the left flank against a possible flank attack from the east.

It had been impressed on the men of the Royal Regiment that the securing of the East Headland known as Le Polet was of vital importance to the operation as a whole. The open main beaches bordering the town of Dieppe were dominated by the East and West Headlands. The Germans had been quick to realise the strategic value of this natural topography and had cunningly arranged heavy gun emplacements on these headlands to make movement impossible on the main beaches.

The Essex Scottish and Royal Hamilton Light Infantry Regiments were scheduled to land on the main beaches at 0520 hours — half an hour after the flanking attacks. The East Headland had to be secured at all costs, or the numerous heavy guns would hurl an impenetrable hail of hot steel and fire against the troops landing there.

The cliffs of the East Headland rose almost vertically — 150 feet above the sea. It was considered impossible for a large assaulting force to scale them in a surprise attack. The only possible method of assault was to land on the tiny beach opposite the village of Puys some 1500 yards to the east of Dieppe. Here nature had carved a gully out of the cliff face. Unfortunately, this beach was only 250 yards long. To lead and direct a large amphibious assault force on to this tiny spot required navigation of a very high order; to add to the difficulty, the landing on a strange coast had to be made in total darkness without the benefit of navigation lights or beacons of any description. At high tide, when the assault was to take place, the beach stretched only 50 yards from the water's edge to the foot of the cliff. To complicate an already difficult approach, the head of the beach was blocked on the land side by a stone-and-concrete sea wall, some 12 feet high, supported by heavy buttresses on the seaward side and topped with rolls of barbed wire. Two flights of stone steps winding up the cliff from the north-east corner of the beach lead into a lane through a narrow valley into the village of Puys.

The beach is steep and consists of large round pebbles of from two to six inches in diameter, difficult to walk on even in broad daylight. At low tide, the pebbly beach is followed by intermittent patches of sand and flat, slippery rocks that rise gradually on each side of a sea entrance less than 300 feet wide. Any assault landing craft approaching the beach at low tide would be forced to sail through this narrow channel, where enemy guns could lob their shells with deadly accuracy.

On the East Headland stands a lonely church — Notre Dame de Bon Secours. Its tall steeple can be spotted far out to sea on a clear day. On the top of the cliff, not far from the sheer drop, stands a large white house with rows of windows on all sides. Unknown to the Royals and to Intelligence, a concrete pillbox camouflaged as a summer house had been hidden in the front garden of the house. The main fire slit of this pillbox had been carefully designed to cover the approaches from the beach and the top of the 12-foot high wall at very short range. On the top of the cliff were sand-bagged machine-gun and mortar positions. On the other side of the gully, another house had also been converted into a German strongpoint. As a final touch of genius, a pillbox had been mounted directly on top of the sea wall to cover any frontal attack from the sea.

All of these obstacles and defences had been designed to provide a death trap for any amphibious assault force foolish enough to attempt a landing on the tiny beach at Puys. If the preliminary air reconnaissance had been carried out more systematically, the massive and impregnable defences on Blue Beach would have been detected and measures taken to destroy them before the landings. Quite possibly, the landing would have been transferred to some other point on the coast and a massacre averted. If the securing of the East Headland was considered so vital to the operation, then other plans should have been ready and available to mount an alternate landing in place of Blue Beach. (After the raid the German commander, General Haase, described the invasion as a textbook lesson in map-reading but totally lacking in flexibility.)

Aboard the infantry landing ships *Queen Emma* and *Princess Astrid,* the men of the Royal Regiment had been awakened at 0100 hours, given breakfast and ordered to assemble at their boat stations ready to disembark. Aboard the *Duke of Wellington,* a similar routine took place as the men of the Black Watch and Artillery Regiments prepared for the assault. At 0300 hours the crew had to sail 10 miles in their landing craft after leaving the mother ship and find a tiny beach and gully with pinpoint accuracy on a strange and hostile coast. The moon had waned an hour before.

Once the assault craft had been lowered into the water, they quickly formed up into two columns, nine deep, sailing in line ahead. Motor Gun Boat No. 316 waited patiently for the craft to form up astern of her so that she could lead them into Blue Beach. Aboard her, Lt. Cdr. H. W. Goulding, the senior naval officer, peered anxiously around him as one flotilla of the landing craft sailed suddenly in the opposite direction in the wake of another M.G.B., No. 315. After a delay, the flotilla officer realised his mistake and headed back to take his proper station astern of M.G.B. 316 with the remainder of the assault craft. His mistake was to cost the whole assault group dearly; when they finally set sail, the time was 0325 hours — 20 minutes late.

Suddenly at 0350, the sky was lit up by star shells a few miles to the east, followed by the long graceful trajectories of tracer bullets. A few seconds later they heard the unmistakable sound of heavy gunfire and presumed correctly that Group 5 containing No. 3 Commando had landed in trouble. Many of the stray bullets pinged against the armoured sides of their assault craft, and the men instinctively ducked lower behind their shields. The firing ceased almost as soon as it had started, and the remaining 30 minutes of the voyage continued peacefully.

To complicate matters still further, Goulding decided to head directly for the main beaches at Dieppe, where he hoped to fix his position by the harbour mole and the lighthouse before changing course and heading for Blue Beach to the east. Due to the lateness of the hour, he ordered an increase in speed which, unfortunately, increased the engine noise of the assault group. Sound carries a long way at sea, and it was not surprising that the German defenders ashore were alerted. The signal station at the mouth of the harbour flashed a recognition challenge that went unanswered. A small German convoy was expected at approximately the same time, and at first it was presumed that the approaching vessels were a part of the convoy. When the German signal went unanswered, the harbour lights were extinguished and a general alarm sounded ashore. The men of the Royals were horrified when the probing fingers of searchlights moved in arcs all around them and flares were fired by the defenders. Fortunately their craft remained undetected. The time was 0420 and a general alert was sounded ashore. The element of surprise had now been completely lost; the one remaining chance for a successful landing had been eliminated.

As the Canadians passed the harbour mole and rounded the East Headland, the first grey light of dawn appeared. They could see the lonely French church, Notre Dame de Bon Secours, and the tiny beach of Puys at the foot of the gully through which they hoped to pass.

Now the first wave picked up speed as they altered course to head directly into the beach. The time was 0510; they were 20 minutes late. In the dim light, they could see German soldiers running along the edge of the cliff as they manned their gun positions. Any doubt remaining that they might still surprise the defenders was suddenly and rudely shattered as they were bathed in stark, blue-white light from an enemy searchlight. Like moths attracted to a candle flame, they were held steadily in its beam as they raced for the shore.

In the leading craft, the men of B Company gripped their

71

rifles tightly as they tensed their muscles ready for the touch-down on the beach. They sat in three rows facing the bow. Those sitting to port and starboard were fortunate; they were protected to some extent by the overhanging steel deck above their heads. The centre row was without any overhead protection. The boat designers had not given any thought to possible strafing from the air or from a clifftop.

When they were only 200 yards from the beach, a storm of machine-gun fire raked the leading boats from end to end. Men screamed in agony as their bodies were riddled again and again. Above the sounds of the screaming and the roar of the engines, they could hear the harsh chattering of the machine guns as they traversed back and forth. As the boat grounded on the pebbly beach, the bow ramp was hastily lowered and the men were suddenly fully exposed to the murderous fire pouring down from the cliffs. Inside the boat, the bullets ricocheted in all directions. The entire centre row of men, who were supposed to disembark first, were killed. Company Sergeant-Major MacIver, seated at the rear of the boat on the starboard side, had to step over and on the bodies of his comrades before he could jump down on to the beach. Just ahead he could see the long stone wall at the foot of the cliff and, as the bullets kicked the sand at his feet, he ran for its dubious shelter. Suddenly it felt as though his head had been jerked off his shoulders. A bullet had shattered his steel helmet before passing through and burying itself in his skull, just below his right eye. Staggering to his feet, he shook his head to clear the blood out of his eyes. Just then he saw his friend Sergeant Tommy Preston from Vancouver drop to the beach with a bad leg wound. Forgetting for the moment that he was himself badly wounded, MacIver hoisted Sergeant Preston on his back and, with an almost pathological indifference to the enemy fire, staggered up the stony beach and dropped his burden against the sea wall before passing out.

Private Bill Stevens and Corporal Al MacDonald were buddies. Together they dived for the beach and were both instantly riddled with bullets. Badly wounded, they still managed to crawl across the fire-swept beach for the dubious shelter of the cliff face. Before the day's end, Stevens suffered more than 20 wounds yet survived.

No. 16 Platoon charged out of their craft in the half light and disappeared into seven feet of water. Private Jack Poolton reached the shore totally exhausted and without his rifle. Most of the others drowned.

Private Steve Michell had to roll aside the bodies of his comrades before he could jump onto the beach. As he did so, he noted with horror that one of them was his platoon commander, Lt. Walters. His batman lay at his side with his arms over his officer's body. In this boat too, the entire centre row of men had been wiped out. Blood ran in red streams in all directions before filling the scuppers. Private Michell jumped into chest-deep water and waded into shore with his rifle held high above his head. In the surf he found the very young lad known as 'Smiler' trying desperately to stuff his intestines back through a great gaping hole in his stomach. He was still smiling as he whispered, 'I'm done for, Steve. Look after yourself.' Michell ran for the shelter of the cliff to get medical attention for the lad, but once there, he gazed around in stunned disbelief. Only about a dozen men remained out of B Company of the Royal Regiment of Canada; 12 men left standing out of a company 10 times that number. The slope leading up to the stone wall was littered with the bodies of fallen soldiers. By the stone steps there must have been at least 60 or 70 of them lying dead, piled one on top of another as they had frantically clawed at the barbed wire barring their way to the top. Frozen in grotesque positions with arms and legs spread in all directions, their bones shattered and pulverised by the rain of fire directed from the clifftop, they had died bravely but futilely — a pathetic monument to inflexible planning and inadequate intelligence reports.

There was no escape. The men who had been fortunate enough to reach the shelter of the sea wall still came under fire from the mortars and machine guns on the clifftop. Only behind the sea-wall buttresses that jutted outwards for a distance of four or five feet was there the slightest shelter. The R.A.F. provided some respite when they finally arrived to deliver low-level strafing attacks on the German gun positions. Other airplanes laid a smoke screen, which unfortunately soon blew away. The Luftwaffe quickly picked up the challenge, and scores of dogfights erupted all over the clear, blue sky. Occasionally, a blazing aircraft left the fight to fall twisting and turning into the sea. Sometimes a white mushroom could be seen detaching itself from the plane before it crashed. Far out to sea, the men could see a solitary rubber dinghy bobbing up and down on the waves, one of the lucky ones. Spitfires of the R.A.F. flew around it until a British air-sea rescue launch picked up the pilot.

Lt. Col. Douglas Catto, the commanding officer of the Royal Regiment of Canada, sailed in with the second wave. Even from a distance, the scene of carnage on Blue Beach was dreadful to behold. Sergeant Tom Nicholls, who had been assigned the Colonel's bodyguard, turned to him and said, 'Sir, if we've got any damned sense, we'll get to hell out of here before we get the same!'

Sadly the Colonel surveyed the awful scene. Shaking his head, he turned to Tom and said, 'We have to go in, Nicholls. My orders are to land at all costs, and besides, my boys on that beach need our help.'

So many good men would have been saved to fight on other beaches and in other battles if Colonel Catto had not been forced to land the second wave. There was little point in landing hundreds of additional men to be slaughtered, but the attempt had to be made if the troops landing on the main beaches were not to be wiped out. The batteries of howitzers above Blue Beach were even at that moment firing hundreds of shells in the direction of the main beaches as the Essex Scottish and R.H.L.I. landed at 0520 hours — on time and at the right places.

As the second wave stormed the miserable little beach, they were exposed to the same murderous fire from the clifftop. If anything, the fire had greatly increased and was now reinforced with dozens of heavy mortar bombs and shells. On all sides the water erupted into huge geysers with the occasional direct hit on an assault craft. The craft that survived this initial bombardment reached the beach only to be subjected to a hail of machine-gun fire. Amidst the harsh chatter of machine guns and the whistle and crump of mortar bombs, the steady monotonous crack of snipers' rifles could be heard. Their prime targets were the officers and senior N.C.O.s; secondary targets were the radio operators carrying the number 18 sets. Cumbersome two-man jobs, they were the only means of communication between shore and ship. Without any means of transmitting and receiving, an adequate picture of events would not be received by the headquarters ships, *Calpe* and *Fernie*.

Corporal George Graves hit the beach with his buddy Private Williams. The first burst of machine-gun fire killed his comrade but left him unscratched. To the left of him he saw Private Bubis, the platoon runner, fall seriously wounded and then lie helplessly at the edge of the sea. It seemed impossible for any living thing to survive the whistling storm of bullets and the flying splinters of shrapnel that whined in all directions. George Graves reached the shelter of the cliff where the survivors crouched, many of them wounded. Hastily scanning the faces of the survivors, he found that very few of the men had survived from his platoon. Those who had made it across the beach had suffered one or more wounds. Graves was shocked to find that one of the badly wounded was the boy soldier, Kenny Ingram, from his platoon; he lay quietly on the beach, his face waxen and expressionless, with a great, ugly wound blossoming on his chest. He died shortly afterwards with his head resting on the lap of one of the older men. George Graves looked at the very young face and gently lowering the young head to the ground, he turned to the pillbox in a cold rage and fired round after round at the gaping slit where a machine gun continued its relentless chatter.

Further down the beach Ptes. Ronnie Reynolds and David Thistle managed to set up a Bren gun to give covering fire for the men trying to climb the sea wall. By this time the enemy was becoming quite bold. Leaving the shelter of their sand-bagged strongpoints, the Germans ran along the edge of the cliffs, dropping stick grenades on to the survivors below. Reynolds was lucky. One of the grenades landed smack in between him and Thistle. While Reynolds only got a superficial wound in the elbow from a piece of grenade shrapnel, his buddy lost an eye. Seconds later, Reynolds received a more serious wound in the side. Lt. Stewart, his platoon officer, was badly hit but ignoring his own wounds, crawled over to Reynolds to ask him if he could continue to fire the Bren, which was having some effect against the enemy. Noting that Stewart's leg was almost severed, he grinned an affirmative answer as he squeezed off burst after burst at the house and pillbox on the cliff until he was wounded once more. Ammunition began to run low, and Freddy Corbett was badly wounded as he tried to crawl over with a fresh supply of Bren magazines. A young officer jumped into the breach and managed to crawl to within 10 feet of Reynolds' Bren gun before he was shot through the head. When the ammunition finally ran out, Reynolds retreated to the sea wall, where he was given rough first aid before returning to fight.

Time after time, the Royals attempted to break out of the trap. Many were killed or were caught in the rolls of heavy barbed wire on the sea wall. Lt. W. G. R. Wedd made a brave dash towards the German pillbox mounted on the sea wall, where he managed to toss in a hand grenade, killing all of the German gun crew within, before he was shot dead. His was not an isolated act of sacrifice. Lt. L. C. Patterson and Captain Sinclair assisted by Corporal L. G. Ellis ran across the beach with sections of Bangalore torpedoes to blow the rolls of barbed wire on top of the wall. Once they reached the shelter of the wall, they fitted the lengths together to place them inside the rolls of wire. It is to Catto's credit that he had wisely included Bangalore torpedoes in his assault equipment, even though aerial photographs had not detected the presence of barbed wire. In the face of murderous machine-gun fire, Patterson exposed himself repeatedly to place the charges in position on top of the wall. He was wounded several times as he did so, but continued to work desperately even when his shoulder was shot away; he succeeded in placing the charges only to find that the trigger mechanism was jammed. As he struggled to release it, a mortar bomb landed just behind him and he was instantly killed.

Jumping into the breech, Sinclair and Ellis managed to free the mechanism and after ducking down below the wall, fired the charge at last. Ellis jumped through the gap in the wire and became the first man off the beach. Alone, he raced up the hill to engage the Germans. The men following on his heels found the hole resealed by the enemy, who had quickly concentrated a rain of fire on the opening to discourage others.

On the western end of the beach, Catto had landed with the second wave of the Royals composed of C and D Companies. At the other end of the beach, the Black Watch had managed to land their mortars unharmed. For a brief period of time, they retaliated, before the mortar teams were slaughtered. Their sacrifice gave the colonel and the survivors of C and D Companies time to reach the sea wall. Unfortunately, they had lost their Bangalore torpedoes over the side when transferring from the mother ship to their assault craft. This bungle was to cost them dearly in human lives before a sergeant produced from somewhere a pair of wire cutters. Then began the long, laborious task of cutting countless rolls of barbed wire on top of the wall in full view of the enemy. For a time, their frantic cutting went unnoticed. But suddenly the machine guns traversed back and forth across their section of the wire to discourage any further attempts at breaking out. The men crouched down below the wall to escape the hail of bullets sweeping across the top.

At this moment Lt. Bob Stewart stood up in full view of the enemy machine guns and fired burst after burst from his Bren gun. Under cover of this brave officer's fire, Catto worked desperately to cut the remaining strands of wire. If they failed, they would all be slaughtered.

The hands gripping the wire cutters were torn and bleeding when the final strand parted with a ping. Catto plunged through the wire, closely followed by 14 of his men. As the tiny assault force raced up the hill, Stewart sank to his knees nursing his red-hot Bren gun and wearing a beatific smile in spite of the serious leg wound he had suffered. The time was 0612 hours — they had been ashore for only about 65 minutes.

Corporal Ellis, meanwhile, had already entered two houses on the outskirts of Puys, where he succeeded in killing three snipers before single-handedly engaging a German machine-gun nest with his rifle. After exchanging fire for some time, he decided that perhaps the odds were a little unequal and retreated back to the hole he had made in the wire. He succeeded in wriggling through and dropping back down onto the beach to join the surviving remnants of the Royal Regiment, who now crouched under the wall, hopelessly trapped and protected by the bodies of their dead comrades piled before them.

At the other end of the headland, Catto and his small band of men charged up the hill and quickly overwhelmed one of the fortified houses on the clifftop which had been responsible for the deaths of so many of the Royals' men. They then rushed from house to house to flush out the defenders although many had already been hastily evacuated.

With a larger body of men, the Colonel could have overrun the defenders completely. But when a German counter-attack was mounted against them, he wisely decided that the time had come for a cautious retreat back to the hole in the wire. They had partially succeeded in their task. They had silenced one of the strongpoints, and the enemy fire had been greatly decreased on the western half of the beach. The time was now 0700 hours. When they reached the break in the wire, they found to their consternation that the enemy had closed the escape route by a constant stream of machine-gun fire directed at the opening. Turning aside, they ran for the cover of a small wood, where they remained hidden for the rest of the morning.

On the beach, the Germans poured hundreds of mortar bombs and shells on the few survivors. Many of the men lay motionless, not daring to move a muscle as they feigned death. The intense fire slowly died down. Only staccato bursts sounded as the enemy detected movement among the bodies.

If only there had been a preliminary bombardment or naval fire support from the sea! One heavy cruiser could have annihilated the defenders and saved the Royals. H.M.S. *Garth* was the destroyer detailed to support the landing at Puys. Syd Wilkinson, a Royal Navy telegraphist, had landed with the Royal Regiment as part of a special services unit set up by the Royal Navy to provide communication by portable radio transmitters and receivers between navy ships and the army units landing on the beach. Their specific function was to contact *Garth* sailing off-shore and provide the range, elevation, and targets for her 4-in. guns to bombard in support of the assault troops.

The F.O.O. party reached the shelter of the cliff, but the signalman was killed as he crossed the beach after leaving the landing craft. Unfortunately, Captain Browne, the Forward Observation Officer, followed Catto in his scramble through the wire. Syd Wilkinson and the rest of the team tried to follow but found it impossible after a major and several men of the Royals were badly wounded as they tried to squeeze through the same hole in the wire.

Browne had the code books and maps in his possession, but he was no longer in contact with his team. The wounded major ordered Wilkinson to contact *Garth* and request covering fire to knock out the German guns on the clifftop. The first shells fired by *Garth* landed a considerable distance away on the beach but fortunately did not do any damage to their own troops. The second salvo landed very close to Syd and his team — again on the beach! It began to look as though they would be blown up by their own destroyer, so the major ordered him to signal cease-fire. The little ship complied with the cease-fire order, but for the remainder of that dreadful morning she hovered off the beach, unable to assist the men trapped there. By now the beach was shrouded in smoke provided by the Air Force. Although it provided some measure of relief to the survivors, the smoke also masked the beach from the supporting naval forces so that they were unable to assist with their fire-power.

Bombardier Harry Hancock of the 4th Field Regiment, Royal Canadian Artillery, landed with D Company of the Royal Regiment in the second wave, aboard an M.L.C. carrying over 150 men who were tightly packed in. When the ramp dropped on the beach, the troops could not disembark fast enough because of the dense mass of bodies blocking the exit. The German gunners heavily machine-gunned the troops jammed at the ramp. Many were killed, and those following behind were forced to roll the dead over the side in order to clear a passage. To make matters worse, the naval crew became nervous and backed off the beach before all of the men had disembarked. Some returned to England with the boat, but Bombardier Hancock decided to land and found himself sinking in 20 feet of water. He had generously offered to carry the heavy load of demolition bombs in his own pack when another man had complained about the additional weight. His generosity was now about to drown him. In a frenzied underwater struggle, he finally managed to divest himself of the heavy pack of bombs and struggle to the surface. He gulped in great breaths of air as he swam for shore about 100 feet away. Finally he collapsed on the pebbly beach, totally exhausted. A burst of machine-gun fire narrowly missed his head, lacerating his face with stone chips, but it acted as a forceful incentive to get him to his feet and run for the cliff face to join the remainder of his fellow artillery men.

For the remainder of that dreadful morning, Bombardier Hancock carried the wounded along the beach to a little cave that had been converted into a first-aid station by Captain Robertson, one of the medical officers. As he staggered along the beach with his human burden, he threw smoke bombs behind him so that he wouldn't be shot in the back.

Aboard the headquarters ship, *Calpe*, General Roberts and Captain Hughes-Hallett anxiously awaited news from the Royals on Blue Beach. The first message received at 0620 hours stated, 'Royal Regiment of Canada not landed'. Another version of the same message was received by *Fernie*, the deputy headquarters ship, at 0625 hours, 'Impossible to land any troops on Blue Beach. From navy.' Due to the lack of communication with Blue Beach, the Force Commanders aboard *Calpe* now firmly believed that the Royals were still at sea and unable to land; Roberts therefore sent out a signal to the Royals at 0640 hours directing them to sail to Red Beach and assist the Essex Scottish in their landing. The Force Commanders could not know that the Royals had been almost wiped out. The message reporting that the Royals had not been able to land had most likely been radioed by the Germans. Their task was made easy by the loss of the naval code books carried by Captain Browne when he left the naval signal party on the beach. Any signals sent out by Telegraphist Wilkinson were now in plain language. To complete the confusion, the naval flotilla officer, Lt. Cdr. Goulding, arrived aboard *Calpe* shortly after the puzzling signal had been received to report that the Royal Regiment had successfully landed on Blue Beach!

At 0730 hours, a signal was received aboard *Calpe* from Blue Beach asking for the troops to be evacuated at once. This signal was most likely genuine. A motor boat and two landing craft were directed to Blue Beach to carry out the evacuation but were met by an impenetrable curtain of shell and mortar fire as they approached the beach. The tide was now on the ebb, and the narrow channel through which they were forced to sail was fully exposed. The only craft that managed to reach Blue Beach was the A.L.C. 209, commanded by Lt. N. E. B. Ramsay, R.N.V.R. The survivors on the beach made a mad rush for the boat, which was already badly holed by shellfire. The Germans held their fire until the landing craft, heavily overloaded with wounded and shell-shocked men, had backed off the beach, frantically revving up her engines to escape. Then, when she was 50 yards from shore, the soldiers aboard were cut to pieces by a hail of shrapnel and bullets that poured from the clifftop.

Lt. Ramsay was killed instantly, along with his crew. His ship broke in half and sank. Seconds later, bodies and pieces of bodies were released from the wreckage as a great gush of air bubbled to the surface. Mercifully, the human wreckage showed itself for only a brief moment before sinking from sight beneath the surface of the sea.

On Blue Beach, the firing had finally died down until, at 0800 hours, it ceased entirely. Shortly afterwards, the Germans used a loud hailer to demand that the survivors surrender. For a few moments there was utter silence, and then they received their answer from Regimental Sergeant-Major Murray, senior non-commissioned officer of the Royal Regiment. It was short, terse, and very much to the point: 'Go to hell!' A short time later a second demand for surrender was made. This time there was a much longer silence; the wounded were lying on the beach, many were bleeding to death for want of medical attention, but still they did not wish to surrender. The tide was coming in and one by one, the wounded were being drowned. It was a hopeless situation. When the Germans bellowed, 'This is your last chance to surrender,' one of the officers raised a white flag and German soldiers appeared on the clifftop and even from holes in the cliff where they had been hidden all through the action, sniping continuously. Ladders were lowered to the beach and down they came, the hidden enemy they had never seen.

The Germans were very nervous as they quickly circled around the survivors and forced them back against the cliff face and the sea wall. The order was being bellowed all up and down the beach, *'Hände auf den Kopf. Sofort, sonst werdet ihr erschossen!'* To make sure the men understood properly, several English-speaking German soldiers were bellowing the same order, 'Put your hands on top of your head. Quickly now, or you will be shot!' The men did not require a second warning. The German soldiers were battle-happy. This was certainly not the time to antagonise them.

The men were searched before being forced to climb the ladders off the beach. There was little brutality. Only the occasional ugly incident marred the surrender. Mounting the ladder, one of the prisoners pushed the man above him in his haste to get off the hateful beach. The German waiting at the top of the ladder shot and wounded the unfortunate man who had been pushed over the edge. As he tumbled back, he fell on top of Bombardier Hancock, and both of them ended up at the foot of the ladder. The German officer standing next to the German soldier who had fired drew his Luger pistol and shot him dead! Hancock was then ordered to take the wounded Canadian to the German Field Dressing Station down the road. When he finally arrived there with his wounded comrade, the place looked like an abattoir. The German doctors and assistants were wearing long aprons covered with blood. It gave Hancock a malicious sense of satisfaction to see that the blood that had been spilled was not all Canadian.

Although the Germans behaved with a certain measure of correctness towards the prisoners, they adamantly refused to allow them to return to the beach to bring up the badly wounded. Many men were left on the beach until the next day. The majority died of their wounds, while several others drowned as the tide rose over the blood-stained beach. After the abortive attempt to evacuate the men, the enemy was understandably nervous and firmly believed that a second invasion force would follow, so they were not going to take any chances.

The Canadians able to walk were mustered in a large school courtyard surrounded by high walls. Their guards were not unkind, but they all seemed to mouth the same phrase over and over: *'Für euch ist der Krieg zu Ende.'* 'For you the war is over!' A few minutes later, the war returned to them in all its violence; a British Spitfire zoomed down at housetop level and systematically strafed the prisoners, killing some and wounding a great many more. Corporal George Graves had survived the bloody action on the beach without suffering a scratch. Now he found himself lying on the ground with a bad leg wound — shot by his own side. The seriously wounded were loaded on to trucks and taken to hospital at Rouen, while all those able to walk were marched along the road to Dieppe; one wounded leg or arm was no deterrent.

As the prisoners neared the town of Dieppe, they could hear in the distance the sounds of combat on the main beaches, where their comrades in the Essex Scottish and Royal Hamilton Light Infantry were fighting another unequal battle. Behind them the enemy gun batteries on the East Headland behind Puys added their chorus to the bombardment.

Canadian losses were enormous. The Royals had lost more than any other unit engaged at Dieppe. The regiment's fatalities, including those who died later from wounds and 18 who died while prisoners of war, amounted to 227 out of 554 men who had embarked. Only two officers and 65 men returned to England after the raid, and several of them were wounded. Most of these men had all been in one craft — an L.C.M. that had had engine trouble and had landed much later than the rest. It pulled back off the beach, under murderous fire, after only a few men had landed. The remainder were wounded on board. Not a single man escaped from the Black Watch; all were either killed or taken prisoner. The artillery, signals, and other units attached to the Royal Regiment for the beach landing at Puys suffered a similar fate.

CHAPTER ELEVEN

MASSACRE ON THE MAIN BEACHES

At five in the morning, the sea front at Dieppe lay brooding and hushed. To the casual eye, there were no signs of life. But from hundreds of vantage points all around the sea front, the enemy searched the horizon for the first signs of invasion. They felt it must come soon. To the east and west the sky was illuminated by intermittent bursts of gunfire and tracers. The atmosphere was tense. Nothing stirred except the sea, lapping the shore at full tide. The invasion fleet was then only three miles away from Dieppe and forming up in the darkness for the final approach and touchdown.

The planners had divided the Main Beach into two halves, designating them Red and White Beaches. A battalion of the Essex Scottish Regiment under the command of Lt. Col. Jasperson would land on the eastern half on Red Beach, while the Royal Hamilton Light Infantry under the command of Lt. Col. Labatt would land on the adjoining White Beach. Together they would storm the beach and cross the sea wall before the defenders had had time to raise their heads and face the onslaught. There could be no delay in getting off the beaches and into the town. To assist them in their task, they would be accompanied by 400 sappers (carrying demolition charges), the Calgary Tanks, and the Regiment Fusiliers de Mont Royal.

The tanks were carried aboard tank landing craft, large unwieldy vessels fitted with a forward ramp that would be lowered onto the beach to allow the heavy tanks to land. The first wave of tanks had been ordered to land simultaneously with the infantry to provide maximum fire support and cover in the initial assault. Accompanied by tiny gun boats and motor launches, the assault landing craft deployed into orderly columns and headed directly into the beaches of Dieppe at a speed of 10 knots. They had been led to believe that air and naval bombardment delivered just prior to the touchdown would pulverise the enemy defences and allow them to land with little opposition. In the dim light of approaching dawn, white buildings along the sea front could be faintly seen. Over to the left, the navigation lights on the harbour mole blinked on and off and were then hastily extinguished. Over to the right the lighthouse (Phare d'Ailly) flashed its warning signal. Rapidly they closed the beaches. Pte. Tom McDermott stood in the bow of the A.L.C. with his platoon officer, Lt. Jimmy Palms. Their platoon belonged to D Company of the Essex Scottish Regiment. Tom was a private but a firm friend of his platoon officer. Both men were American citizens. They had crossed the border into Windsor, Ontario, at the outbreak of war to volunteer for the Canadian Army. They were not alone; many other Americans had joined them in the regiment before they sailed overseas.

The sudden ear-shattering roar of low-flying aircraft exploded behind them as Bostons, Spitfires, and Hurricanes dived in to attack enemy gun emplacements ahead. Slowly, the black curtain of night was nudged aside by dawn's left hand. On the horizon, a clear blue sky crept up from the sea. It was going to be a fine day.

The white buildings along the beach were hidden from sight under a dense cloud of smoke laid by friendly aircraft. At 0510 hours — 10 minutes to landing — the destroyers *Garth*, *Bleasdale*, *Berkeley*, and *Albrighton* added their main armament to the bombardment. The air was filled with the curious swish of 4-in. shells passing overhead, followed by distant heavy thumps as they toppled enemy gun positions on the headland. Overhead, scores of planes dived in at rooftop height, strafing and bombing the fortifications. The men hunched forward in their seats, tense and ready to charge off the ramp once it was lowered. They thought of the advice given most forcefully by a British Commando instructor on the subject of leaving a boat and rushing up the beach. 'There are two types of men in the world, the quick and the dead, so you wants to be bloody quick!'

As they neared the shore, fear was slowly replaced by a feverish sense of excitement. Each man had been instructed carefully on his own particular tasks; nervously they did a mental re-run over the details and tried to picture the maps and models they had studied for so long.

Aboard the tank landing craft, the tank crews began warming up the massive engines of their tanks. Earphones were donned as they waited for the terse command. Packed in the narrow space between the tanks and the side of the landing craft, 85 sappers of the Royal Canadian Engineers readied themselves for the touchdown. Each man carried a rucksack that contained a lethal 60 pounds of plastic gelignite plus a tarred bag of incendiaries. Platoons of infantrymen from the Fusiliers de Mont Royal, Essex Scottish, and Royal Hamilton Light Infantry Regiments had been assigned aboard each tank landing craft to assist the sappers and to provide some measure of protecting fire-power while the demolition charges were set.

Sapper Bill Lynch of the 2nd Field Company, R.C.E. from Toronto, stood on the tank treads so that he could poke his head out through the covering tarpaulin for a quick peek. The enemy was fighting back. On all sides, great geysers of water were spouting high in the air as shells exploded among the landing craft. A direct hit and men were flung high into the air amidst clouds of yellow and red flames. Bill hurriedly withdrew his head when a small hole appeared in the tarpaulin close by. The accompanying 'plock' warned him that a German sniper didn't care much for the shape of his head.

The leading craft were now only about 75 yards from the beach. It was impossible to hear what the man alongside was saying amidst the din of battle. The Essex Scottish sailed in line abreast and hit the beach together — on time and mostly in the right spot. Lt. Palms shook hands with Tom McDermott and shouted, 'Good luck!' as he led the charge onto the beach.

Where was the heavy bombing they had been promised? The enemy defences appeared to be whole and deadly efficient. Many had been killed and wounded as they stepped off the landing craft. The initial rush was halted suddenly about 10 yards from the boat by large rolls of heavy concertina wire. The men hugged the pebbly beach and waited for the Bangalore torpedoes to be placed under the wire to clear a path. The Bangalore torpedoes lay at the edge of the surf buried beneath a mass of arms and legs stilled in death. The massacre would have been complete if Pte. McDermott had not suddenly thrown his body across the wire in a brave, foolish, sacrificial gesture. The survivors jumped to their feet and using his body as a bridge, raced across the wire and flopped under the scant shelter of the sea wall. Bruised and cut, Tom McDermott lay passively on the wire almost oblivious to pain until he felt the full weight of a man crash on top of him. Face down, McDermott screamed at the man to get off his aching back, but Stan

Shepley was unable to hear him. He was dead. Tearing himself loose, Tom ran for the sea wall where he could see Lt. Palms standing up in full view of the enemy, trying to cut a way through the second barbed wire barrier along the sea wall. A burst of machine-gun fire tore into Palms' chest and knocked him back — dead.

Lt. Col. Jasperson over on the right had also arrived at the sea wall with the survivors of the Essex Scottish. A Bangalore torpedo placed under the wire on the wall had failed to clear most of the tangled webs and they were left trapped on the beach. By now, they should have been tearing along the esplanade, flushing the enemy out of the gun pits.

Captain Dennis Guest, Company Commander of A Company, Essex Scottish Regiment, also landed on the first wave. Touchdown was about 200 yards to the right of the designated spot so that A Company found itself alongside the Royal Hamilton Light Infantry and to the right of the main body of the Essex Scottish. Captain Guest and his men were also trapped at the first line of wire, but fortunately, it was not very high above the ground. After suffering a number of casualties, Guest took a running jump at the wire and cleared it. The remainder of the men followed in similar fashion. By the time they reached the doubtful shelter of the sea wall, only about 35 men remained out of 108 who had debouched from the boats. Through an unfortunate error, the Bangalore torpedoes had not been loaded aboard the craft when it left England. The wire on the top of the sea wall proved to be quite impenetrable. Corporal Storr struggled desperately to cut the heavy rolls of dannert wire, but without Bangalore torpedoes the task was hopeless. Enemy machine gunners zeroed in on the wire, forcing Guest and his men to dig frantically into the shingle.

Near to the Casino, a mortar bomb landed in Major Hayhurst's lap and blew him to pieces. Harry Bassil, the Sergeant-Major of D Company, Essex Scottish, also hit the beach on the first wave; led by his platoon commander, Lt. Jack Prince, he managed to reach the sea wall with most of his platoon still surviving. The shale had washed up against the wall at this point and he was able to look over the wall into the town. Almost immediately he was wounded in the thigh and right thumb. The bullet that shattered his thumb was meant for his head, his rifle was smashed, but it had served to deflect the

86

fatal bullet. Minutes later, enemy mortars zeroed in to Harry's platoon under the sea wall. Amidst the crump of shells and the moans of the dying, Harry dug frantically in behind one of the timber groynes that ran out to sea from the sea wall. With each fresh explosion the men tried to flatten their bodies even further into the gravel, finger-nails broken and bleeding as they frantically tore at the pebbles and against the shuddering, heaving earth in a vain effort to hide themselves from the rain of red-hot metal whining and pinging all around them. With a terrific bang and flash, the timber groyne next to Harry's head exploded and jammed his steel helmet firmly down onto his eyes. When the stars had cleared, he offered a silent prayer for a fist-sized hole in the timber that had saved his life.

The company radio operator was killed as they landed. His radio equipment had been destroyed by an enemy shell, leaving the regiment without communication with *Calpe* or with their comrades in the R.H.L.I. to the right of them on White Beach. From a highly trained battalion of front-line troops, the Essex Scottish Regiment had been reduced in the opening minutes of the battle to scattered bands of men, many of them wounded, hopelessly trapped and subjected to a murderous fire from an unseen enemy. Many of the senior N.C.O.s and officers had been picked off by enemy snipers as they landed. It was impossible to go forward, impossible to retreat with the sea at their backs. The position appeared hopeless.

The Calgary Tanks, which were supposed to land at the same time as the infantry, arrived 15 minutes late due to an unfortunate error in navigation. The Tanks had been carried over from England aboard tank landing craft – three tanks to each ship. The plan called for the 2nd L.C.T. flotilla to land the first wave of tanks, while the remainder stayed offshore with the 4th L.C.T. flotilla in floating reserve. Also carried aboard these craft were scout cars containing masses of radio communication equipment, signal staffs commanded by Major Rolfe and Brigadiers Lett and Southam with their headquarters staffs.

The firing ashore lessened somewhat as the tank landing craft approached the beaches, but the moment they lowered their ramps a devastating concentration of enemy fire poured into them from all directions. Heavy artillery from the headlands, aided by multiple mortars, pounded them from bow to stern.

L.C.T. 145 was the first to land its three tanks, *Company*, *Calgary*, and *Chief*, on the far left of the beach, but before it could reverse its engines and escape, it was hit by a dozen shells that killed its naval crew and left it burning fiercely before it sank offshore. L.C.T. 163 sailed bravely in to the beach in a suicidal effort to land her tanks. A shell in the engine room had started a massive internal fire, but she continued to head in until the helmsman collapsed, overcome by fumes. The ill-fated ship veered to port. Then another seaman took over the helm and corrected the course until he too was hit. Another rating grabbed the spinning helm from his dying fingers and brought the sinking ship to within 60 yards of the shore before he was also killed. A fourth man brought the brave ship in to the beach, where the tanks were successfully landed. Reversing on her kedge anchor she managed to leave the terrible beach and escape to sea.

L.C.T. 127 had her ramp smashed by shellfire, which set fire to her ready ammunition and magazine. Most of the crew were killed, but her cargo of three tanks, *Cougar*, *Cheetah*, and *Cat*, were seen landing safely on the beach. L.C.T. 159 was put out of action before she began the final run in, and her tanks were unable to land. L.C.T. 126 hit the beach in a sinking condition but managed to land her tanks, *Burns*, *Backer*, and *Bolster*, before she sank off-shore.

Lt. Ed Bennett stood on the turret of his tank *Bellicose* in order to see which way his tank should proceed on the beach. A shell landed aboard and hit the hydrogen cylinders used for inflating the barrage balloon each craft flew overhead. In the holocaust that followed, Ed was severely burned. All his hair was singed away, and one eye was blown from its socket. Brigadier Southam and Major Rolfe were aboard the same landing craft, and some of the all-important radio equipment was destroyed. Staggering to his feet, Ed climbed up on to his tank and dropped down through the hatch ready to direct his troop of three tanks on to the beach ahead.

They had landed right in the centre of Red and White Beaches with the Essex Scottish on the left and the R.H.L.I. on the right. The beach was shrouded in smoke and it was difficult to see which way to head off it. Many of the tanks lay stranded on the beach, half-buried in the shingle with their tracks shot away. It was obvious that they had bogged down in the loose shingle, so Ed Bennett directed his tanks to proceed along the waterline to the Casino where the beach was firmer. Unfortunately, the waterline was dotted with the bodies of comrades and the tanks were forced to pass over them in order to break out. The sea wall near the Casino proved to be much lower than anywhere else due to the shingle that had been washed up by previous high tides. After several trial runs, they made it over the top and found themselves out in the open on the promenade of the Boulevard Maréchal Foch – facing the enemy at last. With the yellow pennant of B Squadron proudly flying, they fired round after round into the enemy-held buildings and strongpoints facing them.

Major Gordon Rolfe, Tank Battalion Signals Officer, had his scout car *Hunter* towed off by the last tank, *Bloody*. As they neared the sea wall, Major Rolfe pulled a lever, disconnecting the towline from the tank. Unfortunately the tank stalled on the edge of a huge anti-tank ditch and then rolled back to crush the front of the scout car. The radio equipment in the rear of the car was undamaged, however, so Rolfe established his tank communication centre right where he was.

Brigadier Southam followed him off the landing craft with copy 37 of the battle orders tucked under his arm and strictly against orders. His signal staff wheeled the brigade wireless communication equipment ashore in a push carriage. They quickly established themselves in a hollow near the Casino and hastily set up the radio equipment to communicate with the regiments on the beach and *Calpe*, the headquarters ship. Almost immediately, a tank crashed down into the hollow, crushing the precious equipment and killing the signalmen. Brigadier Southam then made his way over to Major Rolfe's tank communication centre and arranged for all brigade messages to be sent and received on Rolfe's equipment. For the next seven hours, this would be the sole method of communication between shore and afloat.

L.C.T. 5 beached just alongside the Casino, but she was immediately shelled so severely that her naval crew was killed and the ship set ablaze from stem to stern. Her three tanks managed to reach the beach, but only the first got over the sea wall and on to the promenade. The second tank, commanded by Captain Marcel Lambert, threw a track and bogged down in the shingle to become a helpless target for every German gunner. The third tank also bogged down in the shingle, unable to move for the remainder of the battle.

L.C.T. 6 was the only tank landing craft of the second wave to survive, and her three tanks, *Bob*, *Bert*, and *Bill*, all managed to breach the sea wall and tear up the promenade. Miraculously, her captain was able to leave the beach and head out to sea, even though she was ablaze and holed with shellfire in several places.

L.C.T. 8 brought Brigadier Sherwood Lett and Lt. Col. Johnny Andrews with his tank battalion headquarters staff. Captain Austin Stanton led the troops of tanks ashore, but his own tank bogged down in the treacherous shingle. The sappers of the R.C.E. aboard his craft rushed ashore to assist with chespaling mats, but seven of the twelve were killed as soon as they stepped on the beach.

The landing craft was forced to reverse and seek deeper water, as the bogged-down tank blocked the exit off the ramp for the other two tanks aboard. Brigadier Lett managed to contact Lt. Col. Labatt of the R.H.L.I. by radio communication and informed him that he was again coming into land. 'Don't for Christ's sake!' replied Labatt. 'It's bloody hopeless!'

The enemy fire was reaching a crescendo. Every inch of the beach was swept by bullets and shellfire. Mortar bombs were lobbed in every exposed spot to add their quota of flying steel. As L.C.T. 8 again approached the beach, she was hit repeatedly by shell and mortar bomb. Brigadier Lett was severely wounded. Colonel Parks-Smith, R.M. of Mountbatten's Combined Operations Staff, was killed. The captain, officers, and all but one of the naval crew were killed. The engine-room artificer was blown through a hole in the side of the vessel.

A soldier raced below and managed to control the throttle while a marine took over the helm. Just at that moment a shell hit the ramp, breaking the lowering mechanism; the ramp crashed down into the sea, preventing the L.C.T. from approaching the beach. Lt. Col. Johnny Andrews, thinking that the ramp had been lowered on the beach, headed off the ship and sank in deep water. The crew managed to swim ashore but the enemy machine gunners concentrated their fire on to Andrews and he died in the surf riddled with bullets. L.C.T. 8 now managed to reverse engines and leave. Lett contacted Labatt by R/T and handed over the command of the Brigade to him. Truth to tell, there was little left to command!

Lt. Art Breithaupt of Kitchener, Ontario, managed to get his troop of tanks, *Betty*, *Blondie*, and *Brenda*, off the beach and on to the promenade. Ed Bennett contacted him on R/T and guided him to the low spot over the sea wall near the Casino.

The Churchill tanks had been waterproofed to allow them to land safely in not more than six feet of water. The twin-engine exhausts had been extended upwards to allow the engines to run even though the tank was partially submerged. Trooper Percy Aide was the radio operator in the lead tank on his L.C.T. His buddy, Bill Isbister, was the driver with Len Hudson gunner and Bill Stewart co-driver. Capt. Purdy aboard their tank was the troop commander. As the L.C.T. approached the beach, the cables controlling the forward ramp were cut by shellfire and, when the ramp dropped, it grounded below the ship, bringing it to a halt. Thinking that the ship had correctly beached, Capt. Purdy gave the order to advance and the ill-fated tank dropped into eight feet of water. The horrified crew realised that they were about to be drowned when the lights were extinguished and water started to pour in. After several desperate attempts, Percy Aide managed to free the hatch and the crew escaped in time.

The second tank behind Capt. Purdy managed to reach the sea wall, where it was halted by an anti-tank ditch. The third and last tank was held back because the wooden chocks had not been removed from beneath the tracks. As the tank skidded and reversed, Sgt. Cecil G. Towler, 11th Field Company, Royal Canadian Engineers, shouted to one of his sappers, Blackie Oliver, to remove the chocks. Poor Blackie ran forward to carry out his orders but the driver panicked and tried to gun his engines to force a way through. The tank swerved and Blackie was crushed to death. He became the first R.C.E. casualty aboard the L.C.T. Sgt. Cec Towler and his 85 sappers had still to unload their heavy cargo of explosives and get up the beach.

Of the 24 tank landing craft that had sailed from England, 10 landed a total of 29 tanks. Only 15 tanks were successful in climbing the sea wall and reaching the enemy-held promenade. Two were submerged and another 12 were unable to leave the beach, either because they had bogged down in the loose shingle or had had their tracks shot away.

Most of the crews refused to abandon their immobile tanks and continued to fire their guns throughout the long day of horror and suffering. Although many men were killed on the beach by enemy shells directed at the tanks, it is undoubtedly true that the tanks were the deterrent that prevented the enemy from advancing on to the beach over the sea wall.

Major Brian McCool of the Royal Regiment of Canada had been given the unenviable position of Beachmaster on the main beaches. Assisted by Commander Jeff Lambert, R.N., he was supposed to co-ordinate the movement of men and materials on and off the beaches in an orderly, well-disciplined manner. Special ancillary units were attached to his force to carry out his orders. The military police were represented by the Provost Corps of Guelph, Ontario. A special beach party from the Essex Scottish regiment known as the first Canadian Commandos under Colonel MacGregor had been given several very important tasks, including guarding the radar specialists landing on the main beach, evacuating the wounded, taking over rear-guard duties during the re-embarkation, and, last of all, erecting a series of flagpoles on the beaches with a flag flying from each. These flagpoles were really disguised Bangalore torpedoes, which would blow up the enemy troops as they came down onto the beach.

McCool jumped on to the beach from his landing craft and didn't even get his feet wet. His companion, Commander Lambert, was not so lucky and received a wetting before he followed McCool at a run up the beach to the sea wall. Enemy fire lanced at them from all directions, but both men reached the wall unhurt. As he ran McCool glanced over his shoulder and was shocked and distressed to see that his entire staff lay sprawled in grotesque piles all the way up the beach. He and Lambert were the only survivors. The sun rose above the buildings of Dieppe and blinded the attackers with its dazzling early morning rays. It was impossible to see the enemy. A young naval officer named Robson ran up to report to McCool. He dropped on to one knee to shout his report over the hellish noise. McCool recalls that he was a rosy-cheeked lad with curly hair. Something whipped past McCool's right cheek and suddenly there was a neat round hole in between the naval officer's eyes and he was dead — still smiling. McCool had escaped death by a hair's breadth. Before the day was over, he would describe how the enemy drew 'claret' five separate times — none of the wounds were of a serious nature. Corporal Bob Pearson of Guelph was attached to the Provost Corps under Lt. Oliver. They remained under McCool's orders but in reality there was nothing for them to do except survive. Any movement on the beach was an invitation for an early ticket to heaven.

Pte. Mac Maloy of the Essex Scottish Regiment had landed with Colonel MacGregor and the Special Canadian Commandos. In Maloy's charge was a mystery major who wore a hat with a yellow band. He was one of the radar specialists who were supposed to investigate the German radar equipment ashore. Mac had strict orders to shoot him if capture appeared imminent. The major carried a locked briefcase, and before Mac left the beach he personally burned the papers inside it. During the long day, MacGregor and Maloy made the long perilous trip along the beach several times in order to contact other regiments and to pass along orders. Radio contact between the Essex Scottish and Royal Hamilton Light Infantry was practically non-existent after the first few minutes of battle.

Huddled under the sea wall, Company Sgt. Maj. Cornelius Stapleton seethed with a slow burning frustration; on all sides, his men were being slaughtered by an enemy they couldn't even see to fight. Aided by two of his men, he finally succeeded in firing a Bangalore torpedo under the rolls of concertina wire crowning the top of the sea wall. With a mighty roar of defiance, he leaped over the sea wall and dashed over the Boulevard Maréchal Foch followed by a platoon of his men from the Essex Scottish Regiment. Firing their Bren guns from the hip, they raced along past German-occupied hotels on the sea front, lobbing hand grenades through windows and doors as they passed. Reaching the tobacco factory, they were heartened by the sight of billowing clouds of smoke and flames pouring from every window. British Intelligence had reported that the building was being used as an ammunition dump; in actual fact, the factory contained tobacco, and the townspeople of Dieppe would be deprived of their weekly ration for some time to come. Kicking down doors and racing upstairs, Stapleton and his men wreaked savage vengeance on the enemy gunners before retreating back across the boulevard to report to Colonel Jasperson.

Another party led by Lt. Bill Scott of the Essex Scottish arrived at the sea wall with only one sergeant and four privates remaining from his platoon — all that was left after the murderous crossing of the beach. The sea wall where they finally huddled was very high and under concentrated fire from enemy machine guns. By 0700 hours, after suffering further casualties, they decided to crawl along the beach under the scant shelter of the wall to find a way out of the trap. It was a hair-raising journey but better than being continuously pounded with mortar bombs. After crawling some 500 yards, they came at last to a low spot in the sea wall where the harbour mole provided partial cover. A hasty scramble over the wire, a short dash, and they found themselves on the eastern corner of the tower facing the promenade that ran the whole length of the sea front. Enemy fire forced them to seek shelter in a shop window where all the glass had been blown out. Squatting like tailors' dummies they were pleased to see a German truck loaded with troops rumbling past them. As one, they fired point blank, killing all the truck's passengers. The German truck landed in another store window.

On White Beach, Labatt and his Royal Hamilton Light Infantry were also facing impossible odds. The massive front of the Casino led from the promenade down to the beach, and Labatt realised almost immediately that he had to take the Casino to allow his men to funnel through into the town. The German defenders had also realised this possibility and shortly before the raid had begun to demolish the building. At the moment, it was a very heavily fortified strongpoint, with light machine guns and anti-tank weapons poking out of every window. On the corners of the building pillboxes had been constructed, and from their gun slits a continuous fire swept the beaches from end to end. Captain Tony Hill led a frenzied charge against the massed guns of the Casino, which were surrounded by rolls of heavy concertina wire on all sides. A Bangalore torpedo blew a path through the wire to allow Captain Whittaker to lead a charge against the nearest pillbox. Heavy casualties forced the men to halt in their mad charge, but one man, Private Hugh McCourt, managed to reach the pillbox and ram a hand grenade through the gun port. When the men raised their heads, smoke was pouring from its interior, McCourt was waving a helmet from behind the pillbox to indicate that one problem had been solved and the way was clear!

The time was now 0600 hours, just 40 minutes after the troops had been landed on Red and White Beaches. After C.S.M. Stapleton had reported to Lt. Col. Jasperson that some of his men were occupying one or more buildings along the front, Jasperson had sent a message via the sole remaining radio set to his opposite number, Bob Labatt, and reported that some of his men had succeeded in breaking out of the trap. In turn, his message was intercepted by *Calpe*, along with a further message from Labatt informing General Roberts that his men were attacking the defences of the Casino in order to break out!

Aboard *Calpe*, the message gave a far rosier picture of the situation than was actually the case. General Roberts now firmly believed that beach-heads had been firmly established on both Red and White Beaches. He had also been informed that the tanks had been landed on both beaches to support the troops. An almost total lack of communications had prevented him from learning the truth — that the Essex Scottish and Royal Hamilton Light Infantry Regiments were hopelessly trapped on the beaches and were facing annihilation against murderous and impossible defences and that the Calgary Tanks had been decimated on the beaches with only 11 tanks breaching the sea wall to cruise up and down a promenade from which there was no escape because of cunningly placed tank traps.

Almost at the same time, Roberts received the misleading message from the Royal Regiment of Canada, 'Impossible to land troops on Blue Beach.' It was not possible to say what had really happened on Blue Beach, because the Royals had been massacred. The beach was masked by smoke, and heavy gun batteries made it impossible for any craft to cruise in-shore to give an eye-witness report of the true conditions. General Roberts was forced to conclude from the message that the Royals had failed to land and that they were therefore presently floating off the coast awaiting further instructions. He consequently sent a message to the Royals by radio, ordering them to sail round the East Headland and land on Red Beach to assist the Essex Scottish. It had been decided before the raid that the floating reserves must be sent in before 0700 hours if the evacuation were to take place at 1100 hours. The 10th Panzer Tank Corps would arrive from Amiens by noon. An additional factor was that the planners had calculated that if the enemy defences had not fallen by 0900 hours they would then be able to mount massive counter-attacks that could be disastrous to the small Canadian force. With no news from Green Beach at Pourville and having ordered the Royals into Red Beach after learning that the tanks had landed there, General Roberts now made the momentous decision to throw in the floating reserve, the Fusiliers de Mont Royal commanded by Lt. Col. Menard. Closely following behind them would be the remainder of the tanks lying off-shore in the other tank landing craft. In making this decision, General Roberts hoped to crush the enemy defences with one big knock-out punch now that, as he believed, the troops had broken through the enemy defences.

Long after the Dieppe raid, critics would ask why Roberts did not exploit the successful breakthrough at Pourville and throw in the reserves on Green Beach. It should be remembered that General Roberts did not receive any information from Green Beach until 8 a.m. — two hours after his decision to send the reserves into the main beaches! In addition, the planners had emphasised again and again that if it became a choice of targets to be destroyed — demolitions in the town or the massive torpedo dump under the East Headland — then he should choose the torpedo dump. The war at sea was being won by the U-boat and it was important to deprive it of its weapons. Perhaps the most telling argument against landing tanks at Pourville was the faulty British Intelligence report that the bridges over the Scie and Saane were not strong enough to carry a Churchill tank. At this point also, General Roberts was not aware of Lt. Col. Andrews' death or of the severe wounding of Brigadier Sherwood Lett.

The time was now 7 a.m. Just one hour and 40 minutes had elapsed since they had landed on Red and White Beaches. Those left of the Essex Scottish, Royal Hamilton Light Infantry and Royal Canadian Engineers huddled beneath the sea wall and watched with amazement as the Regiment Fusiliers de Mont Royal emerged from the smoke screen that had just been laid by destroyers. What a brave sight it was — six abreast and four deep, a gallant but futile charge in the face of impossible odds. Lt. Col. Dollard Menard had bellowed his final orders over a loud hailer to his men: 'The mortars will engage the heights behind the old castle. Good luck, boys! Show the enemy what a French-Canadian regiment can do!'

It was planned so that the Fusiliers de Mont Royal would land on Red Beach to support the Essex Scottish but, unfortunately, the navy had failed to take into account the strong westerly set of the current now that the tide was on the ebb. As they emerged from the smoke screen to find the beach 100 yards ahead, they discovered that they had missed Red Beach by almost 1,000 yards! Instead, they were headed for White

Beach. Many of the boats on the extreme right were off the beach entirely and eventually landed on a narrow strip of shingle directly under the sheer cliffs of the West Headland.

The enemy gunners held their fire until the boats were only about 75 yards from the beach. Then, with a sudden belch of flame and anger, every gun and mortar in Dieppe seemed to open fire on the ill-fated Fusiliers de Mont Royal. Two boats were immediately blown out of the water. The remainder were badly holed and many of the men killed and wounded while still at sea. Menard was severely wounded but managed to land and direct the survivors of his regiment.

Corporal Walter Gibson was attached to headquarters section of the F.M.R. As the men emerged from the smoke-screen he was shocked and appalled at the horrible scene of carnage unveiled before him: hundreds of bodies lying all over the beach; tanks lying here and there; helpless targets for German gunners. Under the wall, many men lay or crouched as the mortar bombs burst around them. Some of the survivors under the wall waved frantically at them to go back — to turn around and get out before it was too late.

Gibson's boat struck a sunken landing craft on the way in, and the men were thrown into the shallow water. Capt. Erskine Eaton stood up and bellowed, 'Come on, men, let's go!' The last word ended in a grunt as his head was shattered by machine-gun fire. Now it was every man for himself in the mad scramble for the beach. A weak call for help and Gibson found Pte. Pratt, his friend, with his back wide open like a split kipper.

He stayed with him until Pratt died and then heeded the call of Major Paul Savoy to move forward to the wall. The firing from the West Headland was very heavy but his training served him well. Count to five, and up and forward — down again and hug the ground — count five — up again and forward. Behind him, another cry for help. A quick glance over his shoulder revealed Corporal Grondin, a stretcher-bearer, lying wounded in the surf. Turn around — race back the way he had come, pull him onto the beach. A slap in the arm and a bullet made one arm useless; another bullet hit Grondin straight through the heart. Gibson crawled up the steep beach, a little delirious by now with pain and loss of blood. Ahead stood an abandoned tank. A strong hand hooked into his battle-dress collar and he was hauled the rest of the way by Major Paul Savoy, who was then killed instantly.

Sergeant-Major Dumais found his section heading straight for the Casino on White Beach, where the R.H.L.I. were hammering at the doors; two mortar bombs burst alongside his craft, wounding one of the sergeants and Lance Corporal Taylor. As they hit the beach, Dumais gave the order for his men to head for the Casino and then surveyed the scene all around him. As the bullets started to fan the air close to him he found himself shrinking back until a stronger, more primitive force took over and replaced fear with anger. He turned around to rally his men forward. As he did so, he noticed the landing craft reversing to get out to sea before all of the men and equipment had been unloaded. He drew his revolver and threatened to shoot the officer at the helm if he continued to reverse, but the officer appeared to duck down out of sight to escape Dumais' wrath. He was in fact dead and was sinking to the deck. Leaving the boat, Dumais led his men in a mad dash up the beach toward the Casino. He reached the pillbox that had been cleared by the R.H.L.I. and sank behind the shelter of German sandbags to ponder his next move.

Lt. Robert McRae, R.C.N.V.R., the Commanding Officer of the Canadian contingent of landing craft naval crews at Dieppe, emerged from the smoke screen to find the sheer cliffs of the West Headland straight ahead. The gun-boat that had guided them in had erred! Aboard his tiny R craft he carried a platoon of F.M.R. infantry. Colonel Menard had intended to transfer from the gun-boat to Lt. McRae's assault craft for the final run in, but on the way over from England, the engine had given trouble and the colonel had decided to play it safe and go in on another boat. Lt. McRae's boat came under heavy fire almost immediately from enemy gun positions on the clifftop. The wooden hull was holed in a dozen places by shell and mortar fire. The coxswain, Bob Campbell, stood beside McRae and received a burst of machine-gun fire straight across his thighs, cutting one leg off as cleanly as a surgeon's knife. The boat grounded in the surf and the survivors jumped on to the narrow beach to race for the shelter of the cliff face. They were hopelessly trapped with no way out. The cliffs rose sheer above them; it was impossible to move either to the left or the right. Many other boats were in a similar predicament all along the headland. The German defenders came to the edge of the cliff and looked down into McRae's boat, where he was frantically trying to stem the flow of blood that was rapidly draining Bob

Campbell's life away. McRae looked up into the face of a German *Feldwebel* (sergeant) who stood motionless with a stick grenade raised above his head ready to blast the survivors to pieces. Their eyes met. After a very long pause, the 'enemy' nodded. He stepped back from the edge of the cliff in a singular act of mercy that transcended the horrors of war. For a brief period of time, the war had been halted by a private armistice between two men.

Elsewhere along the narrow beach, the remainder of the proud Fusiliers de Mont Royal were rapidly being decimated as the enemy dropped hand grenades down amongst them where they huddled under the face of the sheer cliff. Their position was hopeless and the end would come soon. At the Casino, the F.M.R. joined forces with their English-Canadian comrades in the R.H.L.I. to storm the seemingly impregnable defences. Labatt fully realised that their one hope lay in overcoming German resistance and funnelling men through the building into the town of Dieppe. Captain Hill and C.S.M. J. Stewart led the men in two flanking attacks on the Casino after units of the engineers had succeeded in destroying the formidable pill-boxes at each end of the courtyard leading into the main building. After bitter fighting the ground floor of the Casino was occupied and the enemy defenders either killed or captured. Sergeant George Hickson of the Royal Canadian Engineers led a party of his sappers to attack the Casino from the rear. Blasting down walls, he flushed out the enemy from room after room, corridor after corridor, until the opposition was finally crushed. Little quarter was given and little asked. It was dirty and bloody fighting at its worst. Emerging from the Arcade at the mouth of the Casino, Hickson was joined by Sapper Albert Brown and a group of survivors from the R.H.L.I. Together, they raced across the fire-swept promenade and burst through the doors of the local theatre where they were immediately surrounded by German troops and subjected to a heavy and continuous fire.

Dumais left his sheltered position and led a party of his men over to the Casino on his left. They entered the building without serious opposition after the R.H.L.I. had silenced the pill-boxes at the entrance and found the survivors under Captain Whittacker fighting a bitter battle within. The large windows had been blown out of their frames, and heavy machine-gun fire was being directed through each window from the castle

99

over on the right. Gathering up a number of his men, Dumais stationed them at each window, armed with Bren guns, and ordered them to keep up a constant covering fire against the enemy positions.

Emerging from the mouth of the Casino arcade, Dumais and his men raced along the Boulevard Maréchal Foch firing their guns from the hip until they were halted by an anti-tank gun at the end of the street. Splitting into two sections of three men each, they succeeded in silencing the gun and killing the German gunners. But in the process, they lost three of their own men. Continuing along the side streets, they reached the Church of St. Remy where Brigadier Bill Southam had hoped to set up his headquarters. Strong enemy opposition forced them to retreat, but not before the corporal in the party had been severely wounded in the leg. He insisted on returning to the beach with Dumais. They arrived back at the Casino without further casualties and reported to Captain Whittaker of the R.H.L.I. for further action.

Sgt. Pierre Dubuc of the F.M.R. led a group over the sea wall to the west of the Casino and charged down the surrounding streets through the road blocks to overcome an enemy machine-gun post. They eventually entered the dock Bassin du Canada where the enemy landing-barges were believed to be moored. Boarding several of the barges, they fought a spirited hand-to-hand action with the German sailors aboard. They had penetrated further into Dieppe than any other Canadian soldiers but it was time to leave. They re-assembled on the dock side and tried to make their way back to the beach but were almost immediately surrounded by German soldiers. They surrendered only because they had run out of ammunition. Their capture posed a problem for the German soldiers who were anxious to get to the beach area as soon as possible. So forcing the Canadians to strip down to their vests and underpants, they posted one soldier to guard them and hurriedly left. Capture and incarceration had not been included in the fiery little Frenchman's itinerary and after distracting the guard's attention for a moment, Dubuc knocked him unconscious with a single blow of his clenched fist. Turning to his men, he ordered them to race back to the beach without further delay. Many were the coarse jokes thrown at them from the windows of the French houses they passed, but return they did.

Back on the beach Dubuc was shocked to find his colonel

propped against the sea wall — severely wounded several times and almost delirious from pain and loss of blood. The enemy fire had increased greatly. Many more troops had entered the town to add their additional fire power to the defenders. Looking around, Dubuc was fascinated by the sight of Colonel Johnny Andrews' tank lying high and dry on the beach now that the tide had receded. Racing across the beach, he dived into the tank to man the six-pounder gun. For the remainder of the morning, he fired at enemy gun positions with telling effect until his ammunition ran out.

By this time, other groups were also emerging from the Casino to enter the town. Captain Hill, Major Lazier, and C.S.M. Stewart had also reached the Church of St. Remy, where they fought a running gun battle against overwhelming odds before returning to the Casino. Some visits to the church are unrecorded. A small stone plaque outside the church acts as a memorial to two unknown Canadian soldiers who, after losing touch with their patrol, hid in the dense branches of a chestnut tree outside the church. Across the narrow rue Bouchard, a lady of ill repute who had been selling her wares to a German officer, spied the men hidden in the branches and gave the alarm. When surrounded by German troops, the men had tumbled down to take refuge in a urinal, which was then riddled with bullets until the two men staggered out to die on the sidewalk.

On the beaches, the enemy fire had heightened. It seemed that no living soul could possibly survive. Enemy fighters and bombers had now added their contribution to the slaughter. Diving almost to the beach, they bombed and strafed the survivors with murderous monotony. From a hundred points along the sea front, enemy mortar teams lobbed their projectiles over every exposed inch of the beach, filling the air with millions of fragments of metal, as sharp as razor blades and twice as deadly. In front of them, all along the sea front, came the clatter and roar of scores of machine guns and anti-tank weapons. With the sea at their backs, they were hopelessly trapped, for now it was impossible for any boats to approach the beach and survive. Their only hope lay in concealment. Friendly aircraft laid heavy layers of smoke all along the beach and waterfront. As the breeze from the Channel nudged it gently aside it was replenished by the survivors' smoke bombs fired from their few remaining mortars.

It has often been said that war brings forth the best and the worst in man. There were those who spent the long day seeking out the badly wounded who lay all across the mile-long beach — unable to move, at the mercy of the enemy and of the sea which was now relentlessly rising up the beach to drown them one by one. Captain Clare and Captain Robertson, the medical officers of the R.H.L.I., worked ceaselessly to save lives. Aided by stretcher-bearers, they risked their own lives time and time again to reach the badly wounded and stem the flow of blood while easing the pain with precious capsules of morphine. Others risked their lives to carry men across the fire-swept beach to improvised first-aid stations, where other doctors battled to save lives as they waited for the inevitable finale. Captain John Foote, the padre of the R.H.L.I., was a big man. Tall in stature and well-built, he could have been mistaken for an all-star football player. A kindly, good-natured man, genial in disposition but possessing a will of iron, his eyes were his most striking feature — large, dark and filled with compassion as he comforted the dying. Many times throughout the long day he picked up men in his powerful arms and carried them across the beach to first-aid posts set up in a hollow of the beach or to the burning tank landing craft that had grounded near the Casino and was used to shelter scores of badly-wounded men.

John Foote won a well-deserved Victoria Cross for his outstanding bravery on the beaches. He lived a charmed life; never once was he wounded although he brushed death every time he carried a man across the beach. Foote would be the first to acknowledge that his Victoria Cross was a joint decoration that recognised other brave men carrying out the same suicidal mercy missions. One was 'Jughead' Harvey, as he was known to the men of the R.H.L.I. The name had been applied to Lt. George Harvey because of the large head with which nature had endowed him. His hat or helmet always seemed to be perched precariously on top of his large ears. After that day on the beach at Dieppe no man who survived would ever laugh at George again. He could be seen throughout the endless day of suffering, walking erect across the beach with a badly-wounded man cradled in his arms on the long trek to the burning T.L.C. first-aid post.

Aboard *Calpe*, Commander Ryder, v.c., reported to Hughes-Hallett that the Royal Marine Commandos had been unable to enter the harbour of Dieppe to capture the enemy landing barges believed to be moored there. The tremendous barrage of shells from the East Headland had formed an impenetrable barrier off the harbour mouth. They could not sail through it without being slaughtered.

In turn, Hughes-Hallett offered the Royal Marine contingent to General Ham Roberts. It must be remembered that communications between ship and shore were practically non-existent and a clear picture could not be obtained of conditions on the beachhead. Roberts had been led to believe that the Essex Scottish had broken through the enemy defences on Red Beach and were occupying buildings along the sea front. To aid them in their task, he had just ordered the Fusiliers de Mont Royal to land on Red Beach and assist the Essex Scottish. He had also been led to believe that the Royal Hamilton Light Infantry had broken through the Casino and were funnelling troops into the town. He therefore took what he honestly believed to be the right decision and committed the Royal Marine floating reserve into White Beach to assist the R.H.L.I.

With the reserves thrown in on both beaches and a break-through which had already been accomplished, the Canadians could now deliver a knock-out blow — capture the town, destroy essential installations, and leave before 1100. Roberts was not aware of the catastrophe on both Red and White Beaches, which were shrouded from his view by clouds of smoke. Nor was he aware that the F.M.R. had been decimated after landing on the wrong beaches.

'Tigger' Philips formed up his Royal Marine A Commando group some five miles off-shore, then headed directly into White Beach. Almost immediately they came under the fire of heavy German batteries, which surrounded them with huge fountains of water as the heavy-calibre shells burst among them. One boat was blown to pieces while still two miles from the beach. Another boat was sunk shortly afterwards. At a distance of 400 yards from the beach, only seven boats were left of the ten that had started the run-in.

As they emerged from the smoke screen that lay off-shore, the Royal Marines were shocked and dismayed to see the terrible destruction and carnage on all sides. Blazing tank landing craft and tanks were dotted all along the shore. Shells landed on all sides. The deafening thunder and chatter of enemy guns against the inferno of fire and destruction told them the whole story. Too late they realised that they were sailing into a deadly trap. The enemy fire had increased enormously since the first touchdown, and now no boat could possibly land its troops on that terrible beach.

As the enemy turned its fire power against the new threat from the sea, Phillips calmly donned a pair of white gloves so that his signals could plainly be seen by his remaining boats. Standing up to his full height, he turned his back to the enemy and raised his hands above his head to halt the advance. At the same time he shouted, 'Go back! For God's sake go back!' His warning came almost too late. Scores of mortar shells landed among the remaining seven boats. Two were sunk immediately, but the other five boats turned about and escaped, wounded but still afloat. Enemy machine-gun fire cut down this gallant man a few seconds after he stood up to warn his men to go back.

The Royal Marines who did manage to land were cut to pieces in the surf. Only a handful reached the shelter of a burnt-out tank and under the command of Lt. Smale, R.M., they engaged the enemy with Bren guns in a brave but futile act of defiance as they awaited the end. One of the boats that had turned about after Phillips' warning returned once more to the scene of carnage to pick up the survivors. Under the command of Captain R. R. Deveraux, R.M., they dragged the Royal Marines aboard before they fell victim to enemy sharp-shooters.

Some were given the thankless tasks, the dirty jobs with few accolades, that required a special brand of courage under fire. The primary purpose of the raid could be said to be demolition. The infantry regiments had been ordered to attack and capture the port of Dieppe for a few short hours to enable the Royal Canadian Engineers to carry out extensive demolitions of torpedo dumps, railway rolling stock and tunnels, gas works, radar stations, and perhaps most important of all, spiking heavy gun batteries that surrounded the town on all sides.

Under the command of Major B. Sucharov, three field companies of the R.C.E., the 2nd, 7th, and 11th, had been specially trained on the Isle of Wight. Just prior to the raid, Sgt. Bill Lee of Second Field Company, R.C.E., was taken blindfolded and under guard to a secret Combined Operations Headquarters. There he was placed in charge of a group of sappers assembling the various demolition charges to be used on the raid. The plastic gelignite charges were placed into backpacks of from 40 to 60 pounds in weight and numbered according to the section and man in each team. On the night before the raid, when they were ordered to collect their equipment and embark on the tank landing craft, each man collected the backpack bearing his section and number. Aboard the tank landing craft, 309 sappers crouched alongside the tanks, waiting to jump ashore and carry out their assignments.

Lee landed with his section on White Beach and immediately suffered casualties as they put out the huge rolls of wood and wire known as chespaling, used for the tanks to gain traction on the treacherous shale. They succeeded in landing all three tanks, but at what a cost! Only Lee and Corporal Cousins reached the slim shelter of the sea wall; the other 14 men in the section had been killed. Sapper Don Wilson lay badly wounded with his pack of high explosive blazing away on his back; when freed from his deadly cargo he was dragged to safety and managed to survive. Flipper McGee, a pleasant young boy from the Gaspé peninsula, had been shot through the thigh and later bled to death for want of medical attention. 'Peace River' Elliot had been shot in the back and lay dying with his head cradled in Sandy Shusterman's arms and his stomach in his pants. Collie Shaw, known affectionately by the boys as Cauliflower, had been killed outright, along with four privates. The remainder of the section was badly wounded.

Sgt. Rod MacKenzie's section landed alongside Bill Lee and suffered equally heavy casualties as the men struggled to land their tanks. The fire was coming from three directions at once. Sapper Bill Lynch headed for a gap in the wire and prayed that he would make it in one piece. Russell, Collinsaw, Johnson, and Brown were mowed down as they hit the beach. A few yards further on, three more of the men in his section were killed — Schargo, Barnes, and George. Through the deafening roar of mortar bombs, he dimly heard MacKenzie bellowing to the men to spread out to the right and not to bunch up as an easy target. He flopped into a shell hole between two tanks, lying forlornly on the beach with their tracks shot away. There he was joined by Sapper Larry Kennedy. They both hugged the heaving beach as enemy shells pounded the tanks on either side of them, causing shrapnel to whiz around like hail. Both men were hit in the face before Bill Lynch felt something tearing through his hip pocket and realised that the morning trip to the toilet would be something of an ordeal in future. Just in front of him, he could see Bill Broom lying across the wire, badly wounded with his pack of explosives on fire. The enemy gunners were attracted to the fire and smoke like moths to a candle flame and round after round thudded into the smoking conflagration until a life was mercifully snuffed out.

Above Bill, the rubber water-proofing surrounding the tanks had been set on fire and was giving off acrid, choking fumes. They sucked pebbles to relieve their thirst as they waited for the inevitable end. Each shell created a wind that snatched at their clothing with a foul breath of noxious gases; pieces of the tanks were being fragmented to join the rain of metal above them as their clawing hands feverishly scraped at the pebbles beneath them in a vain effort to hide from the devilish reverberation. They were roused in the midst of the flaming insanity by Rod MacKenzie who had returned from the safety of the sea wall to bring them out. Helped by Norm Pender, they limped up to the wall to join the other survivors.

Under the direction of Lt. Shackleton, R.C.E., Syd Cleasby and Bill Lee, aided by Sapper George Barless, piled a large number of satchel explosive charges against the sea wall, at that point over seven feet high. Warning the men to bury their heads in the gravel, Cleasby fired the massive charge and succeeded in blowing a large hole through which the tanks could at least succeed in leaving the beach and mounting the promenade.

When the plans for the Dieppe raid had been drawn up, it had seemed a straightforward matter to include sappers aboard each tank landing craft to land the tanks after chespaling had been laid on the beach. Once the sappers had performed this chore, they would be free to move up the beach carrying Bangalore torpedoes to clear a path through the barbed wire. The remainder of the sappers would then proceed to the sea wall, where they would be regrouped under their N.C.O.s and despatched to various key enemy installations under the protection of the infantry. They could set their charges before returning to the beach, where they would be re-embarked under the protection of an infantry rear guard. It was not to be so straightforward.

After the debacle at Dieppe, engineers landing in future raids would be protected within special armoured vehicles. But future planning would not help the survivors of the R.C.E. who now huddled under tanks, in shell holes, and under the sea wall, unable to leave the beach, shocked at the awful slaughter that had thinned their ranks to a mere skeleton force, but angry that poor planning had prevented them from achieving their objectives.

Aboard *Calpe*, a wounded Royal Marine officer stood swaying before General Roberts and Captain Hughes-Hallett as he delivered his report. After the misleading messages from Red and White Beaches, General Roberts was shocked to learn that not only had the Essex Scottish and Royal Hamilton Light Infantry Regiments been pinned down on the beach, but that the landing of the reserves had also been a failure. He had been about to order in the reserve tanks, which were still aboard the remaining tank landing craft off-shore. The Marine officer convinced Roberts that conditions on the beaches were so bad that a further landing by tanks would only invite another massacre. Giving the order to cancel the reserve tank landing, Roberts decided to land on the beaches himself to assess the situation. Hughes-Hallett refused to supply a naval craft to convey the general on such a suicidal mission and, instead, urged him to evacuate the survivors as soon as possible. Reluctantly, the general agreed. Any further delay could only lead to further loss of life. Unfortunately, the evacuation, codenamed Operation Vanquish, could not be carried out without an adequate air umbrella from the R.A.F. in England. Air Commodore Cole, the Air Force Commander's representative aboard *Calpe*, informed Roberts that adequate air defence could not be provided before 11 a.m. The word was passed to Major Rolfe, the signals officer ashore on White Beach, and he in turn passed the message to Brigadier Southam and Lt. Col. Labatt. Lt. Col. Jasperson on Red Beach was also given the message — not by radio, but from a verbal report delivered by a runner who had managed to cross the mile-long stretch of beach unhurt.

On the promenade, the few tanks remaining in action also received the message over their earphones and made preparations to return to the beach. Ed Bennett, in his tank *Bellicose*, fired a few last bursts at the enemy trenches, then headed towards the sea wall. By now his remaining eye had closed from the severe burns he had received, and in total disregard for his own personal safety, he poked his head out of the hatch and directed his tank by holding the swollen eyelids open with his fingers. He reached the sea wall and teetered on the edge, fearful that he would crush the survivors below, but, thankfully, he completed the operation without further loss of life. Art Breithaupt, in his tank *Betty*, had been safely extricated from a tank trap by the other two tanks in his troop, only to be disabled finally when the tank tracks were shot away. Running over to *Brenda* commanded by Bill Olive, he managed to scramble through the side door of the tank after cutting away the rubber water-proofing. A burst of machine-gun fire narrowly missed his head as he did so. Inside there was little room for passengers, but Ed managed to curl up in the rear of the tank after taking off his revolver. Some time later, he thanked his guardian angel that he had removed it.

On the beach, the word passed swiftly along that the boats would be coming in at 11 a.m. Hundreds of men surveyed the horizon for the first glimpse of the life-saving boats. The few tanks still operative after returning over the sea wall formed a perimeter to fight a rear-guard action. There was no doubt that the Germans were preparing for an all-out assault on the beach. Scotty Mavin of the R.H.L.I. was ordered by his sergeant to stay behind until the very end and provide cover for the men being re-embarked off the beaches. He was given six smoke cannisters and 30 pounds of Bren-gun ammunition, plus a few dozen hand grenades.

On White Beach, Lt. Prince gave the order to lay smoke bombs on top of the wall, ready to be activated once the boats arrived. Pte. Al Duxstraff of D Company, Essex Scottish, hoisted a dead body on top of the wall and then climbed up to lie behind it to catch the first glimpse of the boats coming in. Tom McDermott looked around at the awful scene: bodies and pieces of bodies on all sides as far as the eye could see. A nude major lay dead with sightless eyes staring up at the blue sky; by some freak explosion he still wore his tartan tie around his neck. A headless corpse lay near him in full uniform with hardly a button disturbed. All along the mile-long sea wall, the survivors tensed their muscles ready to make the marathon run to the boats when they arrived. The officers were detailing off a rear guard to hold off the enemy with Brens and grenades for the few precious minutes necessary for the main body of men to scramble aboard. Pte. Jim Bowman and his buddy Pte. Utman gathered ammunition and smoke bombs from the many dead comrades around them and prepared for a siege.

In the Casino, an all-officer rear guard remained behind to prevent the enemy from rushing through the arcade. Upstairs,

Sgt. Maj. Dumais and his men of the F.M.R. waited behind every window for the enemy that was sure to come. On the beach, Lt. Jerry Wood and Lt. Prince were ordering the men to carry the more seriously wounded on their backs to the boats when they arrived. The padre, John Foote, continued his merciful rescue mission — carrying man after man to the shelter of the burning T.L.C. 1, where scores of badly wounded men lay waiting patiently for the boats to Blighty.

Aboard *Calpe*, Roberts and Hughes-Hallett agreed that, in the face of the tremendous enemy barrage, the tanks and equipment must be abandoned. The boats would snatch the survivors off the beach and leave as soon as possible. The tank landing craft would lie off-shore so that the smaller A.L.C. could ferry back and forth.

The tide was now at full ebb, leaving a long stretch of exposed beach. Major Rolfe sent urgent signals requesting the R.A.F. to lay a smoke-screen to give the men a fighting chance. Overhead, the enemy bombers were now arriving in strength, bombing and strafing the survivors. The sea wall, which previously had given some measure of cover from enemy guns, became a trap as the chattering machine guns of air gunners raked in faultless precision along the whole length.

The R.A.F. arrived on time to spread a thick layer of smoke all along the beach. Unfortunately, this action alerted the enemy, who feared a second invasion attempt. Immediately, hundreds of guns and mortars began to fire along fixed lines. All along the mile-long beach, the sea boiled as bursting shells lashed the waves into white foam. The men shuddered at the prospect of crossing the mad maelstrom of fire exploding all over the exposed beach.

Just after 11 a.m., the first four boats arrived at White Beach. A cry of relief was followed by a mad stampede as hundreds of men rushed forward. Survival of the fittest! Three boats got away loaded to the gunwales and in danger of being swamped. The enemy fire died down for a moment, and then as the boats clawed their way to safety, unleashed a tremendous barrage against them. The fourth boat was blown into the sky, leaving its cargo dismembered in the boiling surf.

Another eight boats reached Red Beach, but within a few minutes, six had been shattered and torn by the devastating fire from the East Headland. The remaining two boats succeeded in reaching the tank landing craft and unloading their men. The bravery of the sailors of the Royal Navy and the gunners of the Toronto Scottish was beyond description. Many were killed before the day was out, but unflinchingly they sacrificed their lives one after another to bring help to the beleaguered troops ashore on the infamous beaches of Dieppe.

Labatt ordered the German prisoners to carry the wounded down to the boats on doors torn from the Casino. Only after they had been safely evacuated did he order his officers to accompany him to the last of their boats. As they left the beach, the smoke-screen was blown away by a fresh breeze and they found themselves fully exposed 50 yards from shore and the target of scores of enemy guns. Their boat was quickly holed and sunk, but Labatt and his officers swam back to shore. His adjutant and friend, Herb Poag, was severely wounded as they staggered through the bullet-swept surf. Grabbing a duffle coat and boots from a corpse, Labatt managed to reach the tank landing craft, where Brigadier Southam was organising a last defensive position.

Padre Foote had lifted a wounded man aboard one of the boats and had in turn been dragged aboard himself by eager hands. Calmly climbing back over the side of the boat, he returned to the wounded, whom he felt would need his help in the long years ahead in the prisoner-of-war camps.

Many of the men managed to swim clear as the boats were sunk. Norm Pender adjusted his Mae West life-jacket and slipped over the side of his sinking boat after an enemy bomber had massacred most of the men in it. The naval officer in charge of the boat had disappeared, but he'd left the stumps of his feet in his boots.

Pte. Don Utman of the R.H.L.I. suffered several shrapnel wounds when his boat was blown out of the water but managed to swim around for some time before heading back to shore — naked. Shivering, he looked around for clothes and found no shortage. He took a pair of pants from one corpse, a jacket from another, then headed back to the shelter of the sea wall.

Sgt. Heath reached the shore half-drowned. Staggering over to a shell-hole, he fell on top of a tough little Royal Marine Commando who was firing steadily away at the Germans who were now beginning to show themselves on top of the wall. Leaving his rifle alone for a moment, he pushed Sgt. Heath's head between his knees to force up the sea water and then, with a conspiratorial grin, produced a jar of navy-issue rum that he had rescued from his assault craft as she went down. The fiery liquid drunk out of the marine's helmet did much to revive Heath after his ordeal.

Sgt. Dubuc picked up the badly wounded Colonel Menard and striding easily along, deposited him safely in a boat before returning to the beach to carry other comrades to safety. He managed to board the last boat as it left the beach on its perilous trip back to England. In the Casino, Dumais gave the order to pack all the existing explosive charges together and blow up the building as they left. For some unknown reason, the charges did not fire as Dumais walked down the beach to board the last boat. Over his shoulder he carried a wounded comrade whom he safely deposited over the side of the landing craft just before it hastily reversed its engines and raced out to sea. Dumais was just in time to grab the end of a rope trailing from the bow of the vessel. From deep water he tried to pull himself aboard, but he was heavily loaded with ammunition. He was forced to release his hold on the rope and was promptly washed to the seabed by the boat's wash. As he struggled desperately to unload some of the heavy ammunition, he was mercifully washed ashore by the bow wave of another boat.

For some time he lay in the surf at the edge of the beach, totally exhausted. Machine-gun bullets were whipping the surface of the sea all around him, and he realised that he was doomed unless he could reach shelter quickly. Over to the right, the burning tank landing craft still provided some form of cover for scores of men, many of them wounded. Running through the enemy fire, he reached the landing craft, where he promptly organised the men into a makeshift defence force. *Calpe* sailed right alongside in a last valiant attempt to take off survivors. Many of the men swam out to her and managed to climb the ratlines hung over the side. Under very heavy fire, she at last turned her bow away reluctantly from the beach and headed out to sea. The time was now 1 p.m. This was to be the last rescue attempt by the navy and the men felt a strange sense of loss and loneliness as *Calpe* sailed towards the horizon. On her bridge, Roberts gazed back at the beaches where so many of his men of the Canadian 2nd Division still remained, waiting for a rescue that would not now come. The navy had convinced him that further re-embarkation was impossible and would only lead to further slaughter. He was filled with a great sadness that time would not soften.

General Roberts was not the type of man to shift blame on to other shoulders. He was the Commander of the Land Forces, and he alone would take full responsibility for the defeat. Aboard *Fernie*, Churchill Mann commented to General Truscott, the American observer, 'General, I am afraid this operation will go down in history as one of the greatest disasters.' General Mann had prophesied correctly, and he might have added, 'And somebody is going to take the blame for it.' Who was more convenient than General Ham Roberts? He may have been the whipping boy for the higher command, but the men who took part in the operation absolved him from blame. Their feelings were epitomised by Padre Foote, who simply stated 'Ham Roberts was just a soldier carrying out his orders.'

Unfortunately, he had been forced to carry out his orders under inflexible battle plans designed by others. Impregnable defences that could have been neutralised by the cancelled preliminary bombardment had trapped his Canadian 2nd Division on the beaches. The destruction of radio communications between ship and shore had caused great confusion and had led to the ultimate defeat of the invasion forces. A rigid timetable that took no errors into account demanded that seven separate landings take place with split-second accuracy over a 10-mile front to achieve the element of surprise considered so vital to the success of the operation.

Never again after the debacle of Dieppe would the armchair planners in Britain attempt an amphibious landing on an enemy coast without subjecting it to a heavy preliminary bombardment. The lessons had been learned, but at terrible cost. The overwhelming casualties suffered at Dieppe were to lead to a radical change in amphibious assault planning for the D-Day operation in 1944. If a heavily defended seaport was too difficult to capture, then the assault would have to be made elsewhere on the coast.

As the battered invasion fleet sailed glumly towards England, Captain Hughes-Hallett conceived the brilliant idea of a floating harbour. If it was too difficult to land at a seaport — then they would tow over their own seaport! The D-Day landings would be successful at a later date as a result of the floating Mulberry harbours and the surprise achieved by landing on open beaches where a massive landing was considered an impossibility by the German High Command.

Winston Churchill summed up the success of the D-Day operation by stating that, without the bitter lessons learned at Dieppe, the later landings would not have succeeded.

CHAPTER TWELVE

THE SURRENDER

The Royal Navy had at last turned about and was returning to England. Immediately General Haase gave the order for the Wehrmacht to advance toward the main beaches to end the unequal battle.

For the men on the beaches further resistance could only lead to more bloodshed with no possibility of victory. It was hopeless to continue the fight and impossible to retreat with the Channel at their backs. The navy had tried valiantly, but the deadly German artillery had most effectively cut off their retreat. Hundreds of dead and wounded lay on the pebbled beach. The tide was rising, and men who lay wounded on the beaches would surely be drowned if they were not removed at once. Here and there a body slowly detached itself from the beach and floated face down to join the rest of the flotsam that littered the surface of the sea all around. Occasionally a weak cry for help came from one of the bodies as the tide claimed him. To move from the sea wall was to invite certain death. Better to turn the head, close ears and mind to the suffering. Survive.

In the space of a few dreadful hours, the men had become hardened to the sight of death. After a time the surges of grief and anger at the violent deaths of comrades were reduced to philosophical regret. But hundreds of men remaining under the sea wall were appalled at the scene before them. On one side a solitary figure struggled frantically on the barbed wire lying in great loose skeins. The barbs hooked through his khaki uniform, trapping him like a fly in a spider's web. As he frenziedly tore at the wire with bare hands, lacerated and bleeding, he screamed in fear — a scream suddenly changed to a bubbling bloody sound as the machine-gun fire struck. He hung quivering on the wire for a minute, before folding at the knees and falling face forward on to it. Somebody started to sob, another cursed. Some prayed.

Near the Casino there was one body everyone wanted to see washed away. The intestines lay in grey shiny coils around a torn uniform soaked with blood. The sea breeze wafted the all-pervading smell, sweet and sickly, over to their nostrils.

After conferring with the medical officers and the brave padre, John Foote, Lt. Col. Labatt tied a white rag to a rifle barrel and shoved a German prisoner out into the open with it.

Slowly the firing died, and through the haze of smoke another white flag could be seen fluttering from behind the Casino. Another flew over L.C.T. 1, which had been used as a first-aid station. The surrender had begun, and all along the beach and sea wall men started to destroy their weapons or hurl them out to sea to prevent them from falling into the hands of the Germans.

Over the sea wall they suddenly appeared – the enemy they had never seen. Grim-faced, they slowly advanced with rifles ready. '*Hände hoch!*' they bellowed. Cautiously the men stood up, hands stretched above their heads, the sour taste of defeat in their mouths. They were being forced to surrender with not even the satisfaction of an accomplished duty.

On the main beaches the roll call was shocking. When the grim casualty figures were added to those sustained on the other beaches, a shocked Canadian nation would learn that 56 officers and 851 men had been killed, 158 officers and 2,302 men wounded and 1,946 officers and men taken prisoner.

Lt. Art Breithaupt left the shelter of his tank and waited with arms above his head as the enemy soldiers advanced towards him. A German soldier stopped directly in front of him and shouted '*Schwein Engländer*' as he smashed his balled fist into Art's face. As he felt the bones crunch and the blood spurt from his broken nose, he instinctively reached for his revolver, only to find the end of an empty lanyard. Later he remembered having left the revolver behind the gunner's seat when he boarded as an extra passenger in the crowded interior. He gave thanks for having done so; the German's companion would most certainly have shot him dead if he'd drawn his gun in anger.

Such incidents were rare. The Germans for the most part behaved correctly, although they all seemed to express the same phrase, '*Für euch ist des Krieg zu Ende.*' For you the war is over.

Major Rolfe calmly piled his papers and radio codes on the beach and set fire to them. As he did so, he noted that Brigadier Southam still clutched copy 37 of the Battle Orders under his arm. He shouted at the general to destroy his secret papers quickly before the Germans reached them, but Southam refused, saying that there might be a use for them yet. At the last minute, he changed his mind and tried to bury them in the gravel, but a sharp-eyed intelligence officer spotted him and recovered the secret orders. This find was to have dire results for all of the men taken prisoner at Dieppe.

Lt. Ed Bennett and his crew had tried to rescue some of the wounded men whose heads could be seen bobbing like corks some distance from the shore after their boats had sunk. His tank driver, Bobby Conellson, was shot dead just before the surrender. As the Germans slowly moved down the beach towards them, Ed took off his pistol and dropped it into the water. At the same time, he felt a body bumping against his legs as a gruesome reminder that things could have been a lot worse.

It was not wise to antagonise the Germans at this time; that would come later. As the survivors shuffled forward, they felt a traumatic sense of shock and degradation. If only they had been given a chance to fight! They felt betrayed. They sensed what lay ahead for them as guests of Hitler's Nazi Germany and were assailed by a great and overpowering nostalgia for the everyday things they had become accustomed to in England. Even the miserable English weather suddenly seemed desirable. The enemy propagandists added fuel to the flames of lowered morale by subtly suggesting to the men that they had been betrayed prior to the raid and that they had been expected.

Lt. Col. Labatt was approached by a German officer, who ordered him to arrange for his men to act as stretcher-bearers to get the scores of badly wounded men off the beach before the rising tide could claim fresh victims. Strong stomachs were required for this job. Severed arms and legs, grey faces on those still alive, yellow or even black faces on the dead were now common sights. Here and there a padre knelt alongside a dying man whose glazed eyes sought solace in an after-life. Tight lipped, badly wounded men puffed steadily at cigarettes as they were carried over the ploughed surface of the beach to the hospital. The stretcher-bearers were bloodied up to their elbows as they applied rough emergency shell dressings to great gaping wounds. From torn uniforms spilled cigarette butts, English pennies, love letters, and photographs. And everywhere there was the sight and smell of blood.

As they left the beach and marched through the town, the men were shocked to see the terrible damage it had suffered. The streets were littered with the debris of hundreds of shattered windows. At one point, they were offered buckets of water by Frenchwomen, but the German guards knocked them over before the men could quench their thirst. They passed the body of a young Frenchwoman lying at the side of the road. On her breast, a small infant mewed like a kitten as its tiny hands searched for her lifeless breast. A fly crawled lazily over her nose. As though on parade, the men averted their eyes sharp left: many had tears in their eyes.

The time was 2.30 p.m. Just a little over nine hours had passed since the men had hit the beach. To many of them, those hours had seemed interminable, a lifetime. With harsh cries of '*'raus! 'raus!*' they were roughly marched along the rue Quai de Lille and rue Thiers to the Hôtel-Dieu — the Dieppe hospital, which had been operated for centuries by the nuns of the Communauté des Augustines. The seriously wounded were taken inside, while the remainder of the men were searched and then made to squat on the grass verge outside the hospital. The lightly wounded had to survive on the treatment provided by companions.

Everything of personal value was purloined and added to a huge pile of 'spoils'. There was a vast and valuable collection of watches, rings, fountain pens, wallets, money, paybooks, pocket knives and tobacco pouches, all considered the property of the guards. At this stage it would have been foolhardy to protest that this thievery was in direct contravention of international laws governing the rules of warfare. No receipts were given and none expected. The men seethed with anger but a short time later they enjoyed a sweet revenge when a young French Canadian tossed a live hand grenade on top of the pile when ordered to empty his pockets. Germans were diving for cover in all directions before they realised that the pin hadn't been pulled and there was no danger of an explosion.

Inside the hospital, the nuns worked their way steadily through the mounting pile of torn bodies. The wards had been rapidly filled and scores of cots lined the corridors. Hundreds of badly wounded men patiently awaited their turn. The tall ceilings and bare walls of the religious sanctuary reverberated with the hollow sound of moaning as these dedicated sisters cut and stitched until the flaring white sleeves of their gowns were red with the blood of Canadians. Sister Marie Monique had hidden a flask of good cognac in her gown — to a man suffering from severe wounds and shock, a nip of cognac was the breath of life. Sister Marie du Sacré Coeur had hidden a number of pieces of bread in her gown, which she surreptitiously slipped beneath the covers to a hungry soldier. In the late afternoon, the nuns were shocked to see a German orderly throw the severed arm of a Canadian soldier on to the rubbish heap. In the dead of night, they crept out of the hospital and, wrapping the arm in a clean sheet, they reverently buried it in the hospital grounds.

The serious cases were moved to the hospital at Rouen. Cec Towler, Ed Bennet, Doug Dunn, and scores of badly wounded men from the main beaches found themselves on the same hospital train as Captain Pinky Laird and Al MacDonald from Blue Beach, along with men from the South Saskatchewan Regiment and Camerons from Green Beach and commandos from the Yellow and Orange Beaches.

At about 5 p.m., the hundreds of men squatting outside the Dieppe hospital were roughly ordered to their feet and formed into long columns. Of the 4,963 officers and men of the Canadian Second Division who had embarked from England, 807 had been killed in action while another 1,154 had been wounded. Although many of the wounded had been evacuated to hospitals in Britain, a total 1,874 officers and men had been taken prisoner. Many of the badly wounded were detained at the hospitals of Dieppe or Rouen, so that the probable number setting out on the march from Dieppe was in the region of 1,600 Canadians plus a considerable number of British commandos, sailors and airmen. The long line of captives was marched through the streets of Dieppe towards the dock area, where they crossed the bridge on to rue National No. 25 leading to the little village of Envermeu some 14 kilometres away.

Many of the officers and men were without shoes; many had lost their uniforms and were wrapped in a solitary blanket. At the head of the column, Padre Foote led the way with Captain Clare, the medical officer. Both men had voluntarily chosen to be imprisoned with the men. The memory of both men would remain forever in the minds of the prisoners.

The sky was still faultlessly blue during the late afternoon, but the men were hardly able to enjoy it. German photographers were busy. Great propaganda material — Churchill's Second Front finished. At frequent intervals, the guards shouted, '*Hände hoch,*' and enforced their orders with the sharp point of a bayonet. When all hands were stretched high in the air, cameras would click like crickets to give visual proof of the Tommies' defeat.

Baldy Fleming of the Essex Scottish gave the men the best laugh of the day. He was suffering from a bad wound in the chest that bled whenever he was forced to hoist his arms. When it hurt, he lowered his arms, only to receive a painful prick in the rear. This pantomime continued for several blocks until a German staff car drew alongside. A German officer sat in the rear, his head swathed in bloody bandages. Baldy very unwisely grinned at the officer, who immediately ordered the car to halt. He stormed over to Baldy, his Luger drawn. Death was very close for poor old Baldy at that moment. Screaming insanely, '*Schwein Engländer*', the officer poked the gun at Baldy's head and was only prevented from pulling the trigger by the German guard behind, who unbelievably stepped forward to bar the way. Still mouthing obscenities, the German officer was driven away from a very relieved Baldy, who turned to his benefactor and said most sincerely, 'Look, friend, I know you don't speak the same language, but I want you to know that, if you want to, you can prod my arse all the way to Berlin!'

It started on the outskirts of Dieppe with a solitary French-Canadian voice singing in a clear tenor, and one after another, all along the long column of prisoners, the men joined in singing the *Marseillaise*. Many of the civilians who lined the sides of the road wept as they stood at attention. It had been a long time since they had heard the sound of their national anthem. The German guards tried to quell the singing, but to no avail.

On the outskirts of Dieppe, a buxom Frenchwoman pushing a wheelbarrow of tomatoes along the side of the road drew level with Hap Summerfield of the R.H.L.I. In a fierce whisper she asked Hap to curse her in French. Hap, puzzled but always ready for a joke, complied, shaking his fist under her prominent nose to give a little emphasis to his swearing. Screaming defiance in a startling French vocabulary, she then commenced to pelt Hap and the boys with ripe tomatoes. Most of them were caught and hidden inside their battledress for a midnight snack. The German guards roared with coarse laughter at the performance and patted the dear old mama on the back to show their approval.

Soon they were in the open country with Dieppe far behind

them. The road was rough with gravel and the barefooted were soon limping painfully with blistered and bleeding feet. The guards were in a hurry and tried to force the pace with their frequent cries of ' *'raus*'; a bayonet prick was the punishment for laggards.

The countryside was beautiful. Fields of lush wheat stretched out on both sides of the road, with dense woods rising on every hill. Herds of fat dairy cattle raised their heads in alarm as the long ragged column passed. Overhead a solitary lark hovered motionless in the sky as it sang its lilting song. Sapper Roy Luxmore watched the bird above with a heavy heart. As one of the 'old' fellows, he'd left a wife and two little daughters back in his home town, Toronto. He prayed that they would soon know that he was alive and unhurt. Pte. Stan Darch of the R.H.L.I. bummed a cigarette from a buddy and limped along the road with ever increasing pain and misery as the sharp gravel cut into the tender soles of his feet. By now, the blisters had burst and pieces of gravel had lodged inside the torn skin, but he knew that if he attempted to fall out to tend them, a beating would most certainly follow.

They passed the Forêt d'Arques, a huge wood on the right-hand side of the road, and on through the tiny picturesque villages of Ancourt, Sauchay le Bas, and Bellengrevillette. A signpost at the side of the road indicated that Envermeu was but three kilometres away over the top of the hill. As they topped the rise, the men thought they were seeing a mirage. A wedding party was walking towards them, the young bride in her white gown and veil, the bridegroom decked out in evening dress and top hat. Behind them came the wedding guests. Monsieur and Mme. Paul Dupuis had just been married in the ancient Norman church, L'Église d'Envermeu. They were fortunate in choosing August 19th, 1942; on the following day the church was occupied by Canadian officer prisoners of war.

The bridal party stopped at the side of the road and watched pityingly as the prisoners passed, the bride with tears in her eyes. The men started to throw money to her — pennies, florins, pound notes, 'Here honey, buy a wedding present,' they shouted as they passed. Years later, Paul Dupuis remembered that the Canadian prisoners were proud and fearless. They had bearing, honour in their defeat, and in their fate. Mme. Dupuis ignored the paper money strewn around her and picked up one English penny as a souvenir of this day.

Stan Darch drew level with the best man, who stood at the side of the road holding the hand of a little boy. The child was only about seven years of age and Stan felt an urge to pick the little chap up and hug him. Instinctively reading Stan's thoughts, the boy gripped his father's hand tighter, and the man, gazing at Stan's torn and bleeding feet, suddenly reached down and unlaced his beautiful brown shoes and handed them to an astonished Stan. The man was M. Robillard and the little boy was his son, Jean Claude. They lived in the little village of Envermeu just around the corner. Stan tried to find words to thank the man but was prevented by the lump that had suddenly formed in his throat.

Suddenly the man was seized by the German guards. He released his little son Jean Claude and told him to run home quickly. M. Robillard was later dragged away and locked in a dark hole under the steps of the Town Hall of Envermeu. The shoes were wonderful and Stan heaved a huge sigh of relief as he put them on. He didn't even mind the boot in his backside as he finished lacing on the shoes. It was worth it!

As they marched through the village of Envermeu, the officers were separated from the men and ordered to spend the night in the village church. The aged priest handed each of them a handful of straw at the door and bade them welcome. He was very surprised at how well the French Canadians could speak his own language. *'Pourquoi êtes-vous venus?'* he asked. *'Ils vous attendaient depuis trois semaines.'* 'Why have you come? They have been waiting for you for three weeks.'

The men continued to march for several more kilometres towards the little village of St. Nicolas d'Aiermont, where their captors had decreed they should spend the night. By now, many of the wounded were in bad condition and were being supported or carried by their comrades. Friendly French peasants brought cans of milk from neighbouring farms, and for a little while, the nearest men quenched their thirst. With great daring, some of the French women passed skirts and blouses to the men before they were chased away. The German officers rode directly into the French civilians in a show of brutality that greatly angered the prisoners. In the confusion, several of the French Canadians donned skirts and blouses and made successful escapes from the ranks. Fortunately, the guards were not too observant and failed to notice the Army-issue boots beneath the billowing peasant skirts.

They were herded into an unused brick factory, a huge shell of a place lacking even the most basic amenities. The floor was rough and uneven but the men flopped themselves down with a grateful sigh of relief after the long day of action. A handful of nettles for a pillow ensured that most slept fitfully throughout the night. Only one hosepipe was available outside the factory for hundreds of men to quench their thirst, and after a short time even this small blessing was cut off. The German soldiers had been replaced by a group of Hitler Youth — arrogant products of a new generation who threatened death to anyone attempting escape.

The wounded were given little or no medical attention, and their sufferings became more acute as milling throngs of prisoners crowded around them. A familiar bellow of authority focused attention on a British Regimental Sergeant-Major of No. 3 Commando. Small in stature, but every inch a soldier, he stood ramrod straight as he addressed the many hundreds of men around him. He introduced himself as R.S.M. Beesley and, as senior non-commissioned officer, he gave a short, friendly lecture on the problems of survival now that they were prisoners of war. Quickly he gave instructions to the N.C.O.s to clear one corner of the ruined building for the wounded so they might be isolated from the main body of men; water was obtained and drunk from steel helmets, and later when minute portions of black bread were issued, Beesley, assisted by the N.C.O.s, divided the shares equally among all the men. Standing up to his full height of 5 feet 6 inches, he instructed them to conduct themselves as soldiers at all times. Under no circumstances should the Germans look upon them as cowardly in defeat. They had been defeated through no fault of their own and had fought courageously under impossible conditions. 'Make your enemy respect you,' was his theme. 'In time they will fear you!'

Many a tired soldier raised his head and squared his shoulders as Harry Beesley spoke. From the very first, he established himself as a leader of men. Many years later, the prisoners would describe him as a special kind of man. They might have lost the battle on the beaches; but from now on a far more insidious battle would be fought behind the lines — a battle of wits that would confuse the captors and bring the ultimate victory a little bit closer.

In the church at Envermeu, the officers curled up on the wooden pews after packing their handful of straw into a makeshift pillow. A few would-be escapers 'cased the joint', but every entrance was well guarded. Major McCool was worried. Rolling around in his battle-dress pocket were a number of dum-dum bullets, which were illegal according to the international rules of war. The dum-dum bullet was nicked or a cross was cut in the nose so that it expanded on impact and inflicted a devastating gaping wound. If the Germans found them in his possession, he would probably be shot on the spot. His eyes roamed around the ancient church for a suitable hiding place and finally he settled on the stone christening font, where he dropped them, one by one, down the drain hole.

The parish priest did his best to welcome the officers and to make them comfortable in his ancient church. But although they were totally exhausted after the battle, few slept. Thoughts turned to comfortable billets in England, only 70 miles away from Envermeu.

Some of the men were still at sea. Many had turned their faces towards England after their landing craft had been sunk and continued the hopeless marathon swim to Newhaven 65 miles away. Some were picked up by friendly ships, others by the enemy, but several continued alone, lost in the grey wastes of the Atlantic as the Channel currents swept them swiftly out to sea. As the hours passed, their leg and arm movements slowly became more feeble, until finally they were forced to surrender to the cold water. The Fusiliers de Mont Royal and several other wounded swimmers managed to board one of these ghost vessels some 10 miles off the coast of France. One of the engines was still serviceable, and in a few minutes they were sailing towards Newhaven and safety.

Pte. Al Richards of the R.H.L.I. dragged himself aboard a landing craft even though his legs had been shattered. The boat was badly holed by shellfire and finally sank about 14 miles from Dieppe. Resolutely turning about, Al began the long, slow swim using his powerful arms while his legs trailed uselessly below him. He arrived back at the beaches late at night.

In Envermeu, the men were awakened at 6 a.m. A small hunk of black bread was their only sustenance for the long march to Verneulles — a French prison camp 20 kilometres from Paris. The officers joined the long column as they passed through Envermeu. The road was still as hard, but Sgt. Maj. Dumais and some of his men had given up their sleep to cut makeshift footwear from the Mae West life-jackets. To a barefoot man, these 'shoes' were a godsend. All that day they marched, in hot sun, with little rest, and even less food and drink. All along the painful pilgrimage, French civilians gathered in groups, waving and making the V sign of victory. Sometimes the men managed to snatch food or cool drinks from civilian well-wishers before their captors chased them off. The plight of the wounded was serious. With little or no medical attention except for paper bandages, their wounds began to smell in the heat of the day and suppurate freely. Many of the men had high fevers and were supported by a comrade on each side as their legs dragged along the endless road.

CHAPTER THIRTEEN

VERNEULLES TO LAMSDORF

They arrived at Verneulles in the early evening and were herded into squalid, overcrowded barrack buildings. The men had been made apprehensive by the macabre silhouette of a number of gallows erected in the camp. Trooper Denny Scott of the Calgary Tank Regiment joked to his buddies about the necktie party ahead but the laughter was forced — they didn't know what lay ahead. In a surgery ward, three Canadian doctors operated continuously around the clock. Captains Clare of the R.H.L.I., Walmsley of the Essex Scottish, and Robertson of the Royal Regiment were assisted by a German surgeon. Three long lines of suffering men lined up all the next day to have their wounds treated. At this stage there was little gangrene, but many of the wounds had formed abscesses from flying shrapnel and stones from the beach. Medical supplies were not plentiful and paper bandages and an aspirin were often the treatment. The odd German medical orderly assisted them in their task, but all serious cases of surgery or amputation were performed by a German doctor, who treated the Canadians with the same unselfish attention and skill he gave to his own men.

His attitude was certainly not reflected in the camp guards. The food was very bad and totally insufficient. Twice a day, the prisoners received a bucket of watery, tasteless soup for each hut of 30 men. As an added bonus, they were given a minute bread ration, 250 grams per day. No eating utensils were issued to them, nor were there any blankets — indeed, there were no beds, and the men were forced to sleep on the hard floors. The whole camp was vastly overcrowded, one reason being that the Germans had not expected so many 'guests'. They could be excused for the overcrowded conditions, but not for the poor and inadequate food and the cruelty of the guards.

Travelling by train, many of the wounded joined up with the main body of prisoners at Verneulles. Sgt. Maj. MacIver, George Graves, and Ronny Reynolds of the Royals, Al Richards and Scotty Mavin of the R.H.L.I., were among the more seriously wounded to arrive. One who was not expected was Sgt. Cec Towler of the Engineers. He was last seen on the beach, his right arm shattered and torn. Now he lay in the hospital at Rouen. A team of German and French doctors had toured the wards telling each of the wounded either, you stay, or you go tomorrow. Cec had been told he would be staying but decided to change those orders after he discovered that he was due for amputation the next morning. Staggering out of bed, he ordered two of his men to help him get dressed. They begged him to stay, but he stubbornly insisted, and when the Germans ordered the walking wounded to muster outside, Cec quietly joined the ranks. He was successful in his deception and arrived at Verneulles with an arm in an advanced stage of putrefaction, painful beyond description, but still attached to his body. In the long months ahead, British and Canadian doctors fought successfully to save the arm and confound medical knowledge in so doing. For five long days and nights they stayed at Verneulles. 'Existed' would perhaps be a better word. On the first night, three men died in Towler's hut; several more died in the days following. Hunger was the number one enemy, and day by day they lost weight on the dreadful diet. On the fifth day they were suddenly marched to the railway station at Verneulles, where each man was given a loaf of black bread and every two men were issued one small can of liverwurst to share, along with some horrible smelling fish cheese.

In a vain attempt to alienate the French Canadians from their compatriots, the Vichy French provided each French-Canadian soldier extra rations and fresh fruit. They accepted the food, only to hand over half shares to their English-speaking buddies. *'Nous sommes une nation de Canadiens et c'est pourquoi nous avons combattu si bien ensemble!'* — 'We are one nation of Canadians and that is why we fought so well together!'

The men were then crowded into wooden box-cars, which were prominently labelled *40 hommes, 8 chevaux*. Over 50 men were squeezed into each box-car. It was impossible to lie down; they were crowded shoulder-to-shoulder after giving up one end of the car to the wounded. Some of the Western Canadians were 'as big as horses'. At one end of each box-car a small barred window allowed in an insignificant amount of fresh air. In the centre of each car, the Germans had placed a large pail for the 50 men to use as a lavatory; it was soon overflowing and added its overpowering stench to the growing discomforts within. The floor of each box-car was covered in filthy straw, fouled by cattle. A single 10-gallon milk can was filled with drinking water; bits of straw floated on the surface. With a macabre sense of humour the German guards had chalked in huge letters on the sides of each box-car, 'Churchill's Second Front Kaput!'

Captain Clare and the other Canadian doctors had worked almost continuously throughout their stay at Verneulles, treating over 250 wounded without equipment. During that time they saved countless lives, but when the order came to move out, they were shocked to find that the serious stretcher cases were to be moved via box-car to Germany. In one small box-car, 21 stretcher cases were crowded with four Canadian medical orderlies and Doctors Clare and Robertson.

The officers had already left for Oflag VIIB at Eichstatt, near Munich. The Germans had little compunction about packing badly wounded men into filthy box-cars, but at the same time, they insisted that the officers travel in regular railway coaches. True, the seats had been removed, but strict protocol demanded that they travel in gentlemanly fashion. Every one of the officers would have volunteered to change places with the wounded if they could.

Many of the seriously injured remained at the Dieppe and Rouen hospitals until they were considered fit to travel to German prison hospitals at Kloster Haina, Obermassfeld, Stradtroda, Hildburghausen, and Egendorf. When convalescent, the men were sent to Stalag IXC at Molsdorf, while the officers were sent to Oflag IXA/Z at Rothenburg.

Jack Poolton decided to escape from the train leaving Verneulles given the slightest opportunity. He was not alone; many other men had determined to make the attempt during the long journey to the prison camps. Jack reasoned that a successful escape had to be made while they were still on French soil; therefore, a knowledge of the French language was vital. Unfortunately, Jack didn't speak a word of French beyond the old army favourite expressions, so he sought out a French Canadian named Pelletier, who readily agreed to join him in his escape. They noticed that some box-car windows had bars, others steel mesh, and reasoned that they had a better chance in bending two steel bars than in trying to break through mesh.

Thus they dodged out of any group headed for the mesh-windowed cars. Several times they received savage blows and kicks from the guards as they dodged from group to group, but they persevered until finally they found what they were looking for. All over the floor were wounded British commandos. Their wounds had received little treatment, and the smell of putrefaction was overpowering within the close confines of the car. One poor chap had received no less than 11 wounds, but he had been laid on the filthy straw with the rest. Jack was amused to find two of the commandos examining the iron bars on the window, and quickly they agreed to join forces.

They waited until dark, and through the open window they could see fields of wheat lit by a brilliant moon overhead. By a superhuman effort, the four men succeeded in bending the iron bars apart. One of the commandos was a little man with a thin chest and spindly legs. He looked more like a half-starved slum child than a member of the tough commandos; but his companion assured Jack Poolton that his size was deceiving. He was as tough as they came, and he proved it in masterful fashion. Helped by his companions, he squeezed through the tiny window to hang by his finger-tips from the roof of the boxcar as it swayed dangerously at a speed of 60 miles an hour. Inside, the men held their breath, waiting for a shot to be fired, but the door was suddenly opened from the outside and the daring little man stepped inside, breathing normally and wearing a wide grin as he dusted his hands.

As they rounded a bend, they noted that five engines were pulling the huge train, and that on alternate cars German guards manned machine guns to discourage potential escapers. They had been warned before they left Verneulles that 10 men would be shot for every one escaping, but this was considered an idle threat posed to discourage them from making the attempt. Later in their captivity they would think differently. Although greatly tempted to jump out there and then, they wisely decided to wait until the train passed through a wooded area where they could quickly find cover. A short time later the train stopped at a railway station and the unlocked door was discovered. Escape plans were shelved for the time being.

Aboard the officers' train, several men made a daring escape by leaping from the windows and trusting to luck not to break an arm, leg or neck. Major Rolfe, the Signals Officer, was joined by Lt. T. M. Baratt of the Black Watch and Lt.

Shackleton of the R.C.E. They were recaptured almost immediately but several other officers did make home-runs all the way back to Britain.

Just outside Brussels, the train drew into a station, where a large party of Belgian schoolgirls waved at and cheered the Canadian officers. Solemnly gathering into a compact group, they sang in good, clear English, 'Will ye no come back again?' Many of the Canadian officers had tears in their eyes as they listened to the words. Just then the German guards waded into the little girls, wielding rifle butts and jackboots to silence the demonstration. There was nothing the officers could do to help. As the train pulled out of the station, they gravely saluted the brave young patriots. At Essen, the platform was crowded with German civilians who jeered and shouted threats to the men as they gasped for air in their fetid box-cars. Showers of stones were hurled through the windows of the cars, injuring men who were already badly suffering from privations and wounds.

At one point, a group of German Red Cross women tried to give food and drink to the men, but the guards and S.S. troops knocked the food out of their hands. Inside some of the box-cars, the situation was becoming acute. In Pte. Mac Maloy's car, his friend Danny MacDonald of the Essex Scottish was in dire need of medical attention; his legs had been shot to pieces and were now in an advanced state of suppuration. He constantly called for water and his comrades tried to help, but Danny should have been in a clean white bed in an intensive-care ward, not in a filthy box-car. In every car of that infamous train, the same conditions prevailed, the same indifference from the guards. Men cursed their captors in low, bitter voices.

They were headed for Stalag VIIIB, reputed to be the largest P.O.W. camp in Germany. Situated a few miles from the little village of Lamsdorf in Upper Silesia near the city of Breslau and the River Oder, they would be neighbours of the Poles and Czechs. After five days and nights of sheer misery, the long train was at last halted at Lamsdorf. With the harsh, raucous cries of their guards ringing in their ears, the prisoners were forced out of the box-cars into the light of day.

What gaunt, emaciated men they were. Cheeks sunken and etiolated, eyes blinking and dazed, by the sudden transition from almost total darkness to brilliant sunshine, they staggered like blind, drunken men. After a few minutes, their eyes adjusted to the new surroundings as they were formed into columns

129

to begin the long march to the prison camp. Not far away, Russian prisoners were unloading ammunition from another train. Bearded skeletons dressed in rags, they were surrounded by German guards carrying bull-whips, which they frequently used with gusto. Did a similar fate await the Canadians?

Regimental Sergeant-Major Beesley ignored his captors and with the other N.C.O.s instructed the men to carry the wounded as gently as possible down the long road ahead. On both sides of the road cherry trees were burdened with ripe fruit, which the men eyed with intense longing but which they dared not touch; they had been warned by the guards that they would be shot if they plucked a single cherry. They neared a cemetery where small, black, dirty crosses stretched as far as the eye could see. One of the Prairie men asked the guard if they were the graves of German soldiers, but before he could answer, the men had read the epitaphs; each represented a soldier from the Allied forces in the First World War — French, British, American, and Canadian. Obviously they had not all died of wounds before they were taken prisoner. Stalag VIIIB had been the biggest prisoner of war camp in Germany in the First War and had developed an evil reputation for ill treatment and malnutrition of its charges.

The road was long and the men weak from hunger and privation, but as the outline of the camp appeared in the distance, they were ordered by their N.C.O.s to lift up their heads and march forward with arms swinging. Men who survived would always remember that moment as one of their finest. One and all, they squared their shoulders and marched in true Aldershot fashion — in step with the next man, line-abreast like a guards' regiment on parade. Many were without clothes; a great many more were barefooted. But march they did and with true and great dignity.

In the distance could be heard the sound of a great baying like a Wembley Cup Final as thousands of British prisoners confined since Dunkirk cheered and waved with great enthusiasm and gusto from behind the barbed-wire fences. 'Good old Canada,' they shouted as the men neared the great gates of Stalag VIIIB know as *Grosses Tor*.

To men imprisoned for years in drab surroundings without adequate news of the war situation after the resounding defeat at Dunkirk, the sight of hundreds of Canadians taken prisoner proved that the war was far from over and that others had joined Britain in her fight. The great and sincere welcome raised the spirits of the Canadians — it was good to know that they had friends within the camp. The British men appeared to be in good health and spirits in spite of their incarceration.

They advanced through the main gate singing. 'The Yanks are coming' to the huge delight of the British troops behind the wire. The guards and officials were puzzled and apprehensive. Beaten armies do not usually march into prison camp with proud bearing and with arms swinging as though on parade.

The hot sun beat down on the Canadians as their captors counted and recounted them monotonously. After a time, the wounded were carried to the camp *Revier* and *Lazarett*, where a team of British doctors was joined by Captains Clare, Robertson, and Walmsley to save as many as possible after their terrible ordeal in the box-cars.

The Germans had made no move to feed them. The only food they had received since capture had been issued five days before at Verneulles. In a spirit of unselfishness, the British prisoners carried out their lunch ration through the inner gates of the camp and, after receiving permission from the guards, handed it over to the Canadians. The lunch consisted of weak cabbage soup served in large garbage pails known as *Kübeln*. No eating utensils were provided, and the men were forced to drink the soup out of their steel helmets or from rusty cans found in the rubbish dumps. The soup was watery with only a few cabbage leaves floating on the top along with a fine collection of grubs and worms, but to men weak from starvation, it tasted warm and soothing.

CHAPTER FOURTEEN

INTRODUCTION TO STALAG VIIIB

After being searched and recounted, each man was photographed and given his new *Kriegsgefangener* (P.O.W.) number, then marched through a second gate into the main prisoner of war compound and checked again. The camp was surrounded by a barbed-wire fence nine feet high with a second barbed-wire fence mounted some six feet inside and parallel to it. Huge rolls of dannert wire were used to fill the space between the two fences. As an added precaution tin cans had been loosely tied to the wire to rattle and give the alarm if any prisoner tried to escape over it.

Three feet inside the second fence, a trip wire had been mounted 12 inches above the ground to form a further barrier. Any prisoner stepping over this trip wire without permission was liable to be shot without warning. Machine-gun towers had been erected at intervals all around the perimeter. Known as 'Goon' huts, they housed a machine gun and searchlight and were manned by keen-eyed guards who kept the compound under constant surveillance.

The camp was divided into three main sections, each separated by a fenced roadway. Every section contained one or two blocks. Apart from the hospital, sick bay, and detention quarters, all prisoners in Stalag VIIIB were housed within 10 of these blocks. Each block contained four long wooden huts or barracks, each divided into two sections by a washroom open to both sections. The washroom was provided with a solitary cold-water tap for 120 men — 60 in each section. At the rear of each block, a long stone building known as the '40-holer' served as latrine for 600 men. Human wastes were collected at intervals from the latrine by a huge tank drawn by horses and commonly called the 'Honey Wagon'.

Such was the prison the Canadians now entered to serve an undetermined sentence. In time they would organise games and sports to occupy their minds and prevent 'wire happiness', but their first initiation into the Stalag was a traumatic one.

Nothing was provided for the unfortunates who were without clothing or footwear. Only a single blanket, threadbare and made of wood fibre, had been issued to each man to protect him from the cold night air. A single spoon was given to everyone, but the guards considered knives and forks dangerous weapons.

The prisoners had been divided into separate groups by the guards and allotted to barrack huts. Sergeant Bill Lee found himself in hut 19b and together with the other N.C.O.s quickly tried to bring about some order. The number of bunks was totally insufficient. The lucky ones managed to lay claim to one of the three-tiered bunk beds. The others had to sleep on the bare floor or arrange to sleep in shifts with a buddy in a bunk.

Each hut was supplied with a single wooden table. Food had to be eaten standing up or squatting on the floor. One stove fitted with a chimney provided the source of heat and warmth for the long hut and food also had to be cooked on its tiny surface. In the winter, when the temperature plunged below zero, the prisoners found to their sorrow that this single stove was totally inadequate either for heating or cooking purposes — especially with the small ration of coal that was issued — 25 pounds per hut per day! In hut 19b, Lee persuaded the men to empty their pockets so that they could pool their resources. Some had combs, others toothbrushes or razors that they had concealed to slip through the searches. All were shared with less fortunate comrades. This type of unselfishness would eventually become a tradition whenever a new man was sent to the huts.

The men were introduced to their new diet — a daily pint of weak cabbage soup crawling with squirmy horrors, augmented by generous portions of dirt. The German captors did not see any reason for washing the cabbage before boiling it. A loaf of black bread was issued to a number of men to be cut into exact portions of 350 grams. This minute ration of bread usually worked out to four slices per day. On Sundays they were given a piece of the vile-smelling fish cheese, which deteriorated to a nasty slime in hot weather, and a small piece of liverwurst, which they were sure could walk. Sometimes a few potatoes were added if a German victory had recently been announced, but the issue was rare enough to be considered a special treat. Liquid refreshment was supplied in the form of mint tea issued after roll-call was over and carried to each hut in *Kübeln*.

Very few knives had escaped the searches, and the dividing

of the bread ration assumed great importance. Sgt. Tom Nicholls found an old door hinge and managed to sharpen it to a knife edge on a piece of concrete. To men starving of hunger, a single crumb is an issue to be debated at length. Taking a tip from their English comrades in the next compound, the Canadians split up into small groups of four for feeding purposes. Each man in the group would be known to the others as a 'mucker', and all things were shared amongst the muckers in the group. In time they developed great skill in dividing the rations in a scrupulously fair manner. At a later date when they received the life-saving Red Cross parcels, or private parcels from home, they shared every item with their muckers, and woe betide the man who took an unfair ration or stooped to steal another man's food!

Ronnie Reynolds joined a mucker group with Don Lazier of the Calgary Tanks. Don had been appointed the controller for the hut by R.S.M. Beesley and his duties included the slicing of the tiny bread ration for over 12 men. Ronnie Reynolds solemnly swore that Don Lazier was the only man in the world who could cut a 'one-sided piece of bread'.

After they had eaten their meagre rations, many of the men collapsed onto their bunks and slept the deep sleep of the exhausted. Others wandered over to the wire separating them from the English compound and managed to borrow a variety of musical instruments for a jamboree, and for some hours, all of Stalag VIIIB reverberated with the unfamiliar sounds of Canadian and American country music! There was more method than madness in this opening party. They had nothing to celebrate; they had suffered a resounding defeat at the hands of the enemy through no fault of their own; they had endured a monstrous box-car ride, and they had just entered a depressing prison. But the music did wonders for the morale of those who were feeling depressed and despondent. Again, the guards were confused by these extraordinary men — a bunch of prisoners celebrating a defeat! A jug of liquor would have livened the party up considerably, but that would come later when the men had learned the secrets of distillation from raisins and yeast.

The bunk beds supported the wood-shaving mattresses on a frame of 12 bed-boards, but the previous occupants had been forced to burn a fair number of the boards to keep themselves warm in the winter. The result was that the poor fellows in the lower bunks were almost compressed by the mattresses bulging through the open spaces above. Furthermore many of the men awoke in the night to find that they were not alone in the bed. Voracious fleas and lice drove their victims frantic with intolerable itching.

Early next morning, they were roused by a raucous screaming ''*raus! 'raus!*' Rolling over with a groan, they were faced with two unpleasant sights; it was still dark outside and the German guards were rushing up and down between the narrow aisles prompting the heavy sleepers with a kick or a blow from a rifle butt.

Hastily throwing on their uniforms, they left the huts to be counted for the early morning roll-call known to their captors as *Appell*. Those who in their innocence hoped to be counted quickly and then dismissed to return to their flea-bags were quickly disillusioned. Usually the roll-call was stretched out for at least two hours as they were counted and recounted, over and over again. In sub-zero winter weather this routine became a nightmare. Clad in threadbare uniforms, many of the men were without overcoats or proper shoes.

The strange new language acquired in the prison camp must have confused the folks back home in Canada. One man wrote home and referred to the roll-calls as *Appell*s. His wife wrote back and said, 'I'm so glad they give you two *apples* a day, they must help out the food situation a lot!' The Germans were no longer Germans. They were 'Goons' and everything German was 'Goonish'. The sentry boxes were Goon huts, the bread, Goon bread. There were Goon rations, Goon news, and Goon guards. The name came from the comical appearance of the guards in their sentry boxes overlooking the camp. In the wintertime, they wore enormous long greatcoats, heavy caps with a scarf wrapped around the neck and lower face, thick gloves, and huge boots. With nothing but their eyes and noses showing, they looked for all the world like Alice the Goon in the old Popeye comics. It may have been a silly name, but it satisfied the prisoners and suited the feeling they had for most of the guards.

The German non-commissioned officer in charge of the Canadian compound was a sadistic man known as 'Spitfire'. From the very first he went out of his way to torment the Canadians. In a short space of time he was hated vehemently by all. In the Royal Air Force compound, the prisoners were blessed with a similar type known as 'Ukraine Joe'. This type of man delighted in bullying prisoners of war who were powerless to defend themselves. To defy his authority meant a long spell in the cooler, but to strike a German soldier, especially an officer or non-commissioned officer, meant a court-martial and a possible death sentence from which there would be no appeal.

For the first month, the Germans were content to starve the Canadians into submission. Later they were forced to labour on farms and in factories outside the camp. By the rules of the Geneva convention, which had been signed by Germany, the officers and N.C.O.s could not be forced to work. Many of the men who had doffed their clothes to swim out to sea at Dieppe had lost their paybooks, the sole documentation that they were private soldiers or N.C.O.s A number of them took advantage of this lack of evidence to assume the mantle of higher rank and became what the prisoners jokingly called 'Stalag' sergeants. The deception was blessed by their own N.C.O.s, who would do nothing to assist the Germans in their war effort.

The dreadful and totally inadequate diet gradually took its toll, and the prisoners began to waste away. It was months before they received their first Red Cross parcels, without which they would surely have died before the end of the war. Perhaps the next most serious deficiency was the lack of mail. When first taken prisoner, they had filled out a Red Cross form and sent a form postcard containing a few brief phrases to assure their families that they were well and had been taken P.O.W.

Boredom was the insidious enemy to be fought at all times, if a prisoner was not to become melancholy and mentally disturbed during his enforced stay. They could understand the possibility of being wounded or even killed. That was a risk they had accepted as front-line soldiers. But they had difficulty adjusting to forced incarceration. It was a thought that had probably never entered their heads. The men who took up a hobby or entered educational instruction under makeshift teachers, or even the men who spent their time playing poker, were fortunate. Their minds were occupied. Anything to stimulate the mind would stave off 'wire happiness'. Those who did not try to keep their minds and bodies active found themselves sinking deeper and deeper into a pit of mental anguish and self-pity from which there was often no escape. It inevitably led to a break-down in normal behaviour and to the ever-ready strait-jacket. During the first few months, more than one of the prisoners was killed as he calmly climbed over the barbed-wire fence in total disregard for the inevitable machine-gun fire from the guard towers.

Some of the more adventurous types were already investigating the possibilities of escape. Regimental Sergeant-Major Beesley called a meeting of the senior N.C.O.s shortly after they had arrived at the camp. He made it very clear that he expected them to plan for escape as soon as possible. It was their duty as soldiers to escape and fight again, he reminded them, and he would help in any possible manner. As senior non-commissioned officer in charge of the Canadian compound, he could not take an official part in such escape plans, but indirectly he would be behind the scenes giving his active support.

While Beesley was the senior N.C.O. in the Canadian compound, two fellow R.S.M.s — Sherriff and Lowe in the British compound — were the officially recognised senior N.C.O.s in charge of the whole of Stalag VIIIB. Both these men had promised Beesley full support and assistance in any planned escapes from the Canadian compound.

Within the British compound a 'racket' compound flourished. Some of the greedier men spent their waking hours bartering and selling watches, rings, cigarette lighters, even English pound notes. These types were often seen moving from hut to hut carrying a small wooden box containing their ill-gotten baubles as they plied their dubious trade. Fortunately, the racket compound was engaged in other, more important business as well. Forgers, tailors, and other experts spent long days preparing false identity cards, railway passes, civilian suits and maps to enable the selected few to escape. R.S.M. Sherriff generously offered the services of his racket compound to the Canadians. A sound word of advice was also included in the offered assistance. All plans for escape attempts or the building of tunnels had to be kept as secret as possible. Past experience, sadly gained by the British, had proved that many such plans had been betrayed to the Germans by traitors in the camp. At a later date, the Canadians also discovered to their chagrin that they had their own special brand of traitors in the Canadian compound.

At the early meetings of the escape committee, various plans were discussed and in most cases discarded as being impractical. Sgt. Larry Palls of the Essex Scottish, who was of Dutch descent, belonged to an intelligence section of the Canadian Army. Initially, he was elected Chairman of the Escape Committee. Bill Lee was to be his assistant. Escape attempts were to be confined to people considered essential to the war effort who could also speak a foreign language, preferably German. Escape from the camp was a difficult accomplishment in itself, but without an adequate knowledge of German, the escaper would most likely be picked up within 24 hours.

A red-headed sergeant named McMurray from the Royal Canadian Engineers was selected to engineer and build an escape tunnel. Under his direction, many men were approached to work on the construction or to dispose of the excavated soil. Other men were chosen as look-outs to be posted at all strategic points and to give advance warning of the approach of a guard.

Sgt. Lee's hut, 19b, was chosen for the entrance to the tunnel because it was the nearest hut to the wire. Taking all precautions, a cunningly disguised trap-door was cut in the concrete floor under one of the bunks, and construction begun.

The shaft was sunk and tunnelling commenced. Tools were non-existent. Improvised trowels, knives, even spoons were used to dig and hack the red soil, which was then packed into Red Cross boxes and handed to the disposal men. Under cover of darkness, the soil was mixed in with the earth in the vegetable patch, which, fortunately, was raised some 12 inches above the ground. The 40-holer latrine was another favourite dumping ground. Periodically, the human waste was carted away in a wagon drawn by two horses. Russian prisoners had been given the hideous job of cleaning out the latrine; they must have wondered at the large amounts of soil in the human waste — perhaps they thought it was due to the unwashed vegetables in the soup.

The shaft constructed by Sgt. McMurray was sunk vertically nine feet beneath the bunk before the tunnel was begun in the direction of the wire, over 100 feet away. The sandy soil provided a very treacherous support for the tunnel, so the leaders approached trustworthy men to sacrifice some of their bedboards; Red Cross string was substituted for the boards. Teams of men worked day and night in rotating shifts. Many of the sappers digging in the tunnel had been hard-rock miners from Timmins; hour after hour they patiently clawed at the soil. Quite a number of them were French Canadians from the

Gaspé peninsula, hard-working men who worked under atrocious conditions without a murmur of complaint.

Light was provided by home-made lamps using pyjama-cord wicks soaked in margarine. The dense black fumes from the lamps soon filled the tunnel with choking carbon dioxide. Work was halted temporarily until some form of ventilation could be provided.

Besides Larry Palls, the head of the escape committee, Bill Lee who would take the escapers through the tunnel, and Sgt. McMurray, the builder of the tunnel, perhaps the most important man was the 'Procurer' — Jimmy Maitland from Sarnia, Ontario. Larry Palls had chosen Jimmy for this special job because it required a great deal of nerve, ingenuity, and cheek. A supply of air required a pump and a pipe. Jimmy sat down and wrote 'Pipe' on a piece of clean paper. The tunnel would be approximately 100 feet long; therefore, opposite the word pipe, he wrote 100 feet. Taking a squad of engineers, he marched them smartly over to the gate to the German sentry and waved the piece of paper under his nose. In the administrative compound, the Germans were erecting some new wooden huts. Gutters on the roofs were connected to down-pipes, each 10 feet long. What better piping could be provided? In calm, detached fashion, Jimmy and the men proceeded to dismantle the down-pipes. On the way back to the Canadian compound, he ordered 'eyes right' and gave the sentry a magnificent salute. The sentry blushed at this splendid example of military courtesy extended to a mere private soldier. With a rattle and a great flourish he presented arms as the men marched proudly past carrying the booty.

A French Canadian named Robichard manufactured the bellows from an old ground-sheet. A make-shift valve was fitted, then connected up to the lengths of down-piping; fresh, clean air flooded down the tunnel. Day after day for the next six months, Sapper Robichard would lie in the terribly confined space under the bunk and pump his bellows at a steady, monotonous rate. Such was his splendid contribution to the building of the escape tunnel.

The supply of bed-boards was running low as the tunnel grew in length. Again Jimmy Maitland came to the rescue with his piece of paper and his 'working party'. By now, the sentries were becoming accustomed to the sight of Jimmy marching his men smartly through the gate. *Der Kanadier* was a good soldier — very smart. This time Jimmy returned with a load of prime oak planks for the tunnel, which was then passing under the roadway and required a firm roof.

Then early on the morning of October 8th, 1942, plans for the escape were suddenly and dramatically shelved.

CHAPTER FIFTEEN

REPRISALS

The men awoke to find their compound ringed with a battalion of German troops. Machine guns had been mounted all around the compound. The German troops had been issued with Tommy guns and stick grenades, which they pointed with obvious menace at the Canadians. Outside along the roadway, armoured cars were stationed with guns cocked as a warning to the prisoners as they rubbed the sleep from their eyes.

Harry Beesley paraded the men in their usual fives, Sgt. Bill Lee, an efficient 'marker' on parade, was number one. Behind him were his friends Bobby Fletcher and Roy Luxmore. In the tense, hushed atmosphere, the prisoners waited for the camp commandant to arrive on the scene. It was obvious that something bad was about to happen, but what? The sight of so many hundreds of heavily armed troops all staring at them with obvious hatred made them fearful of a massacre.

As the German commandant and his adjutant entered the compound, Beesley called the men smartly to attention. The German adjutant handed a long, official-looking document to the interpreter, who proceeded to translate its contents to the thousand and more men assembled before him. In halting English he bellowed the following cryptic message:

> The German Government has always shown the utmost clemency to prisoners of war and accorded them the treatment due to honourable men captured in battle as laid down in the International Agreement signed at The Hague in 1926.

This statement was accorded the derision it deserved. After the appalling treatment during the box-car journey and later in this same prison camp, the words were hypocritical, to say the least. A great murmur arose from the ranks of assembled prisoners. If the commandant understood English he must have recognised some of the more derogatory terms shouted by the men. Pausing for the commotion to subside, the interpreter continued:

After the recent abortive enemy invasion at Dieppe when British and Canadian troops attempted to invade the continent of Europe, many German soldiers were found shot with their hands tied behind their backs!

Now it was out! Obviously the enemy was planning to retaliate by some means. The men shuffled uneasily as they waited for the answer. Beesley wore a stony countenance as the interpreter bellowed the German message in English. With a steely eye he faced the commandant, awaiting the bad news.

This gross cruelty was repeated in a later raid on the Channel Islands by British Commandos. The German Government has demanded an apology from the British Government and an assurance that such inhumane treatment will be discontinued in future.

The British Government has refused to apologise and therefore the German Government has no alternative but to take reprisals against all members of the Dieppe Force!

All along the long lines of men, there was a deathly silence. They had heard about these German reprisals. Lidice was still fresh in their minds. If the Nazis could slaughter 10,000 men, women, and children and wipe out a complete town for the assassination of one German soldier, what chance did they have?

Some of the N.C.O.s and men looked around at the German soldiers surrounding them. If they were going to be shot, then they would at least die fighting! All around them, the massed troops raised their weapons threateningly. The situation was ugly and invited disaster.

The German adjutant gave the order to Beesley to march off the first 10 men into one of the huts for their punishment. Swinging about, he faced Sergeant Bill Lee and his first two rows of men and quietly spoke to them before he ordered them to proceed.

'Men,' he said, in a tightly controlled voice, 'I don't know what's going to happen, but whatever it is, we are going to act like soldiers! First two rows, right turn!'

The surrounding German soldiers tightened their grip on their weapons. They fully expected the Canadians to riot in defiance of the order. Instead, under the quiet discipline of Harry Beesley, they made a smart right wheel and entered the forbidding hut with heads held high and arms swinging. Led by Bill Lee, they shakily whistled 'The Maple Leaf Forever'.

Inside, they were confronted by a number of German soldiers wearing hanks of Red Cross string around their necks. As each man stepped forward, he had his hands securely tied behind his back and was then forced out of a door at the other side of the room. The men waiting in line for their 'punishment', watched the performance with astonishment. Then, as one, they burst into loud peals of nervous laughter. They had steeled themselves to face a firing squad and instead, they were being tied up like a bunch of kids playing cowboys and Indians!

Throughout the long day, the remainder of the men were forced to submit to the tying of hands. It didn't take them long to turn the tables on their persecutors. As each man left the hut after being securely tied, he stood back to back with a buddy so that they could loosen each other's bonds. They then re-joined the long line of men waiting outside the hut to complain that the string had worked loose. Others removed the string entirely before rejoining the line to form an unbroken circle.

Late at night, a group of hysterical guards and their equally hysterical officers staggered from the compound nursing swollen hands after tying thousands of prisoners — a number many times that of the original band of Dieppe prisoners. If they were in any doubt that they had suffered a humiliating defeat, the hooting of the prisoners should have convinced them of the failure of the operation. The Dieppe men had at least turned that into a victory!

At Eichstatt, Oflag VIIB, hundreds of miles to the west, the Canadian officers captured at Dieppe were being accorded similar treatment.

At breakfast time they were startled by a *Sonderappell*, an order over the P.A. system for the officers to fall in for a surprise parade. Once they were mustered outside, the order came for the Dieppe party to fall out in front. Names were checked before they were marched up the incline to the Lagerstrasse. As they moved through the prison gates on to the highway, they were surprised to see a great number of German troops lining the sides of the road. They were all heavily armed and appeared nervous.

After being loaded into two large trucks, they were driven through the streets of the village — guards in front, guards behind, and Tommy guns all around. Lt. Jerry Wood recalled a movie of a revolutionary scene showing a cart-load of condemned going through the streets of Paris. But it was too nice a day for that kind of nonsense. Apparently this area had been a religious centre long ago. Convex window panes of seventeenth century glass were seen in many of the convents and church buildings they passed.

The convoy passed a railroad station. The officers were puzzled. This meant that they couldn't be going to another prison camp.

A short distance outside the village, they were roughly ordered to get out of the trucks and march up a steep incline. Towering above them was the grim fortress of Willibaldsburg Schloss, which commands the heights above Eichstatt. They passed through the tunnel of the outer wall of the castle into a mediaeval inner courtyard.

The gate was shut. 'They are going to shoot us,' said someone with a nervous laugh. This devil-may-care attitude didn't prevent most of the men from feeling uneasy. The grim courtyard, the sphinx-like attitude of the German guards stationed about every two feet around them, the unusual number of machine guns, all added to the tension.

The first four officers were led through a gate into the castle. Somebody facetiously cracked, 'I didn't hear any shots, boys.' From then on, groups went out by fours. It surely had to be an interrogation, the remaining officers thought.

Lt. Col. Bob Labatt was motioned into and along the hall to face the camp commandant, the camp doctor, and several other German officers. Labatt asked the commandant in peremptory fashion why they had been brought away from the prison camp. The commandant, whose attitude to the prisoners had previously been rude, wore a pained expression as he simply apologised for what was about to happen. He stated that he was merely following orders and regretted what he had to do.

Labatt was pushed into another room where two *Posten* (private soldiers), a captain, and the camp adjutant stood silently facing him. Several strands of rope lay on a bed against the wall. The *Posten* seized Labatt's wrists and bound them with a piece of rope stout enough to tie up a horse. 'This is shocking treatment,' he said. 'I can't imagine your men in Canada being treated this way!'

Quite obviously the German officers and men loathed every part of the operation. Labatt was then led down a passageway into a large, barn-like, shadowy room where a number of palliasses filled with wood shavings were laid in rows on the floor. Along the wall, Canadian officers sat on stools with their heads bowed. The boys were ruminating over their sins!

The German doctor examined the bindings. He complained that most of them were too tight. A *Stabsfeldwebel* (R.S.M.) rebound those, and then the men were lined up along one wall as a translator read a long screed from the German War Office outlining how bound Germans had been found dead at Dieppe in compliance with captured British Operation Orders instructing that prisoners be bound. German protests and British denials and assurance of a non-repetition had been followed by another unfortunate incident that had taken place recently on the Channel Islands during a commando raid.

One of the officers now shouted, 'Hurray for the commandos!' The enthusiastic but unwise heckler was quickly silenced by the guards, and the translator continued: the officers would remain tied until Winston Churchill apologised for the incident and gave an assurance that the shameful tying of German prisoners would never again take place!Labatt stood erect and at attention facing the commandant. He spoke for all of the officers present. 'If you are waiting for an apology from Mr. Winston Churchill, you will wait till hell freezes over!'

On the way back to the prison camp, one officer quietly remarked, 'This should convince people that these are our enemies, not our hosts.' Unwittingly, the enemy had helped the cause. They had instilled hatred in the place of apathy. From now on, the prisoners would do anything in their power to goad their captors and to bring escape plans to fruition as soon as possible.

CHAPTER SIXTEEN

THE DIEPPE COMPOUND

Living conditions were deplorable. Since the tying, the men were forbidden to leave the huts. Dysentery was rife, due to the dreadful diet; hundreds of men suffered from chronic diarrhoea but the guards refused to allow them to go alone to the 40-holer. They had to wait in misery until 10 men were in desperate straits; then they were marched as a group with a German sentry at the head of the line and another at the rear. A Canadian medical orderly accompanied them to wipe their behinds afterwards.

With hands tightly lashed together, small tasks such as peeling a potato or cutting a slice of bread required the utmost concentration. Even rolling a cigarette seemed an impossible task, but they learned, and they learned infinite patience. One man held the paper while the second man poured the loose tobacco into it. The third man stood with his tongue hanging out for the first man to wipe the gum edge of the paper over it.

By this time Red Cross parcels should have been supplied to supplement the starvation diet. When R.S.M. Beesley protested, he was informed by the Germans that Red Cross food parcels had been cut off until the British Government sent an apology. Men lay on their bunks to conserve their little remaining energy. One day as a Canadian sergeant doled out the noon ration of soup, the skeleton of a large rat was found in the bottom. The men didn't turn a hair when the sergeant bellowed, 'Meat in the soup today, boys,' and held the skeleton aloft to prove it. Occasionally, when their captors gave a meat ration, it was a horse's head. It was not unusual for some poor soul to receive a staring eyeball for his portion of the issue.

Slowly they were starving to death. It was still possible to obtain food by bartering personal valuables with the rogues from the racket compound. Sleek and well-fed, these men moved daily from hut to hut, bartering with starving men for their last valuables. Harry Beesley was an Englishman but he refused to live in the British compound because he felt that many of the prisoners taken at Dunkirk had lost any desire to escape and fight again. When the racketeering became a serious problem, he formed a unit of 'Camp Security Police' from the Canadians. As the senior N.C.O. he gave them full authority to deal with any soldier, British or Canadian, who did not conduct himself as a soldier.

Three times a day the rations were issued. At 7 a.m. mint tea, used by the prisoners for shaving water or for pouring over their clothes to kill vermin; at 1.30 p.m. the bread was distributed — 350 grams per man or three slices per day if cut thin enough; at 4 p.m. the cabbage or turnip soup was doled out, one ladle to each man.

Twice each week a margarine ration was supplied to each man. It was the size of a patty given in restaurants for one slice of bread. On the remaining days, as a special treat, they were given a one-ounce portion of liverwurst or fish-cheese. Occasionally this treat was supplemented by a spoonful of jam made from sugar beet pulp.

After seven months, the camp was visited by the International Red Cross Commission, whose members told the Germans to provide additional rations in the form of a cereal one day per week. The term 'cereal' was misleading; when it arrived, it was promptly dubbed 'bed-board soup' by the prisoners because it tasted of wood shavings and was quite inedible.

Hygiene was perhaps the next most serious problem after food. The water was only turned on for a short period at 8 a.m. and 3 p.m. Usually there was a mad scramble to fill water cans for drinking purposes before the cut-off time. As a result, personal hygiene became a serious matter. One bitterly cold morning, the whole Canadian compound and the German guards were amazed to see Harry Beesley march smartly across the parade ground and halt at the edge of a large pool of freezing water. The Germans had cut off the water supply. Laying his towel and toilet gear carefully on the ground, Harry stripped to the waist and proceeded to wash himself in the frigid water before shaving. Once his toilet was completed, he wrapped his towel casually around his neck and marched back to his barrack hut. This exhibition was not done to display his toughness; Harry Beesley was not that kind of man. He had done it to demonstrate his contempt for the German guards and to uplift the morale of his men. Shortly afterwards the Germans turned on the water.

The beds abounded with bed-bugs and fleas, which marched in thousands as soon as the lights were turned off. A more serious problem was that of body lice. Several hundred yards away from the main camp at Stalag VIIIB lay a Russian compound. The German treatment of these prisoners was a matter of deep concern to the Canadians. Russia had not been one of the signatories to the international agreement covering the treatment of prisoners of war. The food these men received was far less than the starvation rations given to the Canadians. In the weak, emaciated state, they were prime victims for the typhus bug. An epidemic raged within this compound for months, killing hundreds of Russian prisoners. In the distance they could be seen every morning carrying scores of dead comrades on improvised stretchers out of the camp and dumping them unceremoniously into lime pits — one on top of the other, like dead beasts in a slaughterhouse.

Beesley protested vigorously to the German commandant about this barbaric method of burial. The commandant denied responsibility for the Russian compound but promised to do what he could. The next day, the Russian dead were carried in coffins by their comrades. Unfortunately, the bearers were also seen returning to the camp with the empty coffins.

The mass deaths from typhus in the Russian compound started a large-scale hunt for lice, which carried the disease. The seams of shirts and underpants were favourite nesting places, and the prisoners ran burning matches along the seams to kill them. Hot showers and regular washing of their clothes would have done much to eradicate the vermin problem, but their captors adamantly refused to allow more water for such purposes.

The rumour swept the barrack huts that bed-bugs fed on lice! Corporal Sadoquis of the R.C.E. had previously filled all the cracks and nail holes in his wooden bunk with the German soap — it made an excellent filler but it refused to lather. Frantically now he scraped out the soap to let the blood-thirsty bed-bugs out to feed on the more dangerous body lice. Captain Clare, the medical officer, quickly dispelled the rumours of lice-eating bugs and the soap was again used to seal the odious bedbugs in their wooden tombs.

On December 2nd, the prisoners were again paraded en masse by their German captors. This time the string and ropes were replaced by handcuffs and a chain 15 inches long. At the same time they were delighted to learn from their captors that the British had retaliated by chaining German prisoners in Canada and in Britain. After a short time, however, the British discontinued the practice. The Germans, unfortunately did not follow suit, and the Canadians remained chained until November 21st, 1943 — almost 13 months after they were first tied.

Again the German troops surrounded the compound. The younger soldiers had left for the Russian Front, leaving a sorry-looking home-guard in their place. The whole business was treated as a huge joke by the Canadians, especially after they heard a German officer bellowing, 'Hold your weapons ready, and don't hesitate to use them!'

One of the more enterprising prisoners discovered within a matter of hours that the handcuffs could easily be removed with a key from a bully beef or Klim milk tin. Thereafter, the chaining became a ludicrous affair. Every morning after breakfast, the German guards arrived to chain the Canadian prisoners. The chains were hung on two hooks behind the guards. As each man stepped forward, a guard snapped a pair of handcuffs on his wrists. Passing along, the prisoner would then remove them, using his 'key', and hang them neatly on the second hook!

At the end of an hour when the Germans discovered that not a single prisoner had been chained, the officer would scream at the guards and ask them what they had been doing for the last hour. The guards answered that they had been chaining the prisoners, whereupon the officer, red in the face, screamed, 'Then how is it that the chains are still here?'

The weather was very cold. Those owning overcoats tramped around the wire circuit, hands in the pockets, with a loop of chain passing outside from one pocket to the other but with the cuffs undone. The standard punishment meted out by the Germans if they caught a prisoner without chains was to stand him against the wire or against the side of a hut with his hands tied behind him for eight hours. If he moved at all, he received a 'gentle' correction from a heavy rifle butt.

One day a young soldier was standing naked in the washroom, wearing his chains and washing himself with a cupful of water, when a German guard entered. Screaming insanely at the youngster, the guard rushed for his officer. Obviously, the chains had been removed in order for the man to undress. Hearing the commotion, the rest of the prisoners rushed in and removed the chains hurriedly, dressed him, and replaced the chains before the guard returned with a German officer. The prisoner was now innocently washing his face with all his clothes on. The officer took one look and ordered the guard to report to the guard room under arrest. The charge was 'drunk while on duty'. After this incident, which could have had serious consequences, a careful watch was kept at all times for 'Spitfire' and his guards. Whenever one was seen in the vicinity of the huts, the alarm was given by bellowing, 'Air raid!' and scores of prisoners would hurriedly chain themselves.

To add to their discomfort, winter was now upon them. The first snow storms had swirled through the many broken panes of glass to chill them to the bone, although they soon replaced the missing panes of glass with cardboard or flattened tins. Few of the men possessed winter clothing or greatcoats. Many had entered the camp barefoot and had been issued with wooden clogs. At night they slept fully clothed, shivering under the single thin blanket provided. When they awoke in the blackness before the dawn, the blanket was covered with a layer of moisture from the cold and from the lines of washing strung under the ceiling.

Many became ill with bronchial troubles and the huts rang with harsh, wracking coughs, boding ill for the future; in later years, many would suffer from tuberculosis. In their weakened state, suffering from malnutrition and dysentery, they were easy targets for a score of serious illnesses.

Each barrack hut was fitted with a tiled stove and chimney, but the guards were extremely niggardly in rationing fuel. Every hut was allowed to draw a 25-pound ration of coal for the 24 hour day. In vain Captain Clare and the other medical officers protested at these dreadful heating conditions. Even in the camp hospital, where the seriously wounded men of Dieppe lay, the ration for each room of four patients was one-half of a Red Cross box of coal per day.

The early morning *Appell* at 6 a.m. became a dreaded ordeal under the sadistic Corporal 'Spitfire'. In sub-zero weather he would slowly count and then recount the long lines of shivering men. Deliberately he would make a mistake in the count and start all over again. Some of these roll-calls lasted for hours. When the weather was bad or when some of the men were sick, Harry Beesley would stand up to 'Spitfire' and wade into him like a fighting cock! 'Hurry up, you idiot' he would bawl, 'get these lads counted and get them off parade quickly.' Any other man would have been shot for standing up to the guards in such a manner, but Harry Beesley was feared and respected by his captors.

Cooking facilities in each hut were totally inadequate. Every day of the week, 20 or more men milled around the tiled stove, trying to get a spot on its tiny surface to heat up some kind of mess for the muckers in their groups. Something drastic had to be done.

The British compound came to their assistance and showed them how to construct miniature blowers or forges out of Klim tins and an improvised fan. When a handle was turned, the fan provided a strong current of air through a pipe made of Klim tins fitted end to end. Attached to the other end of the pipe was a bowl in which scraps of cardboard or twigs were burned. When a pan of water was placed on top of the bowl, it was very quickly brought to a boil by the raging forge beneath.

Within a short space of time, every mucker group had constructed a similar type of blower; thereafter, little groups of men could be seen inside and outside the hut cooking their meagre rations and, at the same time, absorbing the warmth into their emaciated bodies.

Although the blowers helped the cooking situation, the heating inside the hut remained a serious problem. When men roamed the compound their eyes were continually searching for the odd scrap of wood or blown twigs. Anything the Germans left around that was combustible was quickly put to use. One day a German electrician entered hut 19b to repair some of the wiring. The poor man should have been warned not to leave his wooden ladder. While his attention was diverted, some of the men chopped up the ladder and popped it into the stove to provide a beautiful roaring bonfire that lasted for over an hour. Needless to say, not one man had seen the ladder disappear.

Eating utensils had not been provided, but then, neither had they been provided to their pioneer Canadian ancestors. Improvisation was the word! Tin cans from British Red Cross parcels were fitted with wooden handles to provide cups. Tin plates and pots were bashed out from Klim tins from the same source.

Slowly they were becoming organised. Encouraged by Harry Beesley, the men started to make their squalid huts more livable. In 19b, the French Canadians painted the walls of the hut with beautiful murals. Each mural represented a separate Canadian province without caption or words to explain which province it was supposed to be. Prince Edward Island showed a beautiful young girl holding an armful of potatoes; British Columbia depicted leaping salmon.

Some extra blankets were scrounged and cut up to provide curtains for the windows. Cleanliness and neatness became the vogue and uniforms were pressed by laying them under mattresses. In all of these matters they were following the advice given by Harry Beesley and the senior Canadian N.C.O.s: 'Make the enemy respect you!'

Almost four months after their capture, they spent their first Christmas in prison camp. The Germans relaxed the harsh rules a little to allow them to receive British Red Cross parcels. Although there was only one parcel shared among every four men, the additional food, which was of far greater nutritional value than what they were accustomed to getting, was received joyfully by the men. As an added concession, the chains were removed on Christmas Eve and not returned for two days. The men were determined to be festive in spite of their squalid prison life. From the Red Cross parcels, they saved the silver paper from cigarette packages to make tinsel decorations. A bottle of wine would have helped, but some of the Red Cross parcels did contain the traditional Christmas puddings. Hour after hour they sang Christmas carols and hymns.

The padre, John Foote, organised a Christmas service for the men. Men of many faiths gathered together to hear John Foote and other padres communicate the word of God. The opening words of the service were, 'Men, we will have a regular service that everybody will understand.' In the congregation were Jews, Lutherans, Presbyterians, and Anglicans. Popular hymns such as 'Stand up, stand up for Jesus' were sung by all denominations at the top of their voices.

Every Sunday afterwards, Padre Foote held a regular Church service. The men enjoyed them. Apart from the spiritual comfort they provided, they enjoyed the communal atmosphere. It was also several degrees warmer in the church than in their freezing barrack huts.

Throughout the long prison days, John Foote did much to uplift morale; without him many of the men would have become mentally ill. His door was always open to a man deeply troubled or worried by bad news from home. Very often his letters, written late at night after listening to a troubled soul, solved a problem or smoothed over difficult situations at home.

Foote's services did not end with spiritual guidance and morale uplifting. Many times during the prison life he had voluntarily entered, he would harass the Germans for better treatment for the men. Towards the end of the war, he became an obvious target for the Gestapo and his life was threatened.

Work on the tunnel continued all through the winter. Under the expert direction of Sergeant McMurray, the tunnel sloped gradually upwards to a spot some 20 yards from the wire and behind a clump of bushes. Surveyors' tools were non-existent and the gradient had to be engineered by crude but effective methods. A long rod was carefully pushed through the roof of the tunnel to the surface of the compound. The man pushing the rod had a piece of string attached to his leg. Keen-eyed watchers in the barrack hut would signal to other men at the head of the tunnel when the rod was first sighted breaking though the surface of the compound. The rod-pusher would then withdraw the rod and measure the length necessary to break through. McMurray then made the calculations and the decision to slope the tunnel upwards or downwards.

When they finally broke through to the outer air, it was to find that they had surfaced exactly behind the bushes beyond the wire! A cunningly devised trap-door was then built out of wood and covered with soil and turf to camouflage it from prying eyes. Just a few yards away from the tunnel opening, a 'Goon box' reared its ugly head. The work on the trap-door was completed one moonless night under the very noses of the German machine gunners. It was still winter and few leaves were on the screening bushes. After a conference of the escape committee, it was decided to close off the tunnel and suspend operations until the spring.

About this time, the Germans started to send out working parties from the Canadian compound to work in industry and on the farms. By the Geneva Convention, only private soldiers could be forced to work. N.C.O.s had to volunteer, and even then they could only take charge of parties of their own men. As an added inducement, the Germans offered extra rations to those who left for working parties. Many of the privates captured at Dieppe had lost their uniforms and paybooks in the water. They had been advised by some of the more knowledgeable N.C.O.s to claim N.C.O. status when questioned by their captors. The large number of non-commissioned officers compared to the total number of private soldiers must have made the Germans wonder if the Canadian army was composed of all chiefs and no Indians.

While some groups of men were sent to *Arbeitskommando* camps where they lived near their place of work, others left Stalag VIIIB daily to board railway trains at Lamsdorf. Under instructions from Harry Beesley, they left the camp looking spruce and disciplined. Boots were shined to a high gloss and uniforms creased to a knife edge. The smartest uniforms were scrounged from every barrack hut to provide a neat uniform for every man in the group. On the way to and from the railway station they were marched like guardsmen. The German civilians must have drawn an unfavourable comparison with the German guards accompanying them. Invariably they were scruffy in appearance.

Every Canadian carried in his top pocket a propaganda package to lower the morale of the German civilians. Besides letters from home, this package contained bars of precious chocolate and good Virginia cigarettes from Red Cross parcels. When they were paraded on the railway platform, the Canadian N.C.O.s would give the order to stand easy and smoke. Watched by scores of envious German civilians, each soldier would casually fish out a large Player's cigarette and light it, puffing volumes of rich smoke up and down the platform. After three or four puffs, they would throw the cigarette down and grind it under their heels. By the hungry expressions on the faces of the German civilians they judged the propaganda extremely effective. Fortunately the civilians did not realise that the sacrifice of throwing a way a 'whole' cigarette was breaking the prisoners' hearts.

On the passenger trains, they would make a practice of offering pieces of Cadbury's milk chocolate to German children. The little tykes hadn't seen chocolate since the war started. To prevent this largesse the German authorities had spread a rumour that P.O.W. chocolate was poisoned. But the German children laughingly gulped down the chocolate, chanting, 'I'm going to be poisoned!'

In the working compound at Stalag VIIIB, the Germans had erected a board with the various jobs posted on it just like a labour exchange. Each job had a number and a word, such as 'Quarry'. Prisoners returning from such working parties would add their own comments to the description, such as 'Shocking'. If the job wasn't too bad, they would add 'Smashing, this'. In this way many prisoners were able to volunteer for work that wasn't too demanding and that wouldn't tax their remaining strength. Unfortunately, after a period of time some prisoners began adding misleading information to safeguard a soft touch.

Many N.C.O.s who wished to escape wandered down to the working compound to find a suitable 'twin' with whom to change identities. It was easier to escape from a working party than from the camp. Sergeant Wally Dungate of the Commandos wished to escape from Stalag VIIIB. After consulting with Beesley, he contacted a British private who was in the *Strafe* compound awaiting punishment for some misdemeanour. In appearance he looked something like Wally Dungate, so the deal was made. The private wore Dungate's chains and became a sergeant in the Canadian compound, while Wally entered the *Strafe* compound in his place.

Two days later, he was slapped into the 'cooler'. The private had not seen fit to inform Wally that he was awaiting punishment for escaping! After serving his sentence of 28 days, Wally was sent to Oppeln to work in the cement factory as the private. Some weeks later, he received the mail from England addressed to his 'twin'. To keep up the masquerade Wally had to open and read the letters from the other man's wife, in which she tearfully confessed that she was pregnant. Wally saw an opportunity to get his own back for being forced to serve a sentence for his 'twin' and wrote an angry letter to the wayward lady condemning her for her questionable behaviour!

For the senior N.C.O.s such as Beesley, Sherriff, and Lowe, and intelligence officers such as Larry Palls, the war still had to be fought even though they were behind barbed wire. By means that cannot be exposed even today, there was direct communication between these four and the British War Office.

Sergeant Dungate of No. 3 Commando had been ordered by Harry Beesley to exchange identities with a private soldier in order to spy on the enemy strength in the immediate area. His friend, Corporal Pat Habron was ordered to do likewise. Day after day Pat wandered down to the working compound, until he met a private soldier who had the same build and facial characteristics as his. His 'twin' was Private Wally Green of the Camerons who had just returned from a coal mine. The matter of exchanging identities with another man was not as simple as it sounded. Apart from obvious similarities such as physical build and features, many facts regarding the other person's background and family life had to be memorised. Every day when the working parties left the camp, they were questioned on these facts by a guard scanning the prisoner's personal dossier. Many a man was caught because of such obvious physical traits as false teeth or Maple Leaf tattoos. Why on earth would a New Zealander have a Maple Leaf tattoo on his forearm? 'Because I'm a bastard, Sir. You see, Sir, this Canadian sailor met my mother in Wellington before I was born and . . .'

Pat Habron was shipped out to a brickyard near Oppeln, a few miles from Lamsdorf. The rest of the workers were Polish and Russian women who had been brought in as slave labour. After a short time he was joined by another prisoner from VIIIB, Lt. Williams of the British Army. He had exchanged identities with a private soldier in another working party and had eventually been shipped back to Lamsdorf. Three days later, this officer managed to escape from the working party after he had pleaded sickness to stay in the compound. Pat had placed a dummy in the officer's bed to fool the Germans. Unfortunately, Lt. Williams was caught and taken back to the Stalag.

While Pat was working in the brickyard, the first Red Cross parcels arrived. For the first time since they had been captured they were able to eat decent food. The cigarettes and chocolate inside the parcels were received with great enthusiasm; cigarettes could be used to barter for food with the civilian population and were more valuable than money. In payment of their work for Germany, the Germans issued paper money called *Kriegsgefangenen Lagergeld* to the value of one, two, and 10 marks, which could be used to purchase razor blades or toilet gear, but the total amount of money earned each week was extremely small.

The German civilian in charge of the working party was known as the *Meister*. When the Red Cross parcels arrived, he sneered that they were just propaganda and that the British and Canadian civilians were actually starving. Pat and the rest of the prisoners shared their parcels with the Russian and Polish slave workers but their generosity only maddened the *Meister* who then vented his spite on the helpless civilian prisoners.

One Sunday morning the brickyard was visited by some important visitors who requested an inspection of the British and

Canadian prisoners. The brickyard was old-fashioned and lacked modern machinery and equipment. The loads of sand and gravel were brought up from the pit and then carried to the brickyard on a wooden cart pulled by an ancient horse named Foxer by the prisoners. His back sank in the middle and his belly bulged almost to his knees. With eyes hooded and tired after many long years of labour, he retained just sufficient vision to avoid the edge of the pit. His whole appearance was offensive to a lover of horseflesh. But appearances can be deceiving. Old employees would often relate stories of Foxer's past glory when he had been a war horse. On his broad back, a Prussian officer had charged with sword outstretched in the time-faded battles of the last war.

This 'magnificent' animal was the weapon chosen by the prisoners for a propaganda instrument. Before the audience of visitors, a precious bar of scented Lux toilet soap was taken from a recently arrived Red Cross parcel and used to give poor old Foxer a luxurious shampoo. From head to toe he was lathered and scrubbed. He was then rinsed with buckets of water and vigorously rubbed dry with clean towels. To complete the beauty treatment, a meticulous brushing and combing followed. Then his mane and tail were plaited and ribboned.

Foxer slowly swished his tail back and forth as he beamed at the prisoners. Not for many years had such loving treatment and care been lavished on him. As the Germans looked on with disgust, the men patted him on the head for being such a good horse and then fed him a whole chocolate bar. The visitors left in haste after this wasteful demonstration of enemy abundance. Pat and the others collapsed with laughter. The bar of soap and the chocolate were a great sacrifice but well worth it!

Pat Habron spent his working hours casually questioning the German guards and civilians on troop movements in the area. When he was returned to Stalag VIIIB a short time later, he gave a full report to Harry Beesley. Within hours, the report was on its way to Whitehall, informing the War Office which German regiments were due to leave for the Russian front, which regiments were resting in the area, and the locations of anti-aircraft defences, and factories producing war materials.

Sergeant Dungate, Corporal Habron, and the escape committee at Stalag VIIIB were under strict orders not to attempt to escape themselves at this stage. They were still soldiers and under army discipline. Not for them the dream of escape and a successful return to their loved ones. They had been ordered to continue the fight by organising escapes, and that is exactly what they would continue to work towards during their stay at Stalag VIIIB.

CHAPTER SEVENTEEN

THE ESCAPE TUNNELS

The prisoners devised intricate and ingenious methods to aid the escapers. From the information passed from the working parties to Harry Beesley, accurate maps were drawn to scale, time-tables were prepared and updated, and forged documents and passes prepared.

The scholars and linguists in the camp were given the job of reading every available German newspaper and magazine. In the help-wanted advertisements they would find, for example, that a machine-tool manufacturer needed a skilled mechanic. If the ad gave the name and title of the management personnel to be seen for the interview, then so much the better.

In the British racket compound were several excellent forgers. Using fine brushes they would painstakingly 'type' a letter from a Dutch or French worker to a real German company in answer to a current advertisement. Bribed with cigarettes, the German guards could be persuaded to provide real letters from the files or from civilian contacts outside the camp. In this manner the actual letter-heads were copied to the last detail, even to the forged signature of the manager of the company requesting the worker and the initials of the manager's secretary. A worker travelling across Germany had to carry a variety of passes and permits to pass through police and Gestapo checks. The most important document, carried by all civilians, was the *Ausweis*, a card for special identification. In order for any person to work, he also had to carry an *Arbeitskarte* or work permit. When travelling for a company or on business, he had to obtain from the police or civil authorities a *Bescheinigung*, travel document. A similar document, which carried a great deal more weight, was the *Polizeiliche Erlaubnis* or police permit.

Many of these passes were duplicated in the camp on improvised mimeograph machines, which used a broom handle covered with the soft rubber grip from a cricket bat. For the rubber stamps of authorisation and the German eagles added to the documents, they used a rubber heel or half of a potato that had been carved to give an exact imitation of the real thing. The dates were added prior to the prisoner leaving the camp.

Other departments of the racket compound would supply suits tailored from uniforms and dyed so that it was almost impossible to tell them from real civilian suits. Trilby hats and briefcases were either manufactured or bought from corrupt guards.

But all of these elaborate forgeries and preparations were useless if the escaper were not fluent in German. Very few people ever attain fluency in a foreign language without a trace of an accent. Obviously the escaper had to travel as a volunteer worker from one of the occupied countries, such as France. Millions of such workers had been imported into greater Germany during the war, and it was by no means unusual for them to travel across the country to a job or on leave. Therefore, the escaper had to be fluent in another language — his 'mother' tongue. English was obviously not acceptable.

Bearing all of these facts in mind, Harry Beesley and the escape committee decided at an early date that when the tunnel was completed, it should only be used for eligible candidates who were considered important to the war effort.

Previous experience in other prison camps had shown the hazards of organising mass escapes. When a general alarm was sounded, a nation-wide hue and cry alerted many thousands of Home Guard in addition to the Hitler Youth and the regular police force. True, the enemy was forced to garrison a large force within Germany to cope with mass escapes, but very few of the prisoners succeeded in returning to England. For the tunnel to be effective, no more than two men could be allowed to use it at one time, and it was essential to cover their absence for as long as possible to give them a chance to get clear of the area.

In May 1943 the tunnel was re-opened, and Sergeant Bill Lee alerted for the first escape attempt. An English soldier in the British compound was under sentence of death for committing sabotage on a work party. He was smuggled under the noses of the German guards into the Canadian compound, where he was given a pair of Dieppe handcuffs and ordered to remain inside hut 19b and keep his mouth shut.

Although Stalag VIIIB was strictly a camp for other ranks, it was very often used by the Germans as a transit camp for

British officers on their way to Oflag prisoner-of-war camps. Harry Beesley and Larry Palls had been informed by Whitehall that a Colonel Young of the South African Expeditionary Force was being detained in the new prisoner compound in VIIIB. If possible, the colonel was to be assisted in escaping so that he might make his way back to Britain, where he was considered important to the war effort. The directive from Whitehall appeared to be simple enough but in actual fact it was a tall order. The escape committee in the Dieppe compound called a meeting and decided on a plan of action.

Someone had to be substituted for the colonel to avoid an outcry after the escape. The committee approached a Canadian who had the same physical and facial characteristics and asked him if he'd like to be elevated to the rank of colonel for the duration of the war. Readily, he made the switch.

It was quite common for new prisoners to be visited by the older 'lags' who passed on cigarettes and food. The Germans turned a blind eye to the practice, just as they had when the Dunkirk boys had given their lunch ration to the Canadians when they first arrived. A good-will party was organised to enter the new prisoner compound carrying a bunch of treats such as cigarettes, cocoa and meat paste from Red Cross parcels. Sentries were posted to watch out for German guards and the colonel changed clothes with the Canadian. For the next hour they carefully briefed each other on their respective family and military backgrounds before the good-will party wandered back to the Dieppe compound. The colonel, dressed in private's uniform, was attempting a nasal Canadian accent as he passed the guards. The private when last seen was admiring his new uniform and rank in a broken mirror. When the deception was finally discovered, he was severely punished, but for the moment, it felt pretty good to be a full colonel.

Once the two escapers were inside hut 19b, Sergeant Bill Lee took charge of the operation. It had been decided by the escape committee that they should go out in broad daylight to give them a better chance. When the way looked clear, they were instructed to make their way to Lamsdorf station and catch a train that was due just one hour after their escape. When they arrived at Breslau, they were to change trains to Dresden. From Dresden they would follow an escape route using a number of different trains until they reached a little town close to the Swiss border. From then on, they would have to proceed on foot in the dead of night until they finally crossed the border to freedom. Before leaving the camp, they had been provided with an up-to-date time-table indicating the time of arrival and departure for every train; all railway tickets, which had been purchased in advance by men on working parties; detailed maps drawn to a scale of one-half inch; identity cards and police passes, which had been forged and brought up to date — all this supplied by the indefatigable escape committee.

All that now remained was for the escapers to change into the civilian clothes provided for them. The colonel wore a suit of dark blue serge, a dark blue raincoat, and trilby hat. A leather briefcase and a heavy meerschaum pipe were the final touches. The English soldier rescued from his death cell was fitted with a heavy woollen jacket and a pair of khaki trousers which had been dyed a deeper brown with beet pulp. With the addition of an old peaked cap and a pair of steel spectacles, it was difficult to distinguish him from millions of other workers in Germany.

The concrete slab was removed from beneath the bunk-bed in the corner of the hut and willing volunteers dug out the earth packed in the shaft. The earth was stored in Red Cross boxes beneath the bunk-beds, ready to refill the shaft.

Bill Lee and the two escapers wrapped themselves in gunny sacks to keep their clothing clean and then, led by Bill, they dropped down the shaft to crawl on their bellies along the long, narrow tunnel to freedom. From a score of vantage points men stationed themselves to give early warning if Spitfire or any of the German guards approached. If danger threatened, the men had orders to seal the escapers in the tunnel until the coast was clear again. Beneath the bunk, the little French Canadian worked his bellows steadily to send a constant stream of fresh air to the three men.

Outside in the compound, the prisoners started to play tag football. The guards in the 'Goon box' and outside the wire turned their full attention on the game inside the wire. Twenty yards behind them, Bill Lee silently eased the trap-door upwards on its hinge. Inch by inch he raised his head to look carefully around him in all directions. The three bushes screened the opening of the tunnel very effectively, but once clear of the tunnel the escapers would have to cross open ground to reach the shelter of the trees.

The escape committee had foreseen this hazard, and several

of the football players had been given instructions to start a fight to distract the guards. Sapper Roy Luxmore hit his buddy Bill Lynch a great wallop on the side of the jaw. Bill went down with Roy on top of him, wrestling like a madman. Bill got his mouth near to Roy's ear and whispered, 'You son of a bitch, did you have to hit so hard?'

The German guards grinned and nudged each other in delight. The rest of the men gathered around shouting encouragement to one or the other of the fighters, while from behind the bushes, two 'civilians' could be seen creeping stealthily into the forest. Although the Germans frequently searched the huts they never discovered the tunnel entrance in 19b. The trap-door was impossible to detect even at eye level, and when the floors were tapped for hollow sounds, the packed earth in the shaft sounded like any other part of the floor. When the tunnel had been constructed, Jimmy Maitland had managed to 'procure' a bag of cement from a firepool the Germans had been building in the compound. A concrete slab with tapered edges had been cast to make an exact fit for the shaft opening. Whenever the slab was replaced, Jimmy mixed a concrete paste of cement and cocoa to fill in the cracks. Afterwards a layer of dust was brushed over the fresh cement to give total camouflage.

Time after time the tunnel in 19b was used in the same manner. Over a period of six months 36 men were taken out through the tunnel, two at a time. All of the escapers were carefully selected, and at least one man of each pair could speak German fluently. Gradually the word filtered back to the escape committee in VIIIB that 50 per cent of the escapers had managed to return to England. This was a fantastic average, unbeaten in any other prison camp in Germany.

Each time an escape was made through the tunnel, the rest of the prisoners covered up the absence for as long as possible by shifting men into other bunks and informing the Germans that they were sick at roll-call. The guards would go rushing into the huts and find a body in the bunk of the man who had escaped. Another trick the men employed was to dodge to the end of the line once they had been counted and be counted again. Obviously the missing man could not be covered indefinitely, and whenever the Germans realised that there had been an escape they would rush into the compound and empty the huts as they searched for a tunnel.

Although the Germans never discovered the entrance in 19b, they did discover the exit. They then dug up the tunnel for at least 40 feet in search of the entrance but finally gave up. Instead, they filled the trench with excrement to discourage future digging.

After inspecting the tunnel by now complete with railway lines and a little trolley, a visiting German general turned to the prisoners and said in perfect English, 'Gentlemen, I must congratulate you on your truly splendid escape tunnel. How on earth you did it with your hands chained, I shall never understand. I wish I had a million men like you under my command!'

Alarmed, Beesley called a meeting of the escape committee. Larry Palls reported that the Germans had walked directly to the tunnel exit. There was a traitor in their midst. Who was it? The discovery of the tunnel exit was a serious setback to escape plans — but not for long. The next day Sergeant Syd Cleasby of the Royal Canadian Engineers broke the concrete floor under his own bunk to start the second tunnel from Barrack 22b. Soon teams of diggers, carriers and look-outs had been recruited and put to work. Syd was fortunate in having a mucker named George Flint of the Royal Regiment. Past experience had shown that George was an excellent procurer of food from many unexpected sources, and as 'procurer' for the tunnel construction, his abilities were put to good use.

The first item to be obtained was cement for the trap-door. The Germans were using cement and bricks for the construction of a firepool at that time. A German sentry guarded the barracks where the building materials were stored, but George would walk up to him with a forged work order, wave it carelessly under his nose, and enter the barracks. Then he would return past the sentry carrying a bag of cement under his arm, passing the time of the day with him as he did so.

Directly below the entrance trap a large room was dug — 10 feet long by eight feet wide and seven feet high. From the start it was fitted with electric lights tapped from the barrack-room lights. An air pump was built to force air down into the tunnel via a pipe made from empty Klim milk tins fitted end to end. The actual construction of the tunnel was carried out by Syd Cleasby, who used a different principle from that of 19b. The sandy soil was much harder and more compact than before, and therefore the roof could be arched to form its own support without using the precious bed-boards.

Day after day, night after night, men slaved away underground — digging and spooning the dirt as the tunnel crept closer to the wire. The dirt was stored in Red Cross boxes in the underground room at the end of the night shift and carried out by willing volunteers during the day. As in the past, dumping was the problem. Only so much could be emptied down the 40-holer and in the new firepool. The flower beds were now so high they could almost grow coconuts. The compound was unfeasible because the newly excavated soil could easily be detected; winter had again come to Stalag VIIIB, and now snow and ice lay thickly on the ground.

George Flint again came to the rescue. He marched out one cold day with a Red Cross box full of sand on his shoulder and calmly began to spread it over the slippery roadway separating the Dieppe compound from the Air Force compound. When the guards asked curiously what he was doing, George innocently told them that he was spreading sand to prevent the German trucks from skidding! Amazingly they believed him and patted him on the back. From then on, this was where the bulk of the excavated soil ended up. If there were any doubts regarding the wisdom of such a method of disposal, they were dispelled a few days later when an official commendation arrived on the notice board in the Dieppe compound from the German commandant, thanking the Canadian prisoners for their spirit of co-operation in making the paths and roads safe from the hazards of winter!

Eventually the tunnel was completed. It was over 130 feet long and extended well beyond the wire. It was now the winter of 1943 and they had been behind the wire for over a year.

The escape committee decided to wait for spring before planning any fresh escapes. In the meantime, a fresh development was about to force their hand. Larry Palls received a message from Whitehall that a British hussar officer would be arriving at VIIIB. If possible, he was to be assisted in escaping.

The officer arrived and was placed in maximum security in the *Straflager*. Harry Beesley called a meeting of the escape committee to formulate a plan of action. The new tunnel would be used to 'store' the officer until better weather arrived. Syd Cleasby had a cousin in the camp hospital — Tom Cleasby, from Newcastle, England. Although he had often mentioned to the other prisoners that he had a cousin in the camp, nobody had actually seen him except Syd. The British officer could sleep down in the underground room during the night and sit with Syd during the day inside the hut, playing cards and wearing a set of handcuffs. To the curious, he would be introduced as Syd's cousin from England. His British accent would give a stamp of authenticity to the masquerade. When the time was ripe, he would be allowed to change identities with a volunteer private soldier and go out on a working party outside the camp. From there he would escape and return to England.

Larry Palls suggested a brilliant solution to the question of the officer's escape from the *Straflager*. A diversionary escape would be made over the wire in the workers' compound at the same time. The Germans would then automatically assume that the British officer had escaped from his cell and climbed over the wire to the outside!

Sergeant Bill Lee and Jimmy Maitland volunteered to assist a man over the wire during the night. A Canadian Air Force pilot wished to escape as soon as possible and the proposition was put to him. It was a hazardous and very dangerous method of escaping — somebody was bound to be shot. But the pilot cheerfully accepted the risks.

The next night, Bill Lee was awakened by a mysterious messenger who was 'going out' that night from the British compound. It was an eerie experience. He shook Bill and then put his hand over his mouth to prevent him from crying out. He whispered, 'Are you Sergeant Lee?' When Bill said he was, the man asked for his official number and Bill replied, 'B.25310'. The mysterious stranger said, 'Fine, here's a package for you,' and handed over a leather pouch containing a set of steel digging tools and electrically insulated wire cutters. As he left, the stranger asked if there were any messages to go back. Bill shook his head, wondering who the man was and where he'd come from. Again the long arm of Whitehall was showing itself.

The next day the escape committee slipped a hack-saw blade through the window bars to the British officer in the *Straflager* along with a note instructing him to cut the bars as soon as it was dark and climb out at the time indicated.

Jimmy Maitland 'procured' a ladder from one of his seemingly inexhaustible resources, and together with Bill Lee, slipped through the wire fences to reach the working compound. Fortunately there was only a waning moon to illuminate them as they flitted from hut to hut carrying the ladder. By the wire they could see the outline of a sentry marching slowly along the path outside the camp. From the Goon box, the searchlight traversed back and forth. It was all a question of timing and nerve.

Carrying the ladder between them, they made a short dash from the nearest hut to the first line of wire. As the search-light swung over in their direction, they hastily cut the first wire fence to roll through and hide in the ditch on the other side. The ladder they dragged slowly in behind them. Inch by inch they raised the ladder over the rolls of dannert wire to the top of the second wire fence, the one festooned with tin cans.

Around the perimeter an alert sentry marched back and forth. Each move had to be carefully timed with the sentry's movement and the swinging search-light of the nearest 'Goon box'. It was no task for the faint-hearted. At a prearranged time and signal, the air force pilot left the hut nearest the wire and scuttled into the ditch alongside the two men. Leaving his haversack with Lee, he ran up the ladder and over the top of the nine-foot fence to drop with a resounding crash on the other side. Bill Lee was following closely behind with the haversack, which he dropped quickly to the escaping pilot just as the alarm was given and the search-light swung around to bathe him in its dreaded light.

His reflexes worked overtime. The moment the brilliant blue light exposed him, he flipped backwards to complete a couple of backward somersaults that would have done credit to a circus performer. Bullets missed him by inches. Landing in the ditch he scrambled on hand and knees like a greyhound to crash through the door of the nearest hut and lie flat under the first bunk.

When the alarm had finally died down, he crept back to his own hut and collapsed on to his bunk with heaving chest and pounding heart but wearing an ear-to-ear grin.

In the meantime, the alarm gave the British officer ample opportunity to climb out of his cell and join a member of the escape committee, who quickly led him to Barrack 22b in the Canadian compound. Syd and his helpers had already removed the stone slab under his bunk. Handing the officer a couple of blankets and some cigarettes, they quickly helped him down into his dungeon and sealed him in.

The next day, Larry Palls' prediction proved to be correct. The Germans believed that the officer had managed to escape over the fence after cutting the bars of his cell window. After

Appell, Syd helped the officer out of the tunnel, gave him his breakfast from his own rations and introduced him to all and sundry as his cousin Tom from Newcastle.

During the daylight hours or at roll-calls, the officer took refuge in the room below the hut. It was dismal and cheerless, but it did have an electric light and, later on, a radio. The volume turned low, the officer busied himself listening to BBC broadcasts and writing up an information sheet for the benefit of the prisoners. The war had taken a distinct turn for the better, and the news from all battle fronts was extremely encouraging. In the Canadian and British compounds, the war news was monitored from the BBC over well-hidden receivers. Regular bulletins were issued to give the true situation on all war fronts. The Germans would occasionally storm through the huts searching for a radio receiver but they never succeeded in uncovering one. The prisoners were always careful to leave a crystal receiver where it would easily be found during a search.

In the air force compound, the men had drawn a large-scale map and hung it on the wall. Every time the *Sonderlager* — German propaganda announcements — announced a new advance by the victorious German Army they would dutifully pencil in the new front for all to see. The German security officer visited the hut one day and after casually studying the map, suddenly turned it over. On the back he discovered a different map showing the true situation as the BBC had reported it.

Again, the men realised there was a spy or spies in their midst. The problem was how to catch them.

As each long winter month passed, it became obvious that the British officer was showing the strain of being buried alive each night. He never complained, but the escape committee decided to bring in another British officer and hide him as well in the tunnel under Syd Cleasby's bed. The two officers became great chums before they left the camp as private soldiers in a work party. Some time later, word filtered back from Whitehall that both men had reached home base safely.

Forbidden to escape themselves, the members of the escape committee were given a huge boost in morale whenever one of their escapers made it all the way home. Even though they were imprisoned and starving, they were still operating as soldiers and defeating the enemy. Harry Beesley's instructions were being followed to the letter.

CHAPTER EIGHTEEN

FAREWELL TO LAMSDORF

On the Home Front, the war had begun to swing in favour of the Allies. Now that arms and war materials were flooding in by British convoy to Murmansk, the Russians were beginning to fight back with vigour; at Stalingrad, a massive German Army had been routed before surrendering. The British and Americans had finally defeated the Germans and Italians in North Africa, before invading Sicily and Italy. In the Far East, the Japanese were now suffering severe losses after their fleet had been destroyed near New Guinea. On September 8th, 1943, Italy formally surrendered to the Allies and declared war on her former partner, Germany, the following month.

In the air, the British and Americans were bombing Germany by day and by night. At sea the U-boat war was all but over, and war materials were pouring into Britain in a mighty build-up for the eventual invasion of France and Germany.

In the camp, the prisoners were kept informed of daily happenings on all war fronts by the illicit radios and bulletins. Guards and civilians began to change their attitude towards the prisoners. Whereas previously they had bullied and ill-treated them, now they began to moderate their tone. Subtle references by the prisoners to eventual war crime tribunals and hangings after the war may also have had their effect.

After the recent series of resounding German defeats, it is quite feasible that they would have surrendered to the Allies and sought peace if the Allied politicians had not come to the very unwise decision, on January 24th, 1943, to call for Germany's 'unconditional surrender'. With the Russians hammering on their back door and the Allies poised for a stab at the heart, was it any wonder that the Germans decided to fight to the death? What did they have to lose? This fatal Allied blunder was to cost many thousands of lives before the war was finally won. Many of the lives lost would be those of prisoners of war, but at this stage the men did not know that.

With the subtle change in German thinking, the Canadians

began to receive Red Cross parcels at long last. At first it was only one parcel among four men, but even that was most welcome. Within a few months they had graduated to two men per parcel. Unfortunately, the Germans suspected that the various tins of food in the parcels contained escape kits. Thus, whenever the parcels were issued, they insisted on opening every single tin or container for inspection. The prisoners were then forced to eat all of the perishables immediately instead of hoarding them and consuming them in sensible daily portions. Nevertheless, the additional food was a blessing, and many were the weird and wonderful concoctions cooked and served by hundreds of amateur chefs. Inside and outside every hut, blower forges were kept at full blast.

During the first year in captivity, stomachs had shrunk as a result of the totally inadequate diet. The sudden unaccustomed diet caused a rash of stomach and diarrhoea problems before the men grew accustomed to the additional foodstuffs. But they were still hungry. One Red Cross parcel divided among four men for a week was still totally insufficient to maintain a normal diet, but the Red Cross cigarettes helped in more ways than one. The German civilians and guards greatly valued the rich Virginia tobacco, which was superior to their own. Men on working parties traded cigarettes for such delicacies as eggs and meat to add to their rations. In the camp, bartering became a way of life and open-air markets flourished in the Canadian compound. A tin of salmon would be traded for a tin of Spam or a tin of milk powder for a tin of meat paste. The owner of the 'stall' would claim one or two cigarettes as his fee for the transaction, and everybody was satisfied. After a while, it was amusing to see the German guards buying and selling just like the prisoners, or to see a French Canadian haggling with a guard over the asking price of a tin of food.

On September 24th, 1943, the handcuffs and chains were taken away without explanation and not returned until October 15th. One month later, on November 21st, the chains were again taken away, never to be returned. On November 26th, 1943, the Canadians were suddenly informed that a number of their private soldiers were being sent to Stalag IID, near the port of Stettin on the Baltic Sea. It wasn't until the following year, on February 27th, 1944, that the bulk of the Canadians followed from VIIIB. Harry Beesley, Mac Maloy, Jack Poolton, and a number of other Canadian soldiers were either sent out on work parties or retained at VIIIB. The Germans had decided to remove the Canadians from the influence of Harry Beesley. Little did they realise that the Canadian force contained a number of Harry Beesleys. Men of the calibre of Sergeant-Major MacIver and Sergeant-Major Liscombe would stand up to them in exactly the same manner as Harry Beesley had.

They left VIIIB without regrets and without a backward glance. Whatever the future held, it couldn't be much worse than Lamsdorf! Or so they thought at the time.

CHAPTER NINETEEN

STARGARD
STALAG IID

At the railway station they were herded into box-cars for the long journey to Stargard. This was the same station where they had stumbled out of the stinking box-cars almost 18 months before — shell-shocked and wounded, almost delirious from thirst and hunger. Much had happened since that day. They had followed Harry Beesley's advice explicitly. They had fought back against their captors with every weapon at their disposal. On working parties outside the camp, they had sabotaged machinery and war products at every opportunity. Within the camp at VIIIB, they had built two tunnels and assisted over 40 men in escaping. If the Germans thought they were going to avert trouble in the future by splitting up the Dieppe Canadians and sending them north they were greatly mistaken.

On arrival at camp IID they were paraded before the German commandant, who informed them that they had all been sent to this camp because they had volunteered to work for Germany. As *Kriegsgefangene* (P.O.W.s) they must work — non-commissioned officers and men alike. If they worked hard for Germany they would receive extra rations: '*Zum Sieg müssen Räder rollen!*' 'Wheels must turn for victory!'

The prisoners listened politely. Then as the commandant finished speaking, he was greeted with a chorus of cat-calls. But the barrage of noise stopped as suddenly as it had begun when Sergeant-Major Liscombe of the Essex Scottish Regiment stepped out of the ranks and marched forward to slam to a heel-stamping halt opposite the commandant. Staring straight ahead, Liscombe saluted smartly before informing the commandant that the Canadian N.C.O.s would not be going out to work. The commandant bristled like a bulldog as he snapped back at Liscombe, 'Are you refusing to work as ordered?'

'No,' replied Liscombe, 'we are not refusing, we wish to speak to the Swedish Red Cross representative before we go.'

The commandant and his staff glared at the prisoners. They knew that they had no authority to force the N.C.O.s to work. The Geneva Convention was very specific on this point. If an issue was made of this matter, German N.C.O. prisoners in Britain and in Canada would be forced to work in reprisal.

'You have until tomorrow morning to make up your minds,' said the commandant, 'or you will be shipped to Poland.'

Liscombe replied, 'Then you had better arrange for the train, sir. We could do with a ride anyway.' Saluting smartly, he turned about and marched back to his place in the ranks.

For some minutes there was a deathly silence. Liscombe knew that, although he had acted correctly, he might possibly be shot. Suddenly the commandant gave the order to his adjutant to dismiss the parade. The prisoners heaved a sigh of relief, but they knew that reprisals would surely follow. Sure enough, the issue of Red Cross parcels was discontinued, and the German rations deteriorated to an all-time low. Scrounging and bartering were the only alternatives left, and Canadian and British cigarettes became more valuable than gold.

Stargard was a camp of mixed nationalities. New Zealanders and Australians rubbed shoulders with Canadians, Americans, and British. Serbs, Yugoslavs, and Frenchmen bunked with Palestinians, Indians, and Greeks. Many of these prisoners from other nations left the camp every day to go out on working parties. They usually returned in the evening — loaded with contraband obtained from German civilians in return for bartered cigarettes. It didn't take the Canadians long to enter the market and re-barter with the working parties for bread, eggs, and other food-stuffs, but they had to pay many times the number of cigarettes originally traded with the civilians. Obviously the number of cigarettes in each man's possession was limited. Without further Red Cross parcels, food supplies would soon have petered out.

Sergeants Bill Lee and Syd Cleasby, the two tunnel men from Lamsdorf, teamed up with an astonishing character from the French Foreign Legion. Wanted for murder in the U.S.A., he had fought over the years for the French and British in North Africa and spoke any number of languages. 'Pop', as he was called, was the greatest scrounger they had ever encountered.

One day when Bill and Syd dejectedly entered the hut feeling the pangs of hunger, they found 'Pop' stirring a delicious stew. On the side was a hunk of bread he had managed to procure. They wolfed it down with gusto before lying back, holding their full stomachs and inquiring about what exactly they had just eaten. Pop replied in one syllable, 'Dog!' After that, the men never asked about the contents of his culinary masterpieces — especially when they discovered him sitting in the sewer with a home-made spear, stabbing rats.

Except for the poor food, Stargard IID proved to be a much better camp than Lamsdorf VIIIB. Many of the guards were regular soldiers who had served on the Russian front. Knowing these men made the Canadians realise that the guards did not represent the average German citizen.

Padre Foote had accompanied the men to Stargard and was now busy organising their social activities to make life as pleasant as possible under the circumstances. A camp band, supplied with instruments by the International Red Cross, provided many hours of entertainment for the prisoners. John Foote played second trumpet with great gusto. The New Zealanders taught the Canadians to play rugby football and within a short space of time, the Canadians were giving a very credible performance against the 'All Blacks'. In a lighter vein, Syd Cleasby won a singular victory for the Canadians in the international 'peanut pushing race', in which participants crawled on hands and knees, pushing a peanut along the ground by the nose. Canada's team became the world champions.

The British taught them how to play soccer football, but a similar experiment with cricket ended in disaster. By no stretch of the imagination could the Canadians have been called proficient in the ancient and honourable sport. The British soldiers would collapse in side-splitting mirth as they watched their antics before the wicket. A short time later, the Canadians had their revenge when they tried to teach the British the finer points of American baseball! But the biggest surprise came when the city of Calgary sent a full set of hockey equipment. Permission was requested from the commandant for a supply of water to flood an ice rink; it was refused in the usual peremptory fashion.

Undaunted, the next night, Bombadier Harry Hancock of Toronto and a number of other volunteers bribed the guards in the towers to close their eyes while the wire fence to the playing field was cut. All night long the prisoners carried water in soup cans to flood the rink. The next morning, a great sheet of ice faced the early risers, and from then on, the Canadian hockey team played international matches with all challengers.

Some time later, this hockey rink acted as a real tonic to a large band of American soldiers who had been taken prisoner at the Battle of the Bulge. After suffering greatly on the journey to the camp, they were given a tremendous boost in morale when they arrived, fearful and apprehensive, not knowing what lay ahead, suddenly to see an all-Canadian hockey team playing like pros on the ice.

In the next compound, the Russians were struck by a typhus epidemic. Day after day, scores of these poor starved prisoners died and were shovelled into lime pits outside the camp. As at Lamsdorf, the Germans paid little heed to their suffering. Generally they seemed to harbour an age-old hatred and fear of these people. When the Canadians requested permission to feed and look after the Russian sick, the German commandant reluctantly agreed.

Every day thereafter, the German guards would accompany the Canadian prisoners as far as the gates of the Russian compound. Once there, the guards would beat a hasty retreat, leaving the Canadians to feed their Russian comrades and give what little comfort they could. Every morning as the Canadians walked toward the Russian compound, they would pass wagonloads of dead and dying Russian prisoners on their way to the lime pits. Sgt. Cec Towler nursed an emaciated Russian officer who greatly surprised him one day when he grasped his hand and said, 'Thank God for you Canadians. You are good people. It's a pity that one day we're going to be forced to fight you!'

The Russian's face was bathed in sweat and his great dark eyes burned with fever, but Cec realised that he was speaking the words with which he had been indoctrinated. This message was repeated over and over by the Russians: 'Some day we are going to have to fight you!'

Bill Lee and Syd Cleasby had been given orders not to attempt escape while serving on the escape committee at VIIIB. Now that they were confined in Stargard, they felt no such restriction, and together they decided to escape. The simplest method was to change identities with private soldiers and go out from the camp on *Arbeitskommando* working parties, where escape was comparatively easy. Contact was made with two private soldiers who were more than willing to return to the prison camp as Stalag sergeants. It would be a welcome relief from the hard work.

Bill Lee became Private Harold Barnes of Toronto, Syd Cleasby became Private St. Clair from the Cameron Highlanders, and after changing uniforms, they found themselves on a working party on a farm near Klauxine in Pomerania.

Bill Lee was put to work in the blacksmith's shop assisting a great bully of a German in repairing farm equipment. The loft above the forge held the winter's supply of hay — a tempting target for Bill. Within a matter of days, he had constructed an incendiary bomb from a box of matches and a small quantity of muriatic acid obtained from the blacksmith's shop. The acid slowly ate through a spring, releasing a hammer that struck a match head protruding from the end of the box. The blacksmith's shop was destroyed one night in a mysterious fire, believed to have started by spontaneous combustion within the straw!

Bill Lee was then transferred to the *Traktormeister*'s division and after gaining the confidence of his superior, was given the task of changing the engine oil in each of the tractors used to plough the fields. Although under very close supervision, Bill managed to slack off the crank-case nut a thread and a half after filling it with fresh oil. The next day, the tractors seized up in the fields after all the crank-case oil had drained away. The tractors were completely inoperable; the year was 1944 and spare parts were impossible to obtain.

Syd Cleasby was also having fun. The German farmers made a practice of storing the crop of potatoes in a long burrow, 30 yards long by 12 yards wide and 6 feet deep. Each successive layer of potatoes was covered with straw, then a layer of soil, to protect it from the heavy frost. Syd and some of the other prisoners managed to dig down through the potatoes and cut small windows through which the frost could enter and destroy the entire crop. The windows were covered by a thin layer of straw.

As an additional food supply, the Germans bred rabbits in great hutches. After exercise, the rabbits were returned to the cages to breed, but Syd and his buddies made a few significant changes to alter the breeding pattern. The does were placed together in the same cages; the bucks were given similar treatment. The birth rate quickly dropped to zero and mass fights between doe and doe or buck and buck diminished the number of rabbits still further.

Not content with this latest mischief, Bill and Syd managed to attach themselves to a forestry programme, planting thousands of fir seedlings to compensate for the acres of trees chopped down to make pit-props. Here they trained other prisoners in the art of breaking the main roots of each seedling before planting. Long after they had left Klauxine, they received reports of acres of young seedlings left withered and brown in the wake of a mysterious blight.

The local Gestapo became curious — too many mysterious breakdowns were taking place at Klauxine. Bill and Syd decided it was time to move on. Their working compound, surrounded by barbed wire, was well guarded at night. But to old tunnellers, the defences were negligible. They dug a tunnel from beneath a bunk until they reached the cement wall of the building where they had to dig deep to pass beneath the footings. From then on, it was a simple matter to drive upwards and emerge inside a woodshed. The exit was covered with a pile of split logs and the escape planned for a date two weeks later.

Two prisoners elected to go with them — a member of the Royal Canadian Engineers named Fuzzons and an American of French background from Maine who had volunteered to join the Royal 22nd Regiment in Quebec at the outbreak of war.

Bill Lee managed to procure a pair of wire cutters to breach the outer wire and plans were prepared for a break-out. An added complication was the presence of a German watch dog chained outside the compound. At the slightest noise, he would bark loudly and furiously. His lament was picked up almost at once by every dog in the neighbourhood. Obviously the dog had to be silenced or neutralised, but the question was how?

Syd decided on a plan of action. Every night as soon as the moon rose, he leaned out of the window and howled in a sad horrible travesty of an Alsatian's love song. Every dog in the vicinity joined the chorus, until the guards had become thoroughly sick of the noise. They also became accustomed to it. Just before they wormed their way through the tunnel, Syd gave his nightly performance so that when they finally exited through the wire they distinctly heard a guard bellowing, '*Was ist los?*' and the other guard answering, 'No cause for alarm, it's just the crazy Canadian howling at the moon!'

To fool the guards was one thing, to elude pursuit quite another. Each of the men had armed himself with an adequate supply of pepper, which they now sprinkled on the trail behind them. Klauxine was famous for its tracker dogs, and they had no desire to be chased by a pack of voracious Alsatians.

Less than 130 miles from Klauxine lay the major seaport of Stettin. If they could manage to smuggle themselves aboard a ship, they could sail to Sweden across the Baltic Sea to freedom. Using a home-made compass, Bill and Syd set a course directly for Stettin and set off at a swift pace. Fuzzons and the American headed in another direction to lessen the chances of capture. Marching steadily throughout the night, Bill and Syd kept well clear of farms, villages, and highways. At daybreak, they holed up in a clump of trees but awoke wet and shivering after only a few hours sleep. Lack of food and water were their main problems. Before leaving the working compound, they had concocted a mess of biscuits mixed with sugar, oatmeal, and raisins; it was undoubtedly nutritious, but that was all that could be said for it.

For seven more days and nights they followed the same routine — sleep by day, march by night. Syd's feet were bleeding and Bill's legs were swollen and aching from the unaccustomed marching, but their determination to escape kept them going. They had one very narrow escape after they had selected a deer-food distribution point for their haven at daybreak. They awoke to see the gaily-coloured stockings of a game warden not two feet from Syd's head, pushing hay down to the deer. Underneath his arm swung a double-barrelled shotgun. By some miracle they remained undiscovered as they lay in the deep hay.

The next evening they stole a bicycle; for a while then they could take turns riding. By now they were living off the land; raw potatoes and beets, water from the streams were the staples of their meagre diet. Whenever possible they followed railway lines, but if the compass indicated that the course pointed across a stream or a canal, they had no hesitation in swimming across in a direct line.

Then, on the eighth day, they awoke bright and early with an outsize revolver poked under their noses by civilian police. All around the haystack in which they lay, civilians pointed pitchforks and scythes menacingly. But if they expected resistance, they were disappointed. Bill and Syd, in their exhausted condition, couldn't have run 10 yards. The civilians jabbered excitedly at the police to shoot Syd. With his great height and bulk, he had been mistaken for a Russian. Their dog-tags saved them, but they were marched to the nearby town of Pyritz, where they were thrown into the town jail. As they were paraded through the streets of the town, children pelted them with stones; women spat upon them with unerring accuracy.

The situation could have become ugly if they hadn't passed a Gestapo officer. With great presence of mind, Syd called out, 'Eyes right!' to salute him. The Gestapo officer stood to attention to return their salute and then proceeded to upbraid the civilians for their treatment of the prisoners. 'They are soldiers,' he shouted. 'Didn't you see them salute me?'

It was a great disappointment to be captured after being free for eight days, but in a way it was almost a relief. They were exhausted and starving. After two days, two guards arrived to escort them back to IID. On arrival they were sentenced to the normal 28 days in the cooler in solitary confinement.

The cooler was a very small cell, three paces long and six feet wide. Its only source of fresh air was a small window grating in the rear. The door was a solid piece of oak broken only by a finger-hole — the sole means of communication with the world outside. If a prisoner had to relieve himself he stuck a finger through the hole and waited patiently. If the guard was a decent type he would open the door at once and escort the prisoner to the latrine at the end of the corridor; but if he was a sadist, he would either keep him waiting until dysentery soiled the prisoner's pants, or he would nick the outstretched finger with his bayonet.

On the outside of the door, the prisoner's good days were listed — good days being every third day when no complaints had been registered against him. On ordinary days, the prisoner's diet consisted of a cup of ersatz tea for breakfast followed by a one-inch thick piece of black bread for lunch and a small cup of soup for dinner. In the evening another cup of ersatz tea was handed into the cell. No other nourishment was forthcoming until the next morning.

During the day, the prisoners were forbidden to lie down, and at night slept on a wooden board, two feet wide, raised two inches off the concrete floor. No blankets were supplied to keep out the bitter cold.

On 'good' days, an extra piece of bread was supplied during

the morning. For lunch, a larger cup of soup containing a few small potatoes, and in the afternoon another piece of bread with a cup of ersatz tea. One blanket and a straw palliasse were provided every third good day, and taken away the following morning.

Regulations stipulated that each prisoner had to have one hour's exercise in a compound, where he walked in a continuous circle with other prisoners, one meter apart. Conversation was strictly forbidden. The first week was bad, the second, worse. The third week was a nightmare; on the starvation diet the prisoners lacked the strength even to walk around for an hour. It took a very strong man to survive for 28 days.

As they entered the main compound at IID after their incarceration, they were greeted with the tremendous news of a D-Day landing by Allied troops on June 6th, 1944. On the Eastern Front the Russians were pushing steadily westward. Suddenly Germany's borders seemed to be shrinking as strangers hammered on the gates to the east, the west and the south. Almost every day now, the skies were filled with Allied 'planes. The prisoners waved and cheered, knowing that the end was in sight. But they could not carry their enthusiasm too far — they could still easily be shot.

CHAPTER TWENTY

TORUN, STALAG XXA
FALLINGBOSTEL, STALAG 357

On June 28th, 1944, selected Canadian N.C.O.s — Sergeants Cleasby, Lee, and Towler among them — were suddenly packed into box-cars and shipped to Stalag XXA at Torun in northern Poland. The German commandant at Stargard had kept his word.

The camp at Torun was not unpleasant. The barrack huts were more comfortable and the guards were soldiers on leave from the Russian front. The prisoners were good men — Australians, New Zealanders, some of the men from the 51st Division, and a few commandos. The food was more plentiful and of better quality. The prisoners at Torun had organised regular sports affairs before the Canadians arrived and readily lent tennis rackets or rugby football tackle to the Canadians.

But it was impossible to escape. The camp had been built on sand dunes, and tunnelling would have been suicidal. Stalag XXA lay on the west bank of the Vistula river, and the prisoners were awakened one August morning to hear the rumble of heavy artillery across the river. The Russian army was on the move across Poland. Too excited to sleep, the prisoners lay awake watching the night sky to the east lit by the flash and explosion of hundreds of guns. Soon they would be liberated!

All the next day, endless streams of demoralised German soldiers crossed the river in their hasty retreat. On August 12th, 1944, the prisoners were ordered to pack up their belongings and prepare for a train journey. At 6 a.m. they left Torun and marched to the railway station where they were packed in box-cars for the long journey across Poland and Germany to Stalag 357 at Fallingbostel, 25 miles from Bremen.

Fifteen hundred men boarded the long train, crammed like cattle into the box-cars. Fortunately they were well supplied with Red Cross parcels for the journey. On the second night they arrived in Berlin and were shunted into a railway siding just as the R.A.F. launched a massive thousand-bomber raid. The guards locked the box-cars and scuttled into the nearest air-raid shelters.

Hour after hour, while thousands of block-buster bombs and showers of incendiaries battered the capital of Germany, the prisoners were trapped like rats in the locked box-cars. Just one heavy bomb landing on the train would have wiped out 1,500 men. Few of them showed any actual signs of fear, but the latrine can was soon filled to overflowing as men nervously emptied their bladders.

The next morning, the guards scuttled out of their air-raid shelters to board the train, which immediately headed westward out of Berlin. Through the small windows of the box-cars the prisoners could see the enormous devastation and uncontrolled fires raging in all areas of the city. They had been very fortunate.

Camp 357 was a nightmare. It was wet, muddy, and filthy. It was greatly overcrowded with French, English, and Canadian prisoners of war. Food was practically non-existent, and the life-saving Red Cross parcels had not been issued for a long time. The Germans blamed the war situation and the bombing campaign, which was destroying everything moving on the roads, railways, and canals of Germany. It could well have been true. But whatever the reason, the prisoners were back to a diet of watery cabbage soup and minute portions of black bread. The Canadians arrived on August 16th, 1944, in the heat of summer. One month later, on September 20th, they were joined by a large contingent of British and Canadian airborne troops. They had been badly mauled in the Arnhem parachute invasion, and many of them urgently needed medical attention. The Germans provided few medical supplies apart from a limited number of paper bandages and aspirins. Without the help of the Dieppe prisoners, the airmen's plight would have been terrible.

As winter closed its grip around the compound, conditions deteriorated. There was little fuel to be had; the huts were miserably cold. Gradually, under the starvation diet, the flesh began to wither and shrink on their bones, so the prisoners had little or no resistance to the intense cold. Tuberculosis, bronchitis, and rheumatism became rampant throughout the camp, and although the small British medical staff fought desperately to save men, the mortality rate climbed rapidly.

Sgts. Bill Lee, Syd Cleasby, and Cec Towler shared the same barrack hut with Roy Luxmore. All of them were engineers from Dieppe and had been very active in forming escape committees and digging tunnels throughout the long years of captivity. Day after day they watched one another grow weaker. If they weren't released soon, they would surely die.

The final humiliation was heaped on them when they were paraded for a surprise *Appell* one day in mid-winter and informed that their single blanket and wood-shaving palliasse would be taken away forthwith. The reason? The British were supposed to have punished German soldiers in North Africa in like manner.

If conditions had previously been miserable, now they became intolerable. At night, they were forbidden to leave the huts to relieve themselves. To make sure they didn't, savage Doberman Pinschers and Alsations freely roamed the compound each night. Inside the dim hut the men crouched in a circle, fully dressed, wearing overcoats and balaclava helmets to keep out the intense cold. Tensely they listened to the sniffling under the door as the savage dogs searched for food — human or otherwise.

Sergeant-Major Norm MacIver was the senior Canadian N.C.O. in the Dieppe compound at Fallingbostel. In spite of the miserable conditions and lack of food, he insisted on correct soldierly appearance at all times. Shoes and boots were kept clean and polished. Hair was combed and cheeks clean-shaven. It was good for the morale and demoralising to the Germans.

In December of 1944 came an escape from Fallingbostel so daring and imaginative that the prisoners were tremendously uplifted by it. They had been warned to expect a German SS general and his staff for an inspection a week hence. In the air force compound, the escape committee had its tailors working night and day to provide authentic uniforms for an SS general and his colonel. In every tiny detail, the uniforms were perfect, right down to the silver piping and the double zig-zag on the collar.

Promptly at 10 a.m., the SS general arrived with his staff in two huge Mercedes and, after conducting a brief inspection, adjourned to the commandant's quarters to sample his wine cellar. Once they were safely out of sight, the two R.A.F. men walked nonchalantly towards the main gates, watched by hundreds of prisoners. They certainly played the part well, even to the swagger and haughty expression. As they approached, the German sentry snapped to attention before saluting the 'general' and his 'colonel'.

In a peremptory manner, the 'general' ordered the sentry to open the gate at once! When the stammering guard explained to the 'general' that he could only open the gate if ordered to do so by his *Feldwebel*, the daring escape attempt seemed doomed to an early failure. But the R.A.F. man was made of stern stuff. After bawling out the German guard in a torrent of faultness German for being scruffy and unsoldierly, he ordered him to report to the sergeant of the guard and place himself under arrest.

Impatiently, the 'general' tapped his leg with his stick as he waited for the *Feldwebel* to return with the guard. When they both appeared, the 'general' screamed such a torrent of abuse at them that they scrambled to open the gate. When last seen, the two R.A.F. men were marching away down the road to freedom. Some time later, the slow-witted *Feldwebel* remembered that the general had arrived in a staff car and phoned the commandant to enquire why the general had left on foot. The commandant screamed that the general was presently sitting in the commandant's sitting room enjoying a drink.

It was too late, the birds had flown. Some weeks later, they returned to serve a sentence in the cooler. They had reached the port of Bremerhaven after changing into civilian clothes and had been on their way to the docks to board a Swedish ship when they had made a stupid, unconscious mistake which had cost them their freedom. One of them had been out of step with the other and in military manner had automatically changed step. Two Gestapo agents had witnessed the change in step by civilians and had arrested them, thinking they were deserters from the German army.

Unknown to the Dieppe prisoners at Fallingbostel, they were merely the first group to arrive there. In January and February, 1945, other groups would be wending their weary way across Germany to join them. By now, the Dieppe prisoners had been dispersed all over Germany. A great many remained at Stargard, while others had stayed at Lamsdorf, Mulhausen, and Eichstatt. Colonel Merritt and several of the other officers who had attempted a breakout from Eichstatt had been sent to the impregnable fortress of Colditz.

The Allied offensive in the west had almost ground to a halt during the winter months. How long could the Canadians at Fallingbostel be expected to hold out before dying of starvation and illness?

CHAPTER TWENTY-ONE

THE DEATH MARCHES

After the main body of Dieppe prisoners moved to Stargard in February 1943, the remaining Canadians were moved to the working compound. From there they were sent out on working parties throughout the surrounding district. Then early in January 1945, many of them were suddenly returned to VIIIB and warned that they would be moving out in the near future for places unknown. The Russians had advanced by leaps and bounds until their heavy artillery fire could be clearly heard in the distance.

On January 22nd, the prisoners were startled to hear an announcement over the P.A. system. They were ordered to return to their huts forthwith and to stand by for an important message. Amidst the excited buzz and wild speculation, rumours circulated through the camp that they were going to be handed over to the Russians when they arrived at the camp. When the announcement was finally made at 12.15 p.m., these fond hopes were quickly dispelled. A chill of deep apprehension settled on every prisoner of war.

Each of the various blocks in the camp was ordered to march out of the camp at hourly intervals. Each column of prisoners would be composed of 1,000 men and accompanied by one of the medical officers.

Red Cross parcels were divided among the prisoners, who hastily constructed sleighs out of bunks and bed-boards to carry their belongings. Knapsacks were hurriedly sewn together out of rags and used to contain spare sets of socks, underwear, and food. The British and Canadian medical officers warned the prisoners to wrap up as warmly as possible. The weather outside the camp was foul. It was mid-winter. Blowing snow and very low temperatures promised a bitter journey across Germany. Gloves, scarves, and woollen balaclavas were worn by those lucky enough to possess them. Many a girl in Britain or Canada was blessed for the time she had spent devotedly knitting garments for prisoners of war.

Every prisoner had a few precious belongings which he treasured. Among the remaining Dieppe men, Jack Poolton and George Sadoquis packed away their chains and Red Cross diaries as souvenirs. Each prisoner was allowed to take only one blanket. Many ignored the order, only to relinquish the extra load later, when exhaustion took its toll.

As they prepared to leave Stalag VIIIB, the prisoners were unaware that a similar drama was being enacted all over Germany in a score of prison camps. As the advancing Allied and Russian armies squeezed Germany in a death hug, the German army fought its last bitter battle in retreat. Rather than allow the prisoners to be liberated by one side or the other, the German High Command ordered all prisoners to be marched into the centre of Germany.

All prisoners on these marches suffered greatly from hunger and a variety of ills. Frostbite was the main culprit. Many would succumb to its deadly creeping paralysis before dropping out of the march to die at the side of the road, far from their native land in a hostile, friendless country. On many columns, the SS followed in the rear to shoot stragglers or the sick who were forced to drop out.

The roads were packed with civilians. The line of prisoners passed old men, women, and little children, all carrying pathetic bundles of treasured possessions in their frantic flight from the advancing Russian army. Some rode on farm wagons, others pushed baby carriages loaded with household goods. As the trek continued, the white snow on both sides of the road became dotted with many such bundles as people despairingly lightened their loads.

In the distance, the crump, crump of artillery shells could be heard as the parties of advancing infantry engaged the German rear guard. From the immediate rear of the long, straggling column of prisoners and civilians came the occasional crack of a rifle or pistol as the SS shot the civilians who refused to move quickly enough to allow retreating German troops to pass.

On the sixth night they reached the village of Juarnach in the middle of a howling blizzard. No shelter could be found, and they had to march on. Beards and eyebrows were frozen solid. Stalactites hung from frost-bitten noses; the below-zero weather and cutting wind instantly froze the mucus running from their nostrils. In their semi-hypnotic state, reeling from side to side like drunken men, nothing seemed to matter anymore — neither pain nor misery, life nor death. It was all the same; the important thing was to keep going. Pte. Poolton kept up by the simple expedient of repeating over and over again, 'I am on my way home. Every step is a step in the right direction. Don't give up now!'

After another six kilometres they finally reached a roofless barn, which gave partial shelter from the cutting wind. No water was available for cooking or drinking, and the men sat around fires all night long. They knew that if they fell asleep during the terrible night, they would soon die, frozen solid in the sub-zero temperatures.

Many cases of frostbite had occurred after the nightmare journey across the moor. At sick parade, 40 men were pronounced too ill to continue and were sent back to Juarnach the following day. One poor man had his boots stolen during the night and was forced to continue the march the next day with his feet wrapped in rags.

For another five long days and nights, the long column of prisoners continued their trek across Germany. The route was taking them in a westerly direction through the towns of Jauer and Zeichau, Goldberg and Pilgramsdorf to Lowenberg, Welderdorf, and Lichtenau until finally, on Monday, February 5th, 1945, they reached the city of Görlitz, where they were joined by a large group of prisoners from prison camp VIIIA, which lay just outside the city.

For the next 11 days, they rested at Görlitz. Hundreds of sick prisoners were transferred to the *Lararett* in a French camp nearby. Many had fingers and toes amputated after frostbite had destroyed all feeling. Other columns arrived from VIIIB bringing scores of chronically ill prisoners. But by some miracle the first doses of penicillin arrived via the International Red Cross. This was the first time the Canadian and British doctors had used the antibiotic, and many severe cases of pneumonia were assisted over the crisis when previously all hope had been abandoned.

On Thursday, February 15th, those prisoners still able to walk were given a small ration of black bread and forced back on the march, Jack Poolton and George Sadoquis among them. They were not sorry to leave — Stalag VIIIA at Görlitz had been incredibly filthy, the food almost no-existent. But it would be another month before they would end their march. They would march under terrible conditions as far west as the city of Kassel and then turn about and march east to Duder-stadt as the city of Kassel fell to Allied troops.

Dr. Clare, who had accompanied the march, was ordered to load the stretcher cases aboard a train of box-cars for the long journey north to Fallingbostel. French orderlies carried the sick down from the camp *Lazarett* to the railway station. Wood shavings were spread on the floors of the box-cars before the stretchers were laid in rows in each box-car, 14 to a car. By 10 a.m. they were under way, just as a heavy air raid bombarded Görlitz. The following day they passed through the cathedral city of Dresden, burning fiercely from a heavy air raid the night before. They were informed at Dresden that heavy fighting was taking place in Görlitz as the Russians continued their advance on the heels of the death march.

The March from Stargard, Stalag IID

The great majority of the Dieppe prisoners remained in Stalag IID at Stargard until February 2nd, 1945, when they were suddenly given orders to pack up their few pitiful belongings and prepare to move out. The Russians had arrived on the outskirts of Stargard, and fierce fighting was taking place a few short miles from the camp.

There was little time for adequate preparation but some of the men managed to knock together a rough sleigh, using a box mounted on two bed-boards. This started a regular flurry of activity, and in no time there were a hundred sleighs, ranging from a one-man model consisting of the back of an ordinary chair with a Red Cross box on it, to a whole room; they knocked bunks apart and built a large communal sleigh from the bed-boards, side-boards, and posts. The hope was that if the whole room stuck together they could transport a great deal of food and all work at pulling and pushing. In twos, threes, and fours, the boys all got together and made some kind of a sleigh from odds and ends. Some of the tin-bashers even got busy and fashioned tin glides to tack along the bottom of the wooden runners.

The weather was extremely cold; snow drifts had made all side roads almost impassable. All that day they marched in a north-easterly direction. The men plodded along in silence — just the crunch of boots in the snow and the hiss of improvised sleigh runners. They had no idea where they were going or what the German attitude was going to be at the other end. Hour after hour they marched in a long drawn-out column stopping every few hours for a short rest. The sides of the road were soon strewn with cast-off clothing and heavy, useless articles that the men had discarded.

Late at night they neared the port of Stettin, and here they were joined by thousands of civilians all fleeing from the advancing Russian army. One of the prisoners had been having great difficulty lugging a huge home-made suitcase. Every step of the way it banged against his legs until the pain became excruciating. A little boy dragging a sleigh drew level with the column, and the prisoner made frantic signs, accompanied by fragments of 'Stalag' German, to indicate that he wanted to trade two chocolate bars for the sleigh. It was almost pathetic to see the indecision on the little boy's face, but the chocolate won and the suitcase became mobile. After this example of North-American horse-trading, all those who had not constructed sleighs in the camp started to barter for them and soon there was a fine collection all the way from baby-carriage sleighs to large toboggans.

The first evening the prisoners were bedded down in a number of barns and farm buildings on the outskirts of Stettin. Many of them already had problems with frost-bitten toes and fingers. The wiser ones had included several extra pairs of dry woollen socks in their kit. The wet socks were stuffed inside the tunic of their battle-dress to be dried out by body heat.

Just before leaving the camp at Stargard, a large contingent of American prisoners had arrived from the Battle of the Bulge. These men were in poor shape already, and not fit for a forced march in sub-zero weather across Germany. Three years of hardship had toughened the Canadian prisoners in spite of their starvation diet, so that they were better equipped to face the rigours ahead.

Food and shelter would be the major problems. The Germans had forbidden the prisoners to stock up on Red Cross parcels before they left the camp. The daily ration of black bread plus a ladle of weak vegetable soup was totally insufficient for men to keep up their strength after a long day's gruelling march through deep snow and howling blizzards.

Early the next morning they were awakened to the realities of another day's ordeal by the harsh cries of ' 'raus! 'raus!' from their captors. Tardy ones were encouraged by a vicious kick or a swinging rifle butt. After a hasty breakfast of ersatz tea and a scrap of black bread saved from the night before, they were forced back on the march. Padre Foote limped along using a stout stick to support his lame leg. Some of the men offered to carry his knapsack, but he firmly refused.

Day after weary day, the march continued across frozen Germany. Although the general direction was to the west, away from the advancing Russians, very often the march took them to the north or south. Always they steered clear of towns and villages, keeping to back roads and fields. Many times they were unable to find shelter after the long day's march and were forced to sleep in the open fields. Food was becoming a serious problem. For some time, it had been almost impossible to obtain extra rations by trading. The whole of northern Germany seemed to be in the grip of famine. Many fell sick on the march or were crippled by the frostbite. Most suffered from some form of respiratory trouble but comrades forced them to continue the march.

On the thirteenth day of the march, the Red Cross organisation caught up with them. What system of intelligence they used to find out the whereabouts of the marching columns all over Germany will probably never be told but unquestionably they saved many thousands of lives. It only worked out to one parcel for each eight men, but after two weeks of near starvation, even that little amount seemed bountiful.

Ten days later, when almost at the end of their slim resources, they reached the small mediaeval town of Bismark. As the prisoners marched down the winding main street, they were excited by the tongue-watering sight of row upon row of rabbit hutches filled with plump rabbits. Inside the hutch at the very end of the last row, sat a rabbit of enormous size.

For several days the men had had practically nothing to eat. The German guards had threatened to shoot any prisoner caught stealing food, but threats are meaningless to starving men. Ronnie Reynolds of the Royal Regiment was determined to adopt the huge rabbit. A commotion further down the line solved his problem; an intrepid French Canadian had seized a large white goose by the neck and was running down the village street pursued by townspeople and guards. It was the work of a moment for a hungry adventurer to unlatch the door of the hutch and seize the huge beast by his long ears. Covered by Joe Fitzgerald and his other muckers, Ronnie quickly slipped the wriggling, protesting animal inside his battle-dress tunic, and then fastening the buttons all the way up to his neck with much straining and inhaling to make room for the poor unfortunate beast.

Like a cartoon scene, Ronnie resumed the march sporting a magnificent pair of rabbit ears which twitched and turned from left to right like a radar antenna. Although convulsed with laughter and fits of mild hysterics, the prisoners in the immediate vicinity hastily covered the evidence with scarves and woollen hats, licking their cracked lips and gums as they did. It was going to be a glorious feast.

On the outskirts of the town, the guards called a halt for the night. In the mad scramble for dry billets, Ronnie Reynolds and his muckers were indeed fortunate; they managed to secure an upper berth in a hayloft where they could snuggle down luxuriously in the deep hay and rest.

A rabbit stew should have vegetables, and as if in answer to their request, a heavily-laden farm cart passed slowly by. It was loaded with potatoes and swedes and was driven by three Polish women. On the backs of their rough clothes the Germans had stencilled the large letters O.S.T. to identify them as slave workers from the East. Using hand signs and bits of acquired German, the girls willingly gave the prisoners permission to pilfer the wagon and within seconds, several pounds of vegetables had been whisked into the barn in return for a few magical cigarettes.

Sometime later, a wonderful aroma of stewed rabbit floated in the air as Ronnie prepared the precious stew. They were well aware that once the prize rabbit had been missed, a search would be instigated. The contents of the stewpot were cunningly camouflaged with handfuls of herbs and dried leaves. It was fortunate that they did, for a platoon of guards suddenly burst through the door, armed to the teeth. From pot to pot they made their way through the barn in their search for the missing rabbit. Again fortune smiled on the prisoners. The German guard who examined their stewpot was an older, more decent type than his colleagues. As he bent over the pot, the men held their breath and tried to appear nonchalant and carefree. Their innocent expressions changed to horror as a leg, plump and succulent, suddenly floated to the surface to offer damning evidence. With commendable sleight of hand, Ronnie slipped a whole package of cigarettes into the German's palm and was rewarded for his quick thinking by a sly, conspiratorial wink as he turned away to join his companions.

From here they turned northward, and after seven more days of weary plodding, they finally arrived at the town of Lübeck. The last leg of their journey would be completed by train. Over 50 men were pushed into each box-car. Just as they had travelled from Verneulles to Lamsdorf three long years before, they were unable to lie down or to sleep. Jammed almost shoulder to shoulder, they suffered for six long days and nights without being released for an instant to stretch or relieve themselves. The Germans had doled out a loaf of black bread for each three men to share during the long journey. A solitary can of water was the drinking supply for the whole car, while toilet functions were carried out in another can placed in the corner. The can was soon overflowing and covered the floor of the box-car with its malodorous filth. They ate little, having no stomach for food amidst the stench. Many of them had dysentery and were almost too weak to be moved. They just stood or sat in their own excretion and apologised profusely or cursed roundly at the mess they had made. Every time they stopped at a station, they weakly croaked for *Wasser* through the tiny grating above their heads, but their pleas were ignored.

In all those six days and nights, they travelled only 50 miles. Shunted back and forth at the mercy of Allied low-level raids, they finally arrived at the small town of Bremervorde. The doors of the box-cars were unlocked, and those able to walk stumbled blindly onto the platform into the light of day.

It was now the first week of March, 1945, and thankfully, the snow had melted from the roads under a warming sun. From Bremervorde, the prisoners were marched to the small town of Sandbostel, which was a political prison for civilian prisoners who had committed some misdemeanour or crime against the Reich. Through the centre of the camp ran a small-gauge railway. Every morning four or five hundred of the poor starving souls would be gathered up and loaded onto a special train to take them away to Belsen or one of the other extermination camps. The Dieppe prisoners used a small latrine every morning for their daily ablutions, and the death train passed their doorway at a distance of only 10 feet. As it slowly passed, the prisoners were shocked to see bodies piled in the box-cars like neat firewood. At the end of the line, the bodies were dumped into pits and covered with lime. This was the first time the Canadians had been exposed to the horrors of mass extermination. They were shocked beyond belief. The civilian prisoners wore striped pyjama-like uniforms, with rough wooden clogs on their feet. Their heads were shaved, their bodies shrunken and twisted by malnutrition and disease. Their hands and faces were covered with weeping sores. The only feature which seemed to have grown during their terrible incarceration was the eyes — huge and forlorn as they stared forth in soundless horror from the cavernous ruin of their faces. The Canadians had little food, but they threw cigarettes to clawing hands which fought desperately to secure the precious tubes of tobacco. Then the poor dying souls stuffed the cigarettes into their mouths and ate them.

For 44 days the Canadians had been on the march. They had never removed their clothes for an instant. They were indescribably filthy and lousy. But they had survived. After several days in Sandbostel, the Germans suddenly moved them out again. After marching for 15 miles, they were split into different groups before entering separate prison camps. Some went to Fallingbostel to join their Dieppe comrades from Torun. Others entered the naval camp at Tarmstadt Marlag Nord. It was raining heavily as they passed through the familiar barbed wire gate. Through the sea of rain and mud, they could see that their new home was a bleak and desolate place. It had a number of bare wooden shacks, a muddy parade ground, and flat, scrubby land as far as the eye could see. As they stumbled through the doorway of the huts, two dim bulbs suspended from the ceiling provided just enough light to allow them to select a bunk, throw their kit on to it, and then climb wearily up to flop on the wood-shaving mattress and fall asleep, exhausted.

The first weeks at Tarmstadt were extremely bad. It rained almost continuously and it was impossible to keep the rooms or their clothes dry. Many of the men were sick from the privations suffered during the march. The Red Cross had managed to make one delivery of parcels, but the tremendous air offensive made the trucking of parcels across Germany an extremely hazardous enterprise.

The British 2nd Army had slowed in its advance across northern Germany and was presently massing on the western bank of the River Weser, which separated them from Fallingbostel. If they didn't arrive soon, they would be too late to save thousands of prisoners.

In the *Lazarett* in the prison camp at Fallingbostel, Dr. Clare and four other British doctors fought desperately to save lives. Malnutrition, dysentery and disease were finally taking their toll. By Easter the bodies of many prisoners of war were piled up in the mortuary because they were dying too quickly to be buried. Many of the Americans from the Battle of the Bulge had died during the first few weeks of their captivity.

The camp was situated almost directly in the path of the northern air raids. Bremen was only 20 miles away, Hamburg not much farther, and Wilhelmshaven, Bremerhaven, Hanover, and Münster were all in the vicinity. Every day and night now, the bombers flew over in a steady stream on their way to one or another of these cities. The war was drawing to a close, and Germany was being battered into submission.

The guards had long ago given up trying to keep the prisoners inside the barrack huts whenever a raid came over, so the prisoners began to lie out in the open on a blanket to watch the show. High in the sky were the American bombers, hundreds and hundreds of them in beautiful formation. The planes flew in boxes of from 20 to more than 100. On and on they came, until the whole sky was filled with aircraft and the noise was deafening. From time to time, a group would turn off slightly and head for its own special target. All the while, long-range fighters circled and wheeled above the bombers. They could see the fighters only occasionally because they were so small and so high, but the sun would glint off the windscreen during a turn or a vapour trail would streak out from the wings.

At night, the R.A.F. bombed the same targets. Once near Bremen or Hamburg, they would release their 4,000-pound block-busters and the ground would shake even in the camp. Watching the daylight raids was impressive but watching the night raids was exhilarating. The ground for many miles around was flat and the prisoners could clearly see the inferno as bursting bombs and incendiaries fell from Lancasters, Stirlings, and Halifaxes. Pathfinder aircraft dropped yellow flares and, shortly after, green and red target indicator flares lit up the whole countryside. From then on, the night was broken by fires, flashes, explosions, and bursts of anti-aircraft fire. Once in a while, a bomber was hit. When it crashed, it went up with an orange flash that seemed to climb slowly in the sky for miles, then fall back on to itself. Many airmen died during these raids, but the prisoners began to realise that the war was coming to a close. Germany was dying.

The word was passed around to hold on just a little longer. The British were advancing and very soon now, they would be relieved. A deep spirit of optimism began to invade the camp at Fallingbostel.

The rations had been cut during the month of March, so that now the prisoners were living on 1,500 calories per day. Seven men had to share a loaf of bread for the daily ration plus two pots of thin turnip and potato soup. There had not been a Red Cross issue since February 19th, but on Good Friday, mercifully, they received one-half parcel each. Men who had been lying on their bunks all day to conserve their energy now began to feel more cheerful, but a few days later, on April 8th, 1945, they were suddenly marched out of the camp, which was to be evacuated before the British advance.

It was almost more than they could stand — to be forced back on the march in their terribly weakened state when the British army was right on their doorstep, the war all but over.

On April 12th, four days after leaving Fallingbostel, the Germans informed the prisoners of the death of President Roosevelt. Five days later, on April 17th, the Red Cross again caught up with the marching column, and the life-saving food parcels restored many a man near death. By now, Bill Lee and Roy Luxmore were very weak and sick from dysentery and malnutrition. By day they marched slowly across northern Germany. At night, they slept in fields and under hedges. Seldom did they have the luxury of a barn or even a roof over their heads, although the guards were changed every three or four days as they became exhausted.

It snowed and it rained continuously to make their lives even more miserable. At night they spread their blankets under the trees to make a make-shift tent where they could sit all night long waiting for the dawn.

Drop-outs became more numerous as men became too ill to continue. The occasional burst of firing at the rear of the column ended their suffering abruptly.

The British army had crossed the River Weser at the same time that the prisoners crossed the River Elbe. On April 26th the men reached the little town of Cressy just south of Ratzenburg, some 25 miles south of Hamburg. Overhead, the

R.A.F. patrolled steadily. They were well aware that the long column below was that of their own men. They were merely observing the direction in which they were being marched so that they could direct forward reconnaissance units through the back roads to overtake them as soon as possible.

The planes swooped low and waggled their wings to cheer the men and to let them know that they were under observation. Immediately after they had gone, the Germans made the prisoners turn about and march back in the direction from which they had come. After retracing their footsteps for a mile, they then proceeded due north up a long road lined with trees just beginning to bud.

Suddenly the R.A.F. returned. Seeing the long column of men where none had been evident before, they mistook them for a German column and swooped down for the kill. At treetop height, they screamed along the entire length of the column, machine gunning and strafing. For a few terrible moments, the prisoners were too stunned to move. Then as men started to die on all sides, they dived for the shelter of the ditches at the sides of the road.

The strafing was called off almost as soon as it had started. The pilots had suddenly realised they had made a tragic mistake. Eighty-nine men had died in the strafing. The Dieppe prisoners were particularly distressed when they found that one of the dead was Tommy Gage, a sapper from the Second Field Company of the Royal Canadian Engineers and a veteran of the First World War. Alongside Tommy's body lay the shattered remnants of his Red Cross parcel. Syd Cleasby seized a scavenging prisoner who attempted to pick up the food from the parcel.

They gathered up the dead and buried them in neat rows alongside the road before continuing the march. A short time later, the planes returned to wag their wings and let the men know that they had realised they had made a terrible error.

Two days later, on April 29th, the Germans informed the prisoners that they were going to march them only another 12 kilometres before turning them over to British troops. Many of the guards deserted during the night and threw away their rifles. The men were so excited they couldn't sleep.

At 2 p.m. the next day, two light British tanks and a motorcycle rounded a corner ahead of the column. Instantly there was pandemonium! The remaining guards threw away their rifles and fled. Some of the prisoners were quick to snatch them up and fire at their retreating backs. Several were hit.

In their hundreds the prisoners crowded around the tank, waving and cheering hoarsely. It was an advance reconnaissance unit of the Royal Staffordshire Regiment attached to the British 2nd Army. The British army was still about 100 miles behind them. The advance unit was hoping to proceed to Wismar to meet up with the Russian army. At Wismar, they were informed, there was a large German ordnance depot where the prisoners could arm themselves to prevent recapture. Those able to continue on the march followed behind the light tanks until they reached Wismar. To their surprise they found the ordnance depot totally unguarded. It didn't take long to arm fully the remaining prisoners, who then turned about to be led by N.C.O.s such as Cec Towler. The date was May 2nd, 1945, two years and eight months after they had been taken prisoner at Dieppe.

A few miles down the road, the newly armed prisoners surprised some German trucks. After taking the Germans prisoner, they headed back to the British lines at Lüneburg, where they were fed and clothed in royal manner. The sick were flown out from an airfield at Amsdatten to dear old Blighty, where they were whisked into the 14th Canadian General Hospital for careful nursing and diet. The nurses were pretty and the treatment was the best in the world.

The following morning, the Dieppe men sat on the sloping hillside above the town of Lüneburg to witness the official surrender of the German armed forces in northern Germany to Field Marshal Montgomery. As they watched the historic drama unfolding below, their thoughts returned to the beaches of Dieppe where they had been forced to surrender after a hopeless fight. They had suffered greatly in the prison camps and on the death march, but they had never given in. They had followed the orders of Harry Beesley and fought back with every weapon at their command. It had been a battle of wits, of stamina, and of morale.

The once proud and mighty Wehrmacht had been driven to its knees after the Allies had landed on the Normandy beaches. A famous general had said a long time before, that the Battle of Waterloo had been won on the playing fields of Eton. Winston Churchill and Lord Mountbatten would say that without Dieppe there would have been no 'D' Day and no final victory in the Second World War.

The men of Dieppe had earned their place of honour at Lüneburg. It was fitting that they should witness the final surrender.

EPILOGUE

Under the strong but benevolent hand of Harry Beesley, most of the men had survived the worst. There had been times of despair and despondency, and there had been times of great determination when strong wills had continued the fight when all had seemed lost. Above all, they had learned to respect each other and to lend assistance to those in need.

Unfortunately, there were others who returned broken in health; the totally inadequate diet of the prison camps had sapped their strength and their resistance to disease. A large number suffered from tuberculosis or duodenal ulcers. Almost everyone developed some form of rheumatism or arthritis. A great many more were damaged psychologically.

Successive appeals to Canadian Pension Boards for improved pensions for the Dieppe Veterans have met with little success. At the time of writing, the Standing Committee on Veterans' Affairs is studying the Hermann report which may result in an adjustment in pensions. It is to be hoped that the wheels of bureaucracy will turn swiftly to aid these men.

Harry Beesley did not survive. His death remains cloaked in mystery. After the war, the British War Office informed his family living in Staines, England, that he had been killed in a railway accident in Poland. Other survivors have sworn that Beesley was shot by the Russians after he demanded food for his starving men. Exhaustive research and interviews with ex-prisoners and civilians in Poland have failed to unearth the facts. Some day, new evidence may be unveiled and the truth revealed.

Whatever the facts, his death was a tragedy. He helped so many others to survive by giving them the will to live and to continue the fight.

AUTHOR'S NOTE

Some time after the book had gone to the printers, I received the information I had been seeking regarding Harry Beesley's death. In answer to an appeal I launched through the British Commando Bulletin, I received a letter from Mr. Ivor Dunstan of Penryn, Cornwall, England.

He reported that after the Canadian Dieppe prisoners had been transferred to Stalag IID, Harry Beesley was moved to Camp B.A.B. 21 at Blechammer, near the town of Cosel in Upper Silesia. On Christmas Day, 1944, he finally managed to escape, and after travelling through hostile country for several days reached the Polish town of Cracow. The Russian military authorities billeted him while he awaited passage overland to the seaport of Odessa. There, he planned to board a ship for England.

Early in February 1945, R.S.M. Beesley and Mr. Dunstan were ordered on to a train, an old relic of the Czarist regime. Thirty liberated prisoners were crowded into each carriage. The weather was bitterly cold and although each carriage had been fitted with a huge pot-bellied stove, fuel was non-existent. The journey to Odessa was supposed to take five days, but stretched into ten. Desperate for warmth, the prisoners, led by Harry Beesley, made raids on coal dumps whenever the train stopped at a station.

It was during one of these raids that the rear two coaches of the train became uncoupled and started to roll backwards down a steep incline. Beesley immediately ran after the runaway coaches and attempted to apply the hand brake which was fitted to the side of the rear coach. At the bottom of the incline, the coaches jumped the track and toppled onto their left side, trapping Beesley underneath. The two coaches were packed with French slave workers returning to their homeland. Undoubtedly, many of them would have been killed if he had not applied the brakes.

Harry Beesley died as he had lived — helping others.

ACKNOWLEDGMENTS

In the preparation of this book, more than 200 people have freely offered their advice and assistance. Many chose to remain anonymous, but all were anxious to see the facts published. Here then, is a partial list of those who have unselfishly given so much of their time in order to assist me. I am grateful to all of them.

Earl Mountbatten of Burma
Major-General Churchill
   C. Mann
Aide, Percy W.
Anderson, Archie
Anderson, Bernie
Barless, George
Bassil, Harry
Beal, R. F.
Beesley, J.
Bender, David B.
Bennett, Edwin
Blair, N. E.
Bloxham, Bill
Bondy, Ken
Brash, Frank
Breithaupt, Art
Brown, Albert
Brown, Henry, Secretary,
   Commando Association
Bubis, Mr.
Buchanan, G. B., Colonel
Burrows, Russell
Clare, Dr. D. W.
Cleasby, Syd
Coates, Harland
Cousins, Ed
Dalrymple, Wm. R.
Darch, Stan
Darouché, Louis

Dear, W. D.
Douglas, Hugh
Douglas, W. A. B.
Drew, Harry
Dubé, Russell
Dumais, Lucien
Dungate, Wally
Dunne, Doug. A.
Durnford-Slater, Mrs.
Elliot, Jim
Emmott, H.
Emo, Bob
Evans, Stan
Foote, John Weir, V.C.
Gibson, Norman
Gibson, Walter
Giguere, George
Gosselin, Louis
Grant, Wm.
Graves, George
Guest, Dennis
Habron, Pat J.
Hamilton, D. G., Colonel
Hancock, Harry
Hanes, Doug
Harris, S. B.
Heath, Ed
Hodge, Stan
Isbister, Bill
Johns, Russell

Johnston, Wm.
Labatt, R. R., Lt. Col.
Lee, Bill
Linder, Don, R.C.N.
Luxmore, Roy
Lynch, Bill
MacDonald, Al
MacIver, Norman
MacKenzie,
Maloney, Peter E.
Maloy, Mac
Manchester, Harry
Mavin, Scotty
Mayo, Norman
McCarthy, Pete
McCool, Brian, Major
McDermott, Tom
McRae, Donald, Colonel
McRae, R. F., Lt., R.C.N.V.R.
Membury, Roy, R.C.N.V.R.
Merritt, C. C. I., V.C., Lt. Col.
Metzger, F. W., German Army
Michell, Steve
Millward, James
Mulholland, Dave, R.M.
Murphy, Jim
Nicholls, Tom
Pasquale, Jim
Patrick, Harry
Pearson, Bob
Pilote, Marc
Poolton, Jack
Pumphrey, E. N., Captain, R.N.
Ramsey, G.
Reynolds, Ron
Richards, A. G.

Rickard, Cec
Rimes, Slim
Rivers, E. B.
Sadoquis, George
Salmond, Bill
Scott, Dennis
Scott, Ray
Selwyn, John, Major
Smale, Joe N., Major
Smith, Harley
Stanton, Austin, Major
Stevens, Bill
Strang, Mrs. Yvonne
Strickland, Morris, R.N.
Summerfield, Hap
Towler, Cec
Tyminski, Rom Nalecz,
   Captain, P.N.
Utman, Don
Wilkinson, Syd, R.N.
Williamson, John, Colonel
Wood, J. E. R., Lt.
Wootton, Frank W., Brigadier
Young, Peter, Brigadier.

M. Paul Brunet
Mme Denis
M. et Mme Paul Dupuis
M. Georges Guibon
M. Didier Heullant
M. Louis Larcheveque
M. Jean Claude Robillard
M. Raymond le Roy
Sister Marie du S. Coeur
Sister Marie Monique

ROBERT LITTELL

SWEET REASON

The talented author of the bestselling THE DEFECTION
of A. J. LEWINTER has turned his wicked eye away from
the ironies of the cold-war game to take a satirical and
sparkling look at the Navy Lark.

The *Eugene F. Ebersole* is the most clapped-out man-o'
war patrolling the coast of North Vietnam. And her
motley crew the most reluctant. So when an anonymous
pacifist calling himself The Voice of Sweet Reason
starts showering the desks with anti-war broadsheets –
Remember! Nobody can force you to pull a trigger! – they
don't need much reminding. As the ship lurches forward on her momentous mission, the Captain begins a
demented search for Sweet Reason. Sabotage on the
port deck, mutiny on starboard – the *US Ebersole* is a
ship in distress all right. And there's worse to come.

CORONET BOOKS

AIREY NEAVE

THEY HAVE THEIR EXITS

Here is a story of supreme courage, of the daring and resource of men in the bright face of danger. Norman Birkett says in his foreword:

'None of those who have written (about World War II) have had the unique experience that the whirligig of time brought to Airey Neave, and which he has used in this book with such dramatic effect. The young lieutenant of 1940, wounded, captured, imprisoned, suffering intense humiliation, yet lived to be the Major of 1945, who was appointed by the judges at the International Military Tribunal at Nuremburg to a position that brought him into the closest touch with the Nazi leaders when they were, in turn, captured and imprisoned on the collapse of the German Reich.

'It is the vivid contrast of the escaped prisoner of war set in authority over Keitel, Goering, Hess, Ribbentrop and the rest, that gives to this book a quality that no other book of the like possesses'.

CORNELIUS RYAN

A BRIDGE TOO FAR

A BRIDGE TOO FAR is perhaps the most thrilling, moving and powerful work of history to come out of World War II.

Its subject is the battle of Arnhem, the greatest airborne operation of the war, the master-stroke by which Field Marshal Sir Bernard Montgomery, having won over a reluctant General Dwight D. Eisenhower, proposed to end the war in 1944. He planned to drop the combined airborne forces of the American and British armies behind German lines to capture the crucial bridge across the Rhine at Arnhem, subsequently sending a vast army to catch up with them for the drive into Germany.

A BRIDGE TOO FAR is the masterly chronicle of a daring and grandiose operation that ended in bitter defeat for the Allies. The cast of characters includes Dutch civilians, British and American planners, commanders and soldiers, and the German defenders, all of them plunged into a battle that was perhaps the most dramatic of the entire war and that cost the Allies nearly twice as many casualties as D-Day.

CORONET BOOKS

WAR FROM CORONET

All these books are available at your local bookshop or newsagent, or can be ordered direct from the publisher. Just tick the titles you want and fill in the form below.

Prices and availability subject to change without notice.

_____

CORONET BOOKS, P.O. Box 11, Falmouth, Cornwall.

Please send cheque or postal order, and allow the following for postage and packing:

U.K.—One book 22p plus 10p per copy for each additional book ordered, up to a maximum of 82p.

B.F.P.O. and EIRE—22p for the first book plus 10p per copy for the next 6 books, thereafter 4p per book.

OTHER OVERSEAS CUSTOMERS—30p for the first book and 10p per copy for each additional book.

Name ....

Address ....

....